The EVERYTHING®
Aquarium
Book

Dear Reader,

I cannot remember a time when I was not held spellbound by fish and other animals. Growing up in New York City, I had, at my doorstep, institutions that were nothing short of paradise to someone like myself. A long career at the Bronx Zoo and Staten Island Zoo, and countless hours at the American Museum of Natural History provided experiences that continue to enrich my life today.

In following the curious path that has defined my life, however, the foregoing pales in comparison to the support provided by my family. Despite trying financial circumstances at one point, they even encouraged me to follow my heart and abandon a career as an attorney. Burdened by a deep sense of responsibility, I could not have done so without their thoughtful advice. And thus I became one of the fortunate few—living what I love, courting adventure, and becoming, in the process, a better person.

My sincere desire is that the words penned here will assist the reader in discovering new worlds. More importantly, I hope to nurture within you a respectful and caring attitude toward nature. Remember that your concern for animals and their habitats may well influence others to take the process a step further.

Frank Indiviglio

The EVERYTHING® Series

Editorial

Publishing Director	Gary M. Krebs
Director of Product Development	Paula Munier
Associate Managing Editor	Laura M. Daly
Associate Copy Chief	Brett Palana-Shanahan
Acquisitions Editor	Kate Burgo
Development Editor	Rachel Engelson
Associate Production Editor	Casey Ebert

Production

Director of Manufacturing	Susan Beale
Associate Director of Production	Michelle Roy Kelly
Cover Design	Paul Beatrice
	Matt LeBlanc
	Erick DaCosta
Design and Layout	Heather Barrett
	Brewster Brownville
	Colleen Cunningham
	Jennifer Oliveira
Series Cover Artist	Barry Littmann

THE

EVERYTHING®

AQUARIUM BOOK

All you need to build
the aquarium of your dreams

Frank Indiviglio

Adams Media
Avon, Massachusetts

In Memory of Dennis Scauso
His passing on September 11, 2001, was in furtherance of a lifelong mission
to help others—family, friends, and strangers alike.
His ideals remain undiminished, and they continue to enrich our lives.
Thank you.

An Everything® Series Book.
Everything® and everything.com® are registered trademarks of F+W Publications, Inc.

Published by Adams Media, an F+W Publications Company
57 Littlefield Street, Avon, MA 02322 U.S.A.
www.adamsmedia.com

ISBN 10: 1-59337-715-0

ISBN 13: 978-1-59337-715-1
Printed in the United States of America.

J   I   H   G   F   E   D   C   B

Library of Congress Cataloging-in-Publication Data
available from the publisher

This publication is designed to provide accurate and authoritative information with regard to the subject matter covered. It is sold with the understanding that the publisher is not engaged in rendering legal, accounting, or other professional advice. If legal advice or other expert assistance is required, the services of a competent professional person should be sought.

—From a *Declaration of Principles* jointly adopted by a Committee of the American Bar Association and a Committee of Publishers and Associations

Many of the designations used by manufacturers and sellers to distinguish their products are claimed as trademarks. Where those designations appear in this book and Adams Media was aware of a trademark claim, the designations have been printed with initial capital letters.

This book is available at quantity discounts for bulk purchases.
For information, please call 1-800-289-0963.

Contents

Acknowledgments

Any words that I might write here, especially concerning friends and family, will be woefully inadequate. With my apologies for that, I offer my sincerest gratitude to:

Grace Freedson, my agent, for her concern, advice, and sincere efforts on my behalf. Rita Indiviglio, for her thoughtful review of the manuscript, and, more importantly, for everything else. Susan and Frank Schilling, for somehow rendering me semicomputer literate, and for all the support. Jim Berkley, for proving that insomniacs can become excellent authors, thereby offering me hope, and for the friendship. Sylvia Hecht, Marlene Tartaglione, Nao Oguro, Richard Ogust, Robert Shapiro, and all of the wonderful "Friends of Wildlife Conservation" at the Bronx Zoo, for inspiring me by example to pursue my dreams and, most importantly, for their friendship. Dick and Patti Bartlett, for their kindness in sharing so much unique information about animals, and for setting standards of authorship that I can aspire to but certainly not attain. All of the concerned people at Adams Media who played such a vital role in producing this book.

All of the dear friends and interesting people who, by kind act or shared thought, have unwittingly added to my knowledge and abilities.

Top Ten Things You Will Learn in This Book

1. Reasons for keeping an aquarium

2. Feeding, breeding, and medical care of freshwater and marine animals

3. Natural history of many fish, invertebrates, aquatic insects, amphibians, and plants

4. How to obtain aquatic animals and plants

5. How to maintain a freshwater aquarium

6. How to maintain a brackish water aquarium

7. How to maintain a marine aquarium

8. Conservation issues concerning aquatic animals and ecosystems

9. How to participate in research and conservation oriented activities

10. How to learn more and take your interests further

Introduction

▶ This book is, on the surface, something of a how-to manual for those interested in keeping fresh and saltwater aquariums. It should also serve to open your eyes to the wonders of the aquatic creatures and habitats that are to be found all around us and to foster an understanding of why they are important and what can be done to preserve them.

An aquarium can offer insights into worlds far removed from your everyday existence. Through the glass of an aquarium, even children living in the world's largest cities can become intimately acquainted with the lives of creatures that live thousands of miles from their homes. Although complex aquatic systems are discussed in this book, you will also learn about very basic aquariums designed to maintain common, hardy creatures. Something as simple as a glass jar housing a larval dragonfly can open up vast new horizons in your life.

This book reflects an ethical obligation to offer the best possible advice to those seeking to maintain aquatic creatures. Marine and freshwater fisheries the world over are collapsing, taking with them the livelihoods of many people. Species not directly fished are threatened by disruption of the food chain, and also because they are often collected, along with a species targeted by fishermen, as by-catch. Sea creatures that are important to practitioners of traditional medicine are also being harvested at unsustainable rates.

Pollution, industrial development, and the introduction of exotic species devastate both marine and freshwater communities, with coastal sea grass beds, mangrove swamps, coral reefs, and restuaries being particularly at risk. Freshwater habitats, because they are less able to self-clean than the open sea, are being compromised with frightening regularity. Many fishes and invertebrates are limited to very specific micro-habitats. Such species cannot easily relocate, and exterminated populations may not be readily recolonized. The information contained in this book will allow you to contribute to the survival of the threatened creatures of these ecosystems by providing them with proper care and breeding conditions.

On the opposite end of the spectrum, wide-ranging oceanic species are of particular concern because protection in one country does not guarantee safety in another. As you read about the complex reproductive strategies of these species, consider how long these behaviors have taken to evolve, how easily they can be disrupted, and how you can apply your newfound knowledge to help these animals. Each individual removed from its natural habitat is a significant event, and extinctions occur daily. It is possible that the cures for certain diseases are to be found in the body chemistries of aquatic animals—each species lost can therefore have devastating consequences for humanity.

Well-informed hobbyists can contribute significantly to what is known about aquatic animals. This is especially true concerning the less studied species, of which there are many. Scientists and researchers do not even know, to the nearest degree of magnitude, the number of species that exist. The information contained in this book will provide the basic groundwork for keeping a wide range of interesting animals, and will start you on your way to learning more. Especially important is sharing your knowledge with others. Publish your observations in the newsletters of local aquarium societies and cooperate with aquariums, museums, and other such institutions. In these times of decreased budgets for scientific institutions, the help of dedicated volunteers is vital. Conversations with professionals working in your area will often lead to a variety of interesting opportunities.

Above all, enjoy your hobby, continue to learn, and share your passion with others.

Chapter 1

Preliminary Considerations

In the rush of excitement that accompanies embarking on a new endeavor such as aquarium keeping, it is easy to lose sight of certain realities. Before you explore the specifics and the nuts and bolts of this fascinating hobby, you should pause to think about a few related topics. It is important that you consider, for example, the effect of this hobby on the environment, and also that you are aware of certain risks and obstacles that may, if ignored, seriously jeopardize the future success of keeping aquatic animals and plants.

Why Keep Aquatic Organisms?

In the past, it seemed that most people kept aquariums as the result of a long-seated and intense interest in fish and other animals. The difficulties inherent in keeping all but the hardiest of creatures discouraged those with but a passing curiosity.

Today, a wealth of information and technical advances have greatly simplified life for those desiring an aquarium of their own. More and more, people are drawn to the hobby because of the sheer beauty of the animals that can be brought into their homes. Most, if not all, such people soon develop a deeper interest in their charges, and a sincere concern for their well-being.

The Possibilities

However you might come to aquarium keeping, and whether you decide to focus on freshwater or marine animals, or both, you will gain an insight into a world that is largely beyond the reach of humans. Even with the most common of animals in the most basic of settings, you will be privy to the secret lives of a host of fascinating organisms. The thrill of your first breeding success or the observation of a previously unknown facet of animal behavior is one that will further encourage and excite you as you pursue your interest in marine creatures.

ALERT!

More and more we are seeing the destructive effects of human activities on wild animals and the environmental systems that support them. Every bit of information that we can glean about a creature's behavior will contribute, in a very real way, to its future survival in the wild.

The Learning Process

Many of the details of the lives of the world's fish and aquatic invertebrates are virtually unknown. The aquarist who takes the time to properly maintain such creatures has an excellent chance of contributing to a greater understanding of their natural histories. Most aquatic animals (and other animals) will exhibit their full range of behaviors only under ideal captive conditions. It therefore behooves those with a deep interest in such things to learn as much as they can about their charges and to duplicate, as closely as is possible, their natural environments.

Some Less-Expected Rewards

Aquarium keeping readily stimulates deeper interests in a host of related subjects. You, and those with whom you share your passion, will want to learn more and more about the animals that you keep, how they live, what prospects they have for continued survival and what must be done to protect them. For young children, especially those largely isolated from nature, an aquarium can be a call to new worlds and new interests. Many elderly people find such a hobby quite stimulating mentally, and the sense of being responsible for the well-being of other creatures can become an important factor in their lives.

Environmental Ethics and the Law

Most people are aware of the need to maintain wild places in as pristine a state as possible. In many situations, however, protection is not enough. Understanding is required, as many wild places are becoming increasingly cut off from the systems that support them, so much so that human intervention is required if they are to remain viable. Unfortunately, a thorough understanding of an environment is largely impossible when people know so little of the creatures that exist within it. As many aquatic creatures go about their lives largely out of the sight and reach of humans, careful observations of well-housed captive specimens may offer the most practical alternative.

Pollution

Aquatic animals, especially those that live in small freshwater systems, are often affected by pollution more directly than are other animals. With rare exceptions (see "Walking Catfish," at page 76), such creatures cannot leave their environments when conditions deteriorate. Furthermore, animals that live in water are constantly surrounded by and in touch with whatever pollutants are introduced into their environment. They not only live in the water, but also draw it into their bodies as part of their respiratory processes.

Fish and aquatic invertebrates are, in effect, "canaries in the coal mine," in that many begin to suffer or disappear long before the destructive effects of human activities become obvious.

The Effects of Extinctions

It is imperative that people learn as much as they can about the animals for which they are responsible. You should be sure that any animals you purchase have been captive bred. In addition to the ethical concerns involved with damaging an animal population, it is also worth noting that humans have much to learn from our fellow creatures. Nearly all of our medicines have come from natural sources, and no one can be sure where the next important disease cure will be found. The body chemistries of any number of fish, plants, or invertebrates may hold important keys to the future health of our own species. Each extinction closes the door to such possibilities.

ESSENTIAL

Sellers of animals, especially those who ship out of their home base, may not be concerned about the laws in place at the animal's final destination. On a practical level, the eventual purchaser will be held legally accountable for the ownership of protected creatures, even if they were purchased in good faith from a licensed dealer or store.

Legal Restrictions to Animal Ownership

Increasingly, international and local authorities are moving to protect aquatic animals by regulating or prohibiting their capture and sale. Unfortunately, the enforcement of such laws is spotty at best, especially because authorities are often overburdened and occupied with many other concerns.

It is up to each aquarist to be scrupulous in avoiding the purchase of protected fish and aquatic invertebrates while understanding that unscrupulous collectors and dealers are often able to circumvent governmental regulations. An offer of sale at a pet store or, especially, via mail or the Internet, is absolutely no guarantee that ownership of the animal is legal.

Time and Money

The first time aquarist might be in for a rude awakening upon learning the true cost of maintaining an aquarium in the home. Most would probably agree that the cost is well worth the rewards, but before diving headlong into this new project, be aware that the equipment and the animals themselves can be quite expensive. This expense increases, obviously, as one keeps larger and more complicated aquariums. This is especially true concerning marine aquariums. Hidden costs include electricity, medications, and the overall effect of the hobby on your ability to pursue other activities.

A Hobby or a Career?

Very few people are fortunate enough to find a career that allows them to indulge their passion or hobby. When it comes to aquarium keeping, however, you can certainly pursue a career that allows you to enjoy your hobby full-time. Most people are satisfied with indulging their interests in aquariums as a hobby, but those with a deep passion may find little satisfaction in unrelated careers.

Education

Today, education overrides the importance of experience in the hiring policies of most public aquariums. You would do well, therefore, to research and carefully consider your educational possibilities before attempting to build a career working with aquatic animals. Talk with as many professionals as you can, and bear in mind that most started out just as you did, merely with an interest in keeping animals and exploring their worlds.

Volunteering

Find out what sort of research is being done in your area, and offer to help. Most field researchers are poorly funded, and many welcome competent and sincere volunteers. Volunteering is also possible at major aquariums, and organizations such as Earthwatch offer the opportunity to assist in research projects in far-flung corners of the world. Also, contact local governmental agencies to find out what is being done in your specific area of interest.

Contributions You Can Make

Volunteering, as mentioned earlier, will allow you to indulge your passion while contributing to a better understanding of wild animals and wild places. It is very important that you bear in mind that the most basic facts about many aquatic animals are largely unknown. Because of this, just by witnessing your own aquatic pets, you can observe behavior that has possibly never been seen or written about.

Learning by Observing

Interesting and important facts are routinely uncovered by amateurs observing their pets or exploring natural areas accessible to them. The potential for discovering new facts (and even new species) is greatly increased for those with an interest in invertebrates as opposed to vertebrates. We are unaware, even to the nearest degree of magnitude, of their numbers and even more ignorant of how they live their lives. Record everything and anything that you observe as you pursue your hobby. You may wish to employ the help of interested friends and relatives in your observations. People, especially children, are often fascinated by observing live animals and may gladly spend long periods of time watching your aquarium. Such people can serve as your eyes when you are not available and will no doubt surprise you with what they discover.

FACT

Many governmental bodies sponsor surveys of natural places or species of particular concern, and often these are done largely on a volunteer basis. Even if these activities do not lead to a career, you will no doubt thoroughly enjoy yourself and be rewarded with the knowledge that you have contributed to important work.

Special-Interest Groups

Above all, be generous in sharing what you have seen and learned with others. Become involved with special-interest organizations, and publish your findings whenever possible. The fact that an observation first appears as a note in an informal publication may lessen its impact but not its importance. The local newsletters of aquarium organizations are often the starting points for professional researchers interested in particular animals or environments. Don't be trapped into believing that you must be a professional to contribute. As you will discover by reading about nearly any animal, very little can replace direct observation as a means of discovering new information.

Precautions

Although aquarium keeping is, by and large, a pleasant and harmless endeavor, there are a few precautions that you should keep in mind when pursuing your hobby. A few basic safeguards put in place early on will save you a good deal of time, trouble, and expense.

Electricity

Do not ignore basic electrical safety in your rush to provide your pets with ideal captive conditions. Especially where large systems are concerned, an electrician should be consulted to make sure that the equipment you plan to use can be supported by your home's electrical circuitry. Electrical appliances should be operated and installed only as directed by the manufacturer's instructions. (Resist the temptation to experiment with installing electrical appliances yourself!) Likewise, make sure that any extension cords that are added to your system can support the appliance to which they are connected. Some aquarium lights give off a surprising amount of heat, so you must be certain that they are kept away from anything flammable. Lights mounted over aquariums must be securely fastened so that they do not fall into the water, creating an electrical hazard. Be certain, also, that the fixtures in which your lamps are installed can support the wattage of the lamp.

ALERT!

People who maintain aquariums often enjoy keeping other pets as well. If you have any free-ranging pets such as dogs and cats, be sure that they can't knock over lamps or motors. Each year, house fires are started this way.

Floods

Even small aquariums are surprisingly heavy when filled with water and gravel. Be sure to calculate the weight of your aquarium and make sure that the floor below it will support that weight. Also, make sure that the stand or furniture upon which your aquarium will sit can manage the weight of a full aquarium. Floods, especially those caused by large aquariums, can be devastating in terms of property damage to you or your neighbors.

Venomous Animals

The world's fresh and marine waters are well stocked with venomous creatures. As will be mentioned in the various species accounts, the barbs and spines of many species of fish are connected to poison glands, some of which can inject fatal doses of venom. Venomous invertebrates abound as well, and even the highly toxic blue-ringed octopus is offered for sale from time to time.

Avoid keeping venomous animals, even though they may be offered for sale and may appeal to your sense of adventure. Be aware also that not all of the venomous creatures that exist have been identified—some may be unintentionally or unethically offered for sale. Therefore, err on the side of caution in purchasing or handling animals with which you are unfamiliar. Two well-known herpetologists lost their lives after being bitten by snakes formerly believed to be harmless; do not repeat those tragic blunders with your own pets. There are literally millions of bizarre and interesting aquatic creatures that can be kept safely. Think not only of yourself, but of the potential for accidents involving unknowing or reckless individuals as well.

Illness and Disease

Aquatic animals and the water in which they live may harbor microorganisms that are harmful when ingested by people or upon entering a skin wound. Therefore, never clean aquariums or related utensils in sinks that you use to prepare food. Always wash your hands thoroughly after working with your aquarium, and be particularly careful with children. In addition to washing their hands, you must be alert that they do not put anything into their mouths that has had contact with your aquarium or its inhabitants.

Chapter 2

Water and Water Quality

A thorough understanding of the physical characteristics of water and of how water quality affects aquatic life is essential if one is to be a successful aquarist. This is a little difficult for beginners to accept, excited as they often are about the prospect of keeping an array of interesting creatures in their aquariums. It is a common, and almost always fatal, mistake to spend time learning about the habits and dietary needs of aquatic creatures while ignoring the less glamorous aspects of the hobby.

Natural Water

Water, especially seawater, is a highly complex liquid. Although sodium chloride (table salt) is the most abundant compound in natural seawater, trace elements, organic and inorganic compounds, and other chemicals are all present in varying quantities. Seawater and freshwater have calcium carbonate, magnesium sulfate, and elements such as magnesium and zinc. Organic compounds and microorganisms such as plankton give water from different areas unique characteristics.

QUESTION?

Are there certain aquatic creatures that must be kept in natural seawater or freshwater?
Delicate creatures from very isolated habitats (such as caves) where the water has unique chemical characteristics generally do best in water taken from their natural environment. Natural water is useful for raising tiny fry or filter-feeding invertebrates, because it contains the tiny organisms upon which these animals feed.

Although major public aquariums located near the seashore often use natural seawater for their exhibits, this is generally a difficult prospect for the home aquarist. The planktonic organisms found in both freshwater and seawater generally perish in captivity, and their deaths cause harmful chemical changes and an increase in ammonia levels. It is also possible to introduce pathogens, parasites, and disease to your aquarium through the use of natural water. Pollution is, unfortunately, also an overriding concern.

If you do choose to use natural water, collect it from as pristine an area as possible. Generally, seawater collected offshore or from ocean beaches will be safer than that from enclosed areas such as bays and lagoons. The same concept applies to freshwater. Be sure to store the water in containers that have not contained harmful chemicals, which may remain in plastic even after a thorough washing (spring water bottles are a good choice). The safest method of readying the water for the aquarium is to leave it, unfiltered, in a dark area for a week or so, so that the resident microorganisms can die off. Chemical tests should then be performed to determine ammonia levels and pH, and these should be adjusted as necessary. The water should be filtered for at least twenty-four hours before use.

Artificial Seawater and Commercial Freshwater

Fortunately for aquarists, synthetic sea salt mixes are now readily available and provide a very stable and healthy medium in which to raise marine fish and invertebrates. Most come complete with trace elements, which should be replaced periodically per the manufacturer's suggestion.

ALERT!

If you have tap water of poor quality and a large number of aquariums, you might consider the use of a reverse osmosis filter. Salts, minerals, and metals are removed from the water through the use of a fine membrane. These units are, however, quite expensive.

The tap water used to mix the seawater for marine aquariums and for freshwater aquariums must be tested for nitrate and phosphate levels. High levels of either can cause rapid algae blooms. Tap water also contains chemicals such as chloramine and chlorine, which are added to help make the water safe for drinking, but are toxic to many aquatic creatures. Fortunately, commercial preparations that instantly remove both chemicals are readily available. Copper is also toxic to many creatures, particularly invertebrates (copper is often used in medications designed to kill various invertebrate parasites of fish). Water that travels through copper pipes, today usually found only in older buildings, is generally unsuitable for use in aquariums. One alternative if you have tap water of poor quality is to use commercially available spring water. This is generally only an option when you keep a small aquarium. Do not use distilled water, as it is completely free of chemicals and, through the process of osmosis, will cause essential salts and trace elements to leach from the bodies of your pets.

Salinity

The salinity of water is actually an expression of its density, or specific gravity. It is not just a measure of salt, but a reading that expresses the ratio of all of the dissolved salts in the water. Pure water has a specific gravity of 1.000, and the specific gravity of other water is compared to this standard.

Specific gravity is measured with an instrument called a hydrometer. One type of hydrometer is a floating glass tube that rides higher or lower in the water depending upon the specific gravity. The measurement of the specific gravity is read at the water line. Newer types of hydrometers in the form of plastic cases with internal scales are easier to use than are the floating models.

FACT

The specific gravity of water varies with temperature. The original, floating model hydrometers are standardized at a particular temperature, and this needs to be taken into account when using them. A conversion table will be supplied with your hydrometer so that you can make the proper calculation.

Most marine fish survive well at specific gravities of 1.020 to 1.023. Lower specific gravities are gentler on the fish's systems, in terms of maintaining their optimal osmotic body pressure (osmoregulation), but invertebrates generally do not fare well in water with a specific gravity of less than 1.022.

Be sure to research the particular species of fish or invertebrate that you intend to keep in terms of its natural habitat. Animals from estuaries and similar environments may be adapted to specific gravities that are lower than are experienced by purely marine species, due to the influence of freshwater rivers. Such species may also require a fluctuation in the specific gravity if they are to thrive and, especially, if they are to reproduce.

Checking pH

The measurement of water's acidity or alkalinity is called pH. A reading of 7 is termed neutral, with 1 being the most acidic and 14 being the most alkaline readings on the scale. The pH of most seawater hovers around 8, with 8.3 being considered safe for most marine species. In the open ocean, pH is relatively stable, but in aquariums it can change radically, to the detriment of your pets. This holds especially true for coral reef species, because they are adapted to an extremely pH stable environment. Water tends to become acidic due to the respiration of animals (they release carbon dioxide, which becomes carbonic acid). Certain substrates help to mitigate these changes, and these are particularly important in marine aquariums, where an acidic pH is to be avoided. Limestone, dolomite, and coral are very useful in buffering pH changes and in keeping the water on the alkaline side. Effective bacterial filtration is also important in maintaining a stable pH.

Freshwater fish generally do well at a pH near neutral, but many species do best at higher or lower ranges. Freshwater is much less stable than seawater, in terms of pH, and thus it is important to research each freshwater species carefully. Do not to attempt to keep animals from acidic waters with those requiring alkaline conditions.

ALERT!

Ammonia is more toxic to animals at a higher, or alkaline, pH than it is at lower, more acidic levels. Since marine aquarium water is generally maintained at alkaline levels, one must be particularly careful to maintain safe ammonia levels.

The pH of aquarium water will change over time. An accumulation of waste products, uneaten food, and/or dead and decaying plants and animals will lower the pH, while the addition of certain rocks or substrates, such as coral, will cause the water to become more alkaline. Regular monitoring of pH is therefore essential. A number of test kits are available, most of which utilize a color-coded chart that is compared to a water sample that has been treated with a reagent. There are commercial preparations available that will lower or raise the pH of your aquarium, or help to set it at a specific level. While these can be useful in certain situations, it should be noted that the most important factor is to monitor the reason behind the pH changes in your aquarium. Merely correcting the pH without removing the underlying cause of the change will mask the problem and, in the end, will do more harm than good. Also, be sure to make all pH changes very gradually. An animal being maintained in an improper pH may die if suddenly switched to the correct pH without adequate time to adjust.

Fish and other animals that are stressed due to an inappropriate pH level may react by swimming rapidly about, or, in the case of amphibians, by attempting to leave the water. They will also be active at times when they normally would be resting. Eventually, they will become listless and die. Be sure to monitor your animals carefully and learn their normal behaviors so that you can detect such changes.

Oxygen

As a general rule, marine animals are adapted to waters with high levels of dissolved oxygen. Ocean environments are usually well oxygenated by the movement of water and waves and by the large surface area of water that is exposed to the air. Exceptions exist, as in the case of isolated bays and lagoons that do not experience a great deal of water circulation. Freshwater habitats vary more widely in terms of dissolved oxygen levels. Some freshwater fish, such as the lungfish, obtain most of their oxygen from the atmosphere, not from the water.

Aeration occurs when oxygen from the air enters the water at its surface. That fact may, in some cases, influence the shape of aquarium that you want to buy. A long, low aquarium will allow for a greater exchange of oxygen than will a high, narrow aquarium, despite the fact that both may hold the same amount of water. Of course, mechanical aeration can be used to overcome the limitations of tank shape.

The exchange of oxygen is facilitated by water movement. In the aquarium, this movement is created by the flow of water exiting from the filter or by the bubbles that arise from air circulated by a motorized pump through porous aerating devices known as "air stones." The oxygen that is contained in the bubbles created by air stones or other forms of mechanical filtration is lost to the air and does not add to the dissolved oxygen content of the water. By disturbing the water surface, these bubbles and other forms of water movement create turbulence, which allows atmospheric oxygen to dissolve into the water.

When considering how to aerate your aquarium, bear in mind that many aquatic animals are adapted to quiet waters. These species will likely be stressed by strong water currents, because they are unable to feed or swim properly under these circumstances. On the other hand, fish from areas of strong water movement, such as coral reef species, generally require strong aeration and are quite comfortable with fast-moving water. Such species will generally have high oxygen requirements and will perish without proper aeration. Most filters on the market today allow you to control the rate of water outflow into the aquarium, thus enabling you to tailor water turbulence to the nature of the animal that is being kept. For those species that require less water movement, air stones operated by small pumps may be used to provide oxygenation without disturbing the animals.

ESSENTIAL

A power outage that shuts off aerating devices can wipe out your collection. Be sure to have a sufficient number of battery-operated aerators equipped with air stones for use in emergencies. Previously only available in bait stores (used to keep bait fish alive on fishing trips), battery-operated aerators are increasingly being sold in aquarium stores as well.

The ability of water to hold dissolved oxygen is affected by the temperature of the water. Cool water is able to hold more oxygen than warm water. For this reason, be sure to research carefully the habitats from which your pets originate, as those from temperate waters will generally have higher oxygen requirements than will those from tropical waters. Again, there are exceptions to this rule, as in the case of warm-water fish that nonetheless live in areas of moving water that are rich in dissolved oxygen.

You should also keep in mind that the beneficial bacteria in your aquarium and in the filter materials are aerobic, meaning that they require oxygen to survive. The flow of oxygenated water through these materials must be of sufficient strength to support the beneficial bacteria. It is also important that all areas of the filter bed are kept clean, so that water can easily flow through. The buildup of organic material and other detritus will block water flow, creating stagnant pockets where harmful anaerobic bacteria can take hold.

Temperature

As with all water parameters, it is important that you understand your pet's natural environment when considering water temperature. Most marine species have evolved in environments of fairly stable water temperatures. Tropical fish, especially, may experience little in the way of temperature fluctuation in their natural habitats and are not adequately equipped to deal with such in captivity. Even species that live in temperate climates and are therefore subjected to seasonal temperature variations do not fare well when exposed to rapid or frequent changes in captivity. Many temperate species move offshore during times of very cold or hot weather and thus are able to moderate the effect of the seasons.

FACT

Recent research has shown that certain large, active oceanic fish, such as tuna and some sharks, and the leatherback turtle, are able to generate internal body heat. The process is different from that utilized by endothermic, or warm-blooded, animals like birds and mammals, but it does allow these species to enter cold waters where they might not otherwise survive.

Fish and invertebrates are ectothermic, or cold-blooded, and as such are unable to internally regulate their body temperatures. They, like amphibians and reptiles, must instead rely upon behavioral changes to modify the effects of temperature upon their bodies. Free-living animals can move away from areas of unsuitable temperature or burrow into the substrate to escape unfavorable conditions. In captivity, aquatic animals are very limited in their ability to behaviorally regulate their temperature, and so it falls to the pet keeper to be sure that optimum conditions are maintained.

Many fish and other aquatic animals are stimulated to breed by seasonal temperature changes. In captivity, such changes can be mimicked through the use of an aquarium heater's thermostat. The best way of doing this is to study the seasonal variations in temperature in the animal's natural habitat, and to duplicate these changes in the aquarium. Be aware, though, that sudden temperature changes will lead to shock in many species, and also to an infestation by opportunistic parasites that are able to take advantage of the fish's temporarily weakened immune systems.

Unfortunately, aquarium thermometers do not give an indication of impending failure. For temperature sensitive species, thermometer failure during cold weather can lead to illness or death. For this reason, you should always install a second thermometer in your aquarium. This thermometer should be set to the lowest acceptable temperature for the species that you are keeping. In this way, it will come on automatically if the main heater fails.

Keep in mind when monitoring temperature that the metabolism of most aquatic animals increases as the water temperature rises. This, coupled with the fact that warm water holds less oxygen than does cool water, necessitates care on the aquarist's part during periods of hot weather. It may be necessary to increase aeration during these times.

The Nitrogen Cycle

The nitrogen cycle is a critical factor in the establishment of a crystal clear, well-balanced aquarium. This phenomenon is, however, little understood by aquarists. Poor functioning of the nitrogen cycle upon establishing a new aquarium is undoubtedly the most common reason for later failures and losses of animals.

In simplified terms, the nitrogen cycle is the conversion of nitrogen to several organic compounds that are then utilized by various organisms as food. Nitrogen enters aquatic systems via dead animals and plants, uneaten food, and the excretory products of animals. The most toxic nitrogenous compound that is added to aquariums in this matter is ammonia. Ammonia exists in aquatic environments in two forms: ionized ammonia and un-ionized ammonia. The un-ionized compound is extremely toxic to aquatic organisms, and its proportion of the total ammonia increases as temperature rises and as the water becomes more alkaline.

The Role of Bacteria

Two basic types of bacteria control the functioning of the nitrogen cycle. Both of these bacteria species are aerobic, which means that they require oxygen to survive and reproduce. The bacteria develop and thrive on substrates that are exposed to oxygenated water, most especially in the various materials used in aquarium filters, and on the walls of the filters themselves.

The process by which these bacteria convert ammonia to less-harmful compounds basically occurs in two parts. Nitrosomas spp. convert ammonia to compounds known as nitrites. Nitrites, while still dangerous to aquatic life, are less toxic than is ammonia. In the second stage of the process, bacteria of the genus Nitrobacter use the nitrites as food, thus converting them to nitrates. Nitrates are the end product of the nitrogen cycle and are the least toxic of the compounds involved.

Nitrogenous bacteria exist in huge populations in nature and in healthy aquariums. Until such populations are established, the levels of all nitrogen-based compounds in the aquarium will be toxic to most fish and invertebrates.

ALERT!

Water clarity is not a suitable indicator of the functioning of the nitrogen cycle. Ammonia, the most toxic of the nitrogenous compounds, is colorless and odorless and does not cloud the water. The only safe way of monitoring the cycle is frequent testing of the water to determine the levels of ammonia, nitrates, and nitrites.

The period of time from the setting up of the aquarium until the establishment of healthy populations of aerobic, nitrogenous bacteria is often referred to as the conditioning period. As a general rule, one can expect this period to last from one month to six weeks. However the actual timetable varies greatly depending upon the unique characteristics of each aquarium and of the inhabitants therein.

Altering the Nitrogen Cycle

You can shorten the amount of time it takes to condition your aquarium by adding live aerobic bacteria that are now available at pet stores. The freeze-dried and liquid forms seem to work equally well. Alternatively, you can introduce used filter material from a well-conditioned tank into the filter of your new aquarium. Be sure to use material from healthy tanks only, as parasites or their eggs may be present in the filter beds of infected tanks. Natural materials such as rocks or sand often contain beneficial bacteria and offer another option. In the past, it was standard practice to use hardy fish, such as domino damselfish in marine aquariums or guppies in freshwater aquariums, to help hasten the conditioning period. The waste products produced by these fish provide the ammonia necessary to start and maintain the process. Today, however, you can purchase additives that provide food for the bacteria. This is both more effective and infinitely kinder than attempting to use fish to jump-start the process, as most fish subjected to this process did not survive.

When cleaning your filters and changing the filter material, always retain a bit of the old material to add to the clean filtering material. In this way, you will introduce aerobic bacteria into the new filter. These will reproduce rapidly and greatly increase the effectiveness of the filtration.

While commercially available bacteria can be helpful, they do not eliminate the need for a proper conditioning period. The water quality must still be monitored carefully, and new animals should be introduced to the aquarium carefully and in small numbers.

Measuring the Levels of Nitrogenous Compounds

Chemical test kits are essential during (and after) the conditioning period. Ammonia should be tested daily until you notice a rapid decrease. This decrease signals the presence of Nitrosomas bacteria. Nitrate levels will then follow the same pattern once the Nitrobacter bacteria become established. Be sure to regularly check the pH level during the conditioning period, as the water may become acidic at this time. The conditioning period may be considered at an end when the nitrate levels drop substantially. At this point you may begin to introduce fish and invertebrates into their new home. It is still safest to add animals in small quantities, so as not to overwhelm the nitrifying potential of the bacteria present. Observe the new animals and make further additions carefully.

Chapter 3

Filtering Your Aquarium

Filtration is the method by which you maintain the clarity and purity of aquarium water, thereby increasing your chances of success in keeping aquatic animals. Filtration in natural situations is accomplished through the actions of a variety of plants and animals and microorganisms that utilize the waste products and dead bodies of other creatures. While some of these natural processes can be duplicated to a limited extent in the aquarium, you must, except in very unique circumstances, incorporate artificial processes and mechanical equipment as well.

Filtration in General

As you may imagine, the functioning of natural processes such as decomposition and the nitrogen cycle are greatly altered within the confines of a home aquarium. Therefore, a variety of artificial methods, some based upon natural systems, have been developed to maintain the health and vigor of saltwater and freshwater animals kept in captivity.

There are three basic types of filtration available to the aquarist:

- Biological
- Chemical
- Mechanical

Each method of filtration fulfills a specific role, although there is some overlap among them. Of the three types of filtration, biological filtration is by far the most important. If this aspect of the filtration system is not working effectively it will be nearly impossible to keep any but the very hardiest of fish or invertebrates alive. Basically, biological filtration is closely linked to the nitrogen cycle, which is the process through which ammonia and other nitrogenous compounds are rendered less toxic through the action of nitrogenous bacteria (as explained in detail in Chapter 2). Some degree of biological filtration may be achieved with nearly any filter, and several types, such as fluidized bed filters and trickle filters, utilize this method of filtration nearly exclusively.

Mechanical filtration refers to the physical removal of suspended materials from the water. This is accomplished by using a mechanical pump to move the water through materials such as filter floss, pads, or sand. These materials act to trap the suspended particles and must, of course, be periodically rinsed so that they can function at full capacity. Outside and box filters are the best mechanical filters, but nearly all filters perform some degree of particulate removal.

ALERT!

Follow the manufacturer's recommendations about the replacement of the activated carbon in your filter. When activated carbon has exhausted its potential in removing harmful materials, it begins to leach these substances back into the aquarium. This can cause the death of fish and invertebrates, especially if it occurs at a rapid rate.

The removal of proteins and other dissolved organic materials from aquarium water is accomplished using chemical filtration. Such materials impart a yellowish tinge to the water, and their presence creates an unhealthy environment for aquatic animals. A variety of materials have chemical filtration potential. Perhaps the most common is activated carbon, which is extremely effective at maintaining water clarity. Other commercially available products can be utilized to remove ammonia and nitrates from the water. Box filters, outside filters, and most others can accommodate various chemical filtration substances.

Live Rock, Live Sand, and Algae

Before you examine the various types of filters available, you should be aware of what might be called natural filtration systems. The term live rock refers to rocks that have been colonized by various algae, filter-feeding animals, bacteria, worms, sponges, and other flora and fauna. Even a very small piece of rock can harbor a multitude of such creatures.

Live Rock

Live rock provides a few benefits for the inhabitants of your tank. Some filtration is accomplished by the nitrifying bacteria inhabiting the rocks, while the larger species on the rocks assist by metabolizing the waste products of the other inhabitants of the aquarium and by consuming detritus and particulate matter. Some of the animals and plants on live rock may also reproduce in the aquarium, providing a supplementary food source for filter-feeding invertebrates.

Because live rock contains living organisms, it must be introduced carefully into the aquarium. You should test your water for ammonia for a period of time after the introduction of live rock, as tiny creatures may die within the rock and pollute your aquarium. The use of live rock has been most closely studied in marine aquariums, but the same basic principles apply to freshwater systems as well.

Only purchase live rock that has been commercially farmed. The collection of rock and coral is a serious environmental problem that threatens the survival of many species. Also, certain rocks can leach compounds or minerals that can quickly poison animals within the confines of an aquarium. This is less likely to occur if you use farmed rock.

Live Sand

Live sand is similar to live rock in that it is introduced into the aquarium with a full compliment of tiny creatures such as worms, crustaceans, and sand hoppers. Filtration systems that utilize live sand as the sole substrate for the aquarium are sometimes referred to as plenum systems. Occasionally, large outside filters are modified to contain a separate chamber for live sand or live rock. This somewhat lessens the amount of waste material that actually comes in contact with the sand or rock, but it does prevent the aquarium's larger inhabitants from consuming the tiny beneficial creatures that dwell in the sand.

Algae for Filtration

Macroalgae, commonly but erroneously referred to as seaweed, utilizes nitrates, phosphates, and carbon dioxide in its metabolism. Healthy populations of various algae species can go a long way in improving water quality. An algae scrubber is a separate container to house the algae that is used for filtration. Water from the aquarium is directed through this chamber and back into the tank, much in the manner of any other filter. Whether grown in the aquarium itself or in a separate chamber, marine algae require a good deal of light at specific wavelengths. Be sure to purchase lamps specifically designed for growing such plants. Judicious pruning of the plants will encourage new growth and ensure that the uptake of nitrates and phosphates continues at a high level. In freshwater aquariums, plants and algae perform the same role as does marine macroalgae.

Natural filtration methods such as live rock, live sand, and algae are most effectively used as supplemental filtration systems. Although quite a few privately owned aquariums, and even some public aquariums, have been successful in relying almost entirely on natural filtration, such an undertaking is risky at best and should only be attempted by experienced aquarists or professionals. Your first efforts in this area should be with a very small number of hardy creatures in as large an aquarium as possible.

Outside Filters

Outside filters generally take the form of boxlike structures that hang onto the back or side of the aquarium or canisters that rest on the floor below. Water is drawn via an internal motor through a series of filter mediums. In the process, it undergoes biological, chemical, and mechanical filtration. The mechanical filtration—that is, the removal of large particles—is carried out by a number of porous materials such as filter pads, floss, or various cartridges. This is the first step in the filtering process. After this, the water is propelled through activated carbon or other materials that serve as chemical filters. The flow of oxygenated water through the filter material allows for the growth of beneficial aerobic bacteria, thereby providing biological filtration (the breakdown of ammonia to nitrates and nitrates). As mentioned earlier, it is important to replace the chemical filter materials regularly so that harmful chemicals do not leach back into the aquarium. Likewise, the mechanical aspects of the filter must be kept clean so that water can flow throughout the entire system. If blockages develop, the beneficial aerobic bacteria will perish. This interrupts filtration and, if it occurs on a large scale, can quickly raise the ammonia content of the water to dangerous levels. The outflow of water back into the aquarium disturbs the surface and allows for the oxygenation of the water by mixing it with atmospheric oxygen. Most of the newer models of outside filters have diffusers or other means of regulating the outflow of water or directing it to certain areas of the aquarium. This is useful in creating currents that will disturb otherwise neglected areas of the tank, keeping sediments afloat where they can be collected by the filter's intake system.

ALERT!

Always rinse filter materials well before adding them to your filter. Many, especially activated carbon, contain a great deal of dust and will cloud your aquarium water if used straight from the box.

When cleaning filters, it is important to retain some of the old filter material, and to add this to the new when the filter is refilled. The beneficial bacteria contained on the old material will reproduce rapidly and increase the filter's effectiveness. Also, when cleaning the filter box itself, use temperate as opposed to hot water, so as not to kill the bacteria that have become established on the inner surfaces of the filter.

Wet/Dry or Trickle Filters

Originally developed for public aquariums exhibiting tropical reef-dwelling organisms, smaller versions of these effective filters are now marketed for use by hobbyists. The mechanical part of the filtration process is performed by a pad or other material through which the water first passes. The main role of the wet/dry filter, however, is in biological filtration. The area upon which the beneficial bacteria can grow is increased through the use of materials with a large surface area. Most recently, ceramic tubes or partially hollow plastic balls, called bio balls have been used for this purpose. These materials are not submerged, but rather a trickle or spray of water from the aquarium is directed over them. Nitrifying bacteria grow so well in a well-managed wet/dry system that their nitrate production can actually be detrimental to the aquarium's inhabitants. This danger can be lessened by the installation of another chamber that supports anaerobic bacteria. These bacteria convert nitrates, the end product of the nitrogen cycle, to nitrous oxide and free nitrogen. The free nitrogen is then lost to the atmosphere.

Fluidized Bed Filters and Protein Skimmers

Fluidized bed filters work on the same basic principle as do under gravel filters, which they have largely replaced. The unit is a plastic tube that hangs on the outside of the aquarium. The tube is partially filled with sand, through which the aquarium's water is propelled at a fairly high rate. Kept in constant motion, the sand provides an enormous surface upon which the beneficial bacteria can grow. Bacteria growth is further supported by the high oxygen environment within the filter. These filters are strongly recommended for all types of aquariums, and many experienced aquarists consider them a near necessity in the establishment of large marine systems.

Protein skimmers, also know as foam fractionators, rely upon a process known as desaturation to remove organic materials from water. Proteins and other organic materials are attracted to air bubbles that are forced into the protein skimmer. After combining with the bubbles, these materials congeal, forming a surface foam that is then carried to a separate chamber, where it is easily collected and discarded.

Ozone Generators

Ozone generators are another of the advanced forms of water purification that were originally developed for use in public aquariums and that have now been modified for use by home aquarists. Ozone is an unstable form of oxygen, created by energizing air with an electrical current. This process takes place in a machine known as an ozonizer. The extra oxygen atom that ozone contains separates from the ozone molecule and oxidizes microorganisms, thereby killing them. It also breaks down a large number of organic compounds that are routinely found in aquarium water.

The use of an ozone generator might be seen as a safety measure, but not as a requirement, unless you maintain large numbers of aquariums and frequently introduce new specimens. They are, however, a fairly standard item in commercial aquariums and are quite useful to fish wholesalers and importers. In both of these situations, the constant influx of new animals greatly increases the likelihood of the introduction of pathogens and parasites.

FACT

Ozone gas is highly toxic to fish and invertebrates. Water leaving an ozone generator must be passed through activated carbon before it is returned to the aquarium. The specifics of this process will depend upon a number of factors, so the manufacturer's guidelines should be strictly followed.

The effectiveness of ozone in destroying so many types of microorganisms and pathogens is offset by the fact that it is a dangerous gas to use. Ozone is only recommended for serious, adult aquarists with a great deal of experience. Always be sure to follow the manufacturer's directions carefully and seek the advice of seasoned professionals when handling ozone. The gas is also quite destructive to many of the materials that are used in home aquarium, such as plastic and rubber, so be sure to plan for this when installing an ozone generator.

Ultraviolet Sterilizers

Ultraviolet sterilizers are extremely effective in killing most types of bacteria and algae spores. More advanced models can also be used to sterilize aquarium water so that it is free of nearly all disease-causing organisms. When used for the treatment of disease, the sterilizer should be used continually for the entire lifespan of the microorganism being targeted, as ultraviolet light may not kill the eggs of certain parasites. A similar guideline applies to many medications, in that most kill the free-living forms of parasites, but not the eggs or spores.

Ultraviolet sterilizers rely on the use of an ultraviolet lamp, which is housed within a quartz sleeve. Water circulating around the sleeve is irradiated with the light and the organisms are killed. Water should be prefiltered before it enters the ultraviolet sterilizer so that suspended organic material doesn't diminish the light's effectiveness in reaching the desired targets. It also should be noted that, much like many fluorescent lamps, the ultraviolet lamp will remain lit long after its effective life, or the time period during which it emits ultraviolet light, has expired. Therefore, always strictly follow the manufacturer's guidelines as to the effective lifespan of the lamp, and be sure to replace it as recommended.

ALERT!

Ultraviolet light is very harmful to the eyes, and the lamp must never be viewed without appropriate eye protection. Ultraviolet sterilizers are equipped with viewing ports that allow you to safely determine if the light is on and the unit is functioning properly. Never circumvent this safety measure by attempting to open the unit.

Box Filters

Although often viewed as primitive by modern-day hobbyists, box filters have much value and should be considered in certain circumstances. Box filters sit within the aquarium, on the bottom, and are powered by a motorized air pump. Filter floss, or a porous filter pad, functions as the mechanical stage of filtration, while activated carbon or other materials can be used to chemically filter the water. Nitrifying bacteria develop on the filter floss and other filter materials, allowing for effective biological filtration.

Most box filters that are currently available are fairly small, a fact that limits their use to specific situations. Also, because they sit within the aquarium, such filters do detract from the aquarium's overall appearance. Box filters are, however, very useful in quarantine aquariums. In these situations, aesthetic considerations do not matter as much as does function, and these simple filters are easily cleaned. Another useful aspect is that airflow from the pump to the filter can easily be controlled by the use of a mechanical gang valve. This allows you to control the flow rate of the water and air leaving the filter. This is especially useful in situations where you are raising small fish fry or other delicate creatures that will be disturbed by strong currents. Also, because the current is directed upward, large portions of the aquarium water will remain undisturbed and calm.

Sponge Filters

Sponge filters utilize porous, spongelike materials connected to air pumps to perform chemical and biological filtration. Newer models can be fitted with small canisters containing activated carbon, thereby allowing for chemical filtration as well. Suspended materials are removed as water is drawn through the sponge, and the porous surface of the filter allows for the development of huge populations of beneficial nitrifying bacteria.

Much like box filters, sponge filters find their main use in quarantine tanks, where activated carbon and other materials that remove medications from the water cannot be used. They are also quite useful when you are raising small fry or species that require weak water currents. As with box filters, the exiting flow of water and air is directed upward, and the rate of such is easily manipulated through the use of gang valves. When tiny live food items such as newly hatched brine shrimp are used, the airflow can be lessened, so that the food is not drawn into the filter. This is a distinct advantage in raising the young of live-food specialists (animals that eat live food) such as pipefish (see color insert for photo) and seahorses, and in maintaining filter-feeding invertebrates.

Modified sponge filters are available with submersible motors attached. These are more effective at circulating larger volumes of water than are traditional sponge filters, but they do create strong currents. Such filters are, however, quite easy to clean and maintain and are useful in quarantine and hospital tanks and for livestock importers.

Diatom Filters

Usually designed as external canisters with strong motors, diatom filters utilize the fossilized remains of tiny organisms, known as diatoms, as a filter medium. This medium is referred to as diatomaceous earth. The unit's motor forces water through the diatomaceous earth at a high rate, removing even the tiniest bits of suspended matter. Water leaving the filter is exceptionally clear. Most diatomaceous earth filters are equipped with powerful motors that allow for a rapid turnover of aquarium water. This, combined with the extreme effectiveness of the filtration provided, leads many to use such filters on an occasional basis only. Their only drawback is that they clog quickly, because so much material is removed in a very short time.

Most diatom filters are equipped with a reverse flush, which is a system that allows for easy cleaning of the unit. Even so, they generally should not be utilized for long periods of time, especially if they can't be regularly monitored. Diatom filters are, however, useful adjuncts to any filtration system, especially in large aquariums, and are indispensable during emergencies.

Resin Filters

Resin filters are designed for specific functions, the most common being the removal of nitrates or phosphates. The resins are contained in canisters that attach to the outside of the aquarium or sit below it. Water is pumped through the filter, where the resins absorb the nitrates or phosphates. The resins must be replaced or recharged as per the manufacturer's instructions. Recharging the resins often involves the use of toxic chemicals, a process best left to professionals.

Any change to aquarium water should be made gradually. Powerful filtration methods such as resin filters may radically change the chemical nature of aquarium water in a relatively short period of time. While this change may result in a healthier environment for your pets, they may become stressed and die without time to adjust.

For home use, it is preferable to replace saturated resins. You must carefully consider the type of animals in your tank when deciding upon the use of resin filters, or, for that matter, any filtration system. Resin filters, for example, can so completely deplete nitrates and phosphates that certain organisms that rely upon these nutrients will die. They should not, therefore, be used on tanks containing coral, except for short-term use during water quality emergencies. If used regularly, the symbiotic algae required by most corals may perish in the resulting nutrient-poor water.

Other Considerations

In addition to the points already discussed, a number of other factors will determine what type of filtration you should use, and the specifics of its actual employment. For example, you should bear in mind that certain powerful filters, such as protein skimmers, and materials such as activated carbon will effectively remove fish medication from the water. It may, therefore, be necessary to isolate sick animals or to disconnect such filtration during the medication period.

Equally important is the effect of certain filtration methods upon trace elements. We have already mentioned that phosphates and nitrates, while harmful to some creatures in high concentrations, are required by certain algae for their survival. Likewise, a wide variety of minerals, trace elements, and other substances are utilized by many creatures in tiny amounts or, perhaps, only at certain times. Unfortunately, little is known about the specifics of the use of these materials or the exact amounts needed by aquatic animals. Therefore, it is prudent to routinely add commercially available trace elements, especially in marine aquariums, following the manufacturer's guidelines. You may need to do some calculation, and even some educated guessing, to fine-tune the amounts needed in your specific situation. The important point to bear in mind is that trace elements are constantly being removed from your aquarium by the metabolisms of the creatures that live therein, and that the use of certain types of filtration can accelerate this process.

FACT

No matter how effectively your filtration system operates, regular water changes must remain a basic component of your water quality maintenance schedule. Water changes will completely eliminate certain harmful conditions and will also make your filter's job easier, thereby increasing the effectiveness of your filtration system in general.

The type of filter that will be most advantageous is also determined by the specific natural histories of the creatures that you keep. Animals that are notoriously slow to feed or that eat small amounts throughout the day, such as seahorses, will not fare well in an aquarium with a strong filter that quickly removes all the food items from the water column. Likewise, animals that are weak swimmers or those from placid waters will be stressed by strong currents.

Where strong currents can be tolerated, submersible powerheads can be used to create these currents in specific areas of your aquarium. Their location can also be changed regularly to ensure that uneaten food and other debris does not accumulate in undisturbed areas of the aquarium. Strong, alternating currents will stir up such material so that the filter can remove it.

Chapter 4

Light and Heat

When it comes to deciding how to heat and light your aquariums, the factors you must consider are more complicated than merely providing a means to see your animals and finding a device to keep them warm enough, or cool enough, to survive. Of course those considerations are important, but, as you will see in this chapter, creating a proper environment for your pets will encourage normal behavior, reduce stress, and render breeding successes more likely.

Photoperiods in Nature

There are dramatic differences in the light cycles, or photoperiods, experienced by the many types of fish and other aquatic creatures that you might choose to keep. Animals living near the equator are adapted to fairly stable cycles of twelve hours of bright sunlight and twelve hours of darkness each day, while temperate species experience drastically changing amounts of daylight throughout the year.

The intensity of the light required by various animals is also a matter of great importance. Animals from shallow freshwaters or coral reefs will generally require very bright light, while nocturnal species or those living in sheltered waters may be quite stressed by even moderate amounts of light. As you have learned by examining other facets of your hobby, the best way to keep your animals properly is to learn as much as you can about their life histories.

Once you know your animals' light requirements, it is relatively easy to create the proper photoperiod. Light timers can be used to mimic a natural day-night cycle. It is also advisable to provide periods that correspond to dawn and dusk. This can be accomplished by setting a timer to allow a dim lamp to come on before the main lamps, and to remain on after they have been shut off. Alternatively, a room light can be timed to come on and go off an hour or so before and after the main aquarium lights. In addition to providing a more naturalistic environment for your pets, this system will ensure that sensitive animals will not be shocked by a bright light suddenly flooding a dark aquarium.

Lighting in General

Light bulbs are more properly termed lamps. While your lighting choices are significant no matter what type of marine animals you are caring for, the proper quality of light is especially important to those who keep marine invertebrates.

Invertebrate Lighting Requirements

Hard corals are, in general, the most sensitive of the invertebrates in terms of their need for specific light wavelengths. These and other invertebrates often rely upon simple algae known as zooxanthella for their food supply. These algae are extremely sensitive and will not grow unless provided with light of a suitable intensity and wavelength.

ESSENTIAL

Few specifics are known concerning the light requirements of most aquatic animals. You should, therefore, err on the side of caution and provide full-spectrum light in natural cycles. The absence of such may help explain the poor captive breeding records of many creatures.

Fish and Lighting

Those seeking to keep freshwater or marine fish and not invertebrates still need to be concerned about light, but less so. Although intensity and wavelength will not likely be as important as it is for marine invertebrates, fish certainly do best when provided with a lighting regime that approximates that of their natural habitat. As a safeguard, natural photoperiods should be provided if breeding is desired.

The Qualities of Light

The main qualities of light that you need to know about when setting up and maintaining your aquariums are the color temperature, intensity, and wavelength. Each of these qualities should be considered, and what products you choose will depend on the types of marine animals you have.

Light Color Temperature

The color temperature of light is expressed in degrees Kelvin, with a higher reading describing light that appears to be white and a lower reading corresponding to light that appears red or yellow in color. Light shining into water is filtered out by the water at varying rates, depending upon its color temperature. Red light is filtered out first, while green and blue light penetrate the water more deeply than do other colors. Modern lamp manufacturers take these factors into consideration in designing their products, so that your animals and plants can be shown to their greatest advantage.

Light Intensity

Light intensity is measured in units called lumens. Light intensity is important to consider for viewing purposes and is critical to the survival of hard corals and certain other marine invertebrates. Plants also have specific light requirements and will only thrive if provided with light of suitable intensity. Light intensity is not, as is commonly believed, related to the wattage of the bulb in question. Wattage merely expresses the amount of electricity that is needed to turn the lamp on.

Light Wavelength

The wavelength of the light entering the aquarium is also of critical importance in maintaining plants, marine invertebrates and macroalgae. The effect of wavelength on the health of fish has not been well studied, but it is likely that future research will reveal it to be a consideration for many of these creatures.

Types of Lamps

The aquarium hobbyist today is presented with an almost overwhelming number of options when it comes to lighting the aquarium. Fortunately, most manufacturers take great care in describing the qualities of their lamps. Bearing in mind the considerations that have already been discussed, such as photoperiod, wavelength, and light intensity, it should be relatively easy to locate a lamp that suits your particular needs.

Metal Halide Lamps

Metal halide lamps are mainly used in saltwater aquariums, and their introduction into the hobby has revolutionized the keeping of marine animals, particularly light-sensitive hard corals. These lamps provide the high-intensity light necessary for many creatures that originate on coral reefs. The use of metal halides is particularly important in deep tanks where the lighting from even the strongest fluorescent tubes would be nearly filtered out before it reaches the bottom of the aquarium. Light entering the aquarium is lost in a number of ways, including through the glass, through refraction from the water's surface, through diffusion by particles in the water, and through a loss of intensity by absorption into the water, where it is converted into heat energy. Properly sized metal halide lamps largely eliminate these considerations.

FACT

Metal halide lamps that emit light in the range of 10,000 to 14,000 degrees Kelvin are the best choice for most marine aquariums. Marine fish and invertebrates display colors to their best advantage within these ranges.

An additional benefit of metal halide lamps, and other lamps of high intensity, is that the growth of potentially harmful dark green and red algae is discouraged. These types of algae thrive only in dim light. Once established, they spread rapidly, and they frequently smother coral and other sessile invertebrates.

The disadvantages of metal halide lamps are the relatively high cost and the huge amount of heat that they generate, but their price has begun to drop as more and more aquarists purchase them and additional manufacturers enter the field. Concerning heat, it is essential that strict safety precautions be in place. All flammable material should be kept far from these lamps, and children must be prevented from touching them. Metal halide lamps are generally suspended at least 12 inches above the aquarium so that the heat generated does not adversely affect the aquarium's water temperature. It is imperative that they be installed by a professional, because poorly anchored lamps can fall into the aquarium and cause an electrical hazard.

Be sure that your aquarium's lamp is installed in an aluminum aquarium reflector. Well-designed reflectors will deflect up to 50 percent of the lamp's light back into the aquarium.

Fluorescent Lamps

There have been great advances in the development of fluorescent lamps for aquarium use in recent years. Several models are now available that provide the light wavelengths most suitable for plant growth in both freshwater and marine aquariums. One of the most useful lamps for marine aquariums is the triphosphor lamp. These emit light in the wavelengths required by most invertebrates and macroalgae, and they are calibrated to take into consideration the effect of the changes in intensity that light experiences as it travels through water.

ALERT!

Be sure to read the manufacturer's guidelines concerning your lamp's effective life. Many lamps will remain lit after they have ceased producing light of wavelengths suitable for plant and invertebrate health. A triphosphor lamp, however, retains all of its qualities until the lamp itself no longer functions.

Actinic blue fluorescent lamps produce the ultraviolet light that is required by many invertebrates and possibly by fish as well. They are also very useful for nighttime viewing of your aquarium's inhabitants. The presence of a blue light does not seem to disturb the animals as they go about their nightly activities. Actinic lamps may also be used to create a dawn and dusk period if they are set to go on before and turn off after the aquarium's other lamps.

Temperature

Although temperature was briefly touched upon in the discussion of water quality, a brief overview of the various types of heaters and methods of controlling temperature in the aquarium is essential. In considering temperature, always keep in mind that you will do well to re-create, as closely as possible, the natural temperature cycles that your pets would experience in the wild.

Natural Temperature Cycles

Tropical animals will, as a rule, be adapted to temperatures that vary little from season to season, while animals native to temperate climates are more tolerant of, and may even require, temperatures that vary throughout the year. Certain temperate species may experience enough in the way of temperature fluctuation if their tank is kept at normal room temperatures throughout the year (assuming that the aquarist lives in a temperate climate area). For others, hot and cool cycles may be regulated through the use of aquarium heaters.

Standard Aquarium Heaters

The standard aquarium heater equipped with a thermostat, more properly termed a heaterstat, is familiar to most aquarists. Most of the models available today allow for precise temperature control. Of course, you must choose a heater that is appropriate for the size of your tank. Follow the manufacturer's suggestions regarding appropriate wattage. Remember that the actual amount of water that is in your aquarium will likely be less than the tank's capacity. For example, a 55-gallon aquarium will generally hold considerably less than 55 gallons of water once substrate, rocks, and coral are added.

Large aquarium systems might best be serviced by heaters plumbed directly into the filter's return outlet. Another option is to heat the room containing the aquarium. Supplementary tank heaters can be used for those species that require slightly higher temperatures.

Canister Heaters

Canister filters with heaters already incorporated within the unit are becoming very popular. Many, however, are designed for freshwater use only, because they contain metal parts. Marine animals are quickly poisoned when saltwater comes in contact with most metals, so be sure to check this point carefully before deciding upon a canister heater. A variety of more advanced systems are available for those with complicated or large aquarium systems.

Aquarium heaters do not give any warning of impending failure, so be sure to always include an extra one, set at the lowest acceptable temperature for your animals, within your aquariums. In the event of a failure of the main heater, the supplementary one will come on as the temperature drops. External heat sensors equipped with alarms and computerized systems are also now available for those who desire a safety net or a greater degree of control over the temperature of their aquariums.

Chillers

As will be discussed concerning coldwater aquariums, chillers are now readily available to the aquarist. Be sure to purchase a chiller that is designed for aquarium use, because other types may bring the water into contact with potentially harmful metals or chemicals. Also be sure to check that the unit is appropriate for marine aquariums, because many models are designed for use with freshwater systems only.

Chapter 5

Setting Up Your Aquarium

Perhaps the most important aspect of setting up your aquarium is the initial planning and preparation. Mishaps or failure at this stage of the process are very hard to correct later on. It is, therefore, important that you read about the subject, visit well-run public aquariums, join aquarium societies, and speak with experienced aquarists whenever possible. In this chapter, we will examine the important considerations necessary for success in establishing a freshwater or marine aquarium. Although not absolutely necessary, experience with freshwater aquariums will prove very useful for those seeking to keep marine aquariums.

5

Types of Aquariums

People decide to keep aquariums for a wide variety of reasons, and it is important that you identify those that have compelled you to take up this hobby. If you simply want some beautiful fish to watch after a stressful day at work, you will approach the hobby with a different perspective than someone who wants to breed endangered species or whose main interest is in learning about the secret lives of aquatic invertebrates. Whatever your motivations, the enjoyment you find will no doubt encourage a greater appreciation of aquatic animals and the places they inhabit.

Considering Environmental Stability

Marine habitats usually provide animals with environments of extremely stable conditions, in terms of temperature and water chemistry. Coral reef animals, for example, experience very little in the way of environmental changes. Therefore, these animals have not evolved mechanisms to cope with the often drastic fluctuations in water quality and water chemistry that may occur in the home aquarium. Fish and invertebrates from large rivers or lakes are similarly unsuited to coping with change. For this reason, such creatures may be extremely difficult to keep in captivity unless environmental stability can be guaranteed. Similarly, freshwater animals from unique, isolated habitats, such as caves, will not thrive unless their specific requirements are met in captivity.

Instability in Nature

Animals, both marine and freshwater, that thrive in unstable conditions in the wild are generally resilient creatures in captivity and make excellent first choices for the new hobbyist. In the ocean, such creatures would include those that are found in tidal pools, subjected as they are to daily changes in water depth, temperature, and oxygen levels.

Perhaps the hardiest of all aquarium candidates are freshwater animals that dwell in small freshwater ponds. Such animals have evolved unique methods of coping with the frequent fluctuations in temperature and water chemistry that occur regularly in their native habitats. Consider, for example, lungfish, which withstand drastic changes in water quality and can live under the mud for up to three years without food or water, breathing atmospheric oxygen only.

ALERT!

The incredible advances made recently in aquarium life-support systems, may, in some ways, hinder the new aquarist. With so much high-tech equipment available at once, one may miss the basic steps in learning why certain techniques work and others do not. Read about the basics, and consider starting simple setups before attempting more complex aquariums.

Aquarium Size

You should also consider the time and expense that aquarium ownership and maintenance will entail. Complex setups generally require much time and maintenance, and marine aquariums will, in general, be more expensive to establish than freshwater tanks. However, remember that larger aquariums confer more stability upon the captive environment. Small changes in water chemistry and the like will be much more drastic in a 10-gallon aquarium as opposed to one that is 55 gallons. In most cases, it is wisest to start with the largest aquarium that you can afford and reasonably maintain. Marine animals are generally more sensitive to environmental changes than most freshwater species. Unless you are keeping only the hardiest of species, it is best to begin with a marine aquarium of at least 40 gallons in size.

Types of Animals and Communities

The type of animals that interest you will also influence the time and expense that you will need to devote to your aquarium. Animals that need to consume a wide variety of tiny, living food items (like pipefish) are more difficult to maintain than are goldfish, which will thrive on a diet of commercially available flakes. Although a well-established community of animals and plants will actually lessen the hobbyist's work in the long run, the initial stages of establishing such systems will take more time and effort than will single-species tanks. Similarly, if you are seeking to keep invertebrates or to keep fish with invertebrates, you will need to spend a good deal of time in research and in observing your pets' interactions with each other.

The Key to Success

It cannot be stressed enough that the hobby should be a source of enjoyment to you, and not a job. Keep this in mind when deciding how to approach aquarium keeping. A system that is manageable and pleasurable will enable you to learn and to share your observations with others. An aquarium that is beyond your means, in terms of expense and expertise, will be a source of frustration and will likely result in the loss of animals and in you abandoning the hobby.

QUESTION?

How many fish can I keep in my aquarium?
The usual rule is that you should allow 4 gallons of water for each 1 inch of fish (excluding the tail). This rule is, however, is extremely general. The true answer will be determined by many factors, including fish species that you keep, tank design, and the nature of your life-support systems.

Aquarium Shape

When considering shape, remember that a large water surface is helpful in allowing for the effective exchange of oxygen and carbon dioxide between the air and the aquarium. In practical terms, this means that long, low tanks will usually allow you to house more animals then will short, high tanks of the same volume. The wide variety of "designer" tanks that are now available can be extremely tempting, but they may not allow for the establishment of suitable environments for most animals. You might consider using such tanks for a particular individual animal or species that is amenable to the tank's shape. A high hexagonal tank, for example, might be planted with eelgrass and stocked with animals such as shrimp and seahorses, or those that will utilize the shape of the tank in their wanderings, such as snails or sea stars.

Glass or Acrylic?

Aquariums are now available in either glass or acrylic. Each of these materials has its advantages and disadvantages. Glass is more likely to break than is acrylic, but it is far less likely to scratch. Acrylic generally provides superior light transmission, but it is usually more expensive than glass.

Those who keep marine aquariums are fortunate in that most of the associated life-support systems are now manufactured in corrosive proof materials. Saltwater spray is, however, extremely corrosive and seems to have a way of spreading from even the tiniest of openings in your aquarium's cover. In establishing a marine aquarium, use only equipment specifically designed for use with saltwater. Be sure that any supplies made of metal or other corrosive materials are kept well away from the aquarium. In the event that you must use metal or other such objects, be sure to paint them with three to four coats of polyurethane varnish and to seek the advice of an expert before attempting to waterproof.

Aquariums for Specific Situations

It is important to consider exactly what type of animals you wish to keep, and your reasons for doing so. The following discussion of aquariums designed for specific purposes, such as mixed-species aquariums, nursery aquariums, or quarantine aquariums, may help you in this regard.

Mixed-Species Aquariums

One of the most fascinating aquarium types is that containing mixed species of fish or mixed species of invertebrates and fish. Often termed community aquariums, such displays can be both beautiful and interesting. The chance to observe the interactions of various groups of different creatures in a setting mimicking their natural habitat is one not to be missed. Unfortunately, many people do not realize that mixing various species complicates aquarium keeping. In no event should animals be selected for their looks or other desirable characteristics. Community aquariums should, ideally, be based on natural assemblages of animals and plants. It is important to consider such factors as territoriality and social structure when establishing such an aquarium. Also, you must realize that animals that coexist in the wild may not necessarily thrive together in captivity.

It is often a bad idea to house animals from different parts of the world in the same aquarium, even if they get along well, because one may be unusually susceptible to minor maladies of the other. Microorganisms that do no harm to an African fish may, for example, kill a related species from South America.

You must also consider the feeding methods of the creatures that you plan to keep together. For example, methodical, live-food specialists such as seahorses will starve to death in aquarium with more active fish, despite the fact that they may live together in peace. Similarly, filter feeders such as clams will need special attention in terms of diet and light in a community aquarium, even if other animals in the aquarium do not directly compete with them.

Quarantine or Hospital Aquariums

Although time-consuming and expensive to set up in the beginning, serious aquarists know the value of having a quarantine aquarium up and running at all times. Especially if you keep delicate, rare, or expensive creatures, you may wish to establish new animals in a separate tank before introducing them to the rest of your collection. The downside of this is that the newly arrived animal must endure two separate acclimatization periods. The stress of this can be lessened if the water chemistry of each aquarium is kept essentially the same.

Although some medications can be used in aquariums housing healthy animals, it is sometimes necessary to remove sick creatures to a separate aquarium to treat them for disease or parasites. Fish medications, especially those designed to kill parasites, will usually be fatal to any invertebrates that you may keep. Such medications may also kill the beneficial bacteria in the filters, resulting in a crash of the entire system.

Nursery Aquariums

It is often nearly impossible to raise baby fish in an aquarium containing adults. Of course, many fish parents protect their eggs and care for the young, but eventually the fry must live on their own. These tiny fish also require different types and quantities of food than do adults. It is therefore often easier to raise baby fish in a separate aquarium. Many young fish have incredibly large appetites and must be constantly surrounded by food that is easily located. In complex setups, they may not be able to obtain all the nourishment that they need. Many do well in fairly simple aquariums with bare bottoms, so that food can easily be found. This is especially true for those species that feed upon living animals like brine shrimp.

Most young fish are weak swimmers and would quickly be swept into the intake tubes of your main aquarium's filters. Sponge filters allow for effective filtration without posing a threat to tiny fish. Also, the outflow of water and air from the filter goes straight up, so that strong currents, which small fish cannot navigate, are avoided. Sponge filters are operated by simple air pumps, and gang valves can be installed to moderate the amount of air entering the filter.

FACT

Most growing fish require huge amounts of food. Baby seahorses, for example, may consume up to 3,000 individual brine shrimp each day. As newly hatched fish are often not very mobile, and are not adept at hunting, they must be literally surrounded by food if they are to thrive.

Specific Habitats

One of the most fascinating undertakings in aquarium keeping is to attempt to re-create a specific habitat within your tank. You might choose an area of particular interest, or a local habitat where you can actually collect what is needed to establish the environment in your aquarium. The list of possibilities is endless—African rift lakes, tidal pools in the northeastern

United States, coral reefs in the Philippines. Any of these will provide life-long opportunities for adventure and enjoyment.

Actually, nearly all animals will do better if they are housed in some approximation of their natural habitat. Some species will not survive at all unless they are kept in fairly natural situations. In attempting to re-create a specific habitat in your aquarium, research and planning is indispensable. Be sure to investigate not just the animals that interest you, but their entire environment as well. Learn all that you can about light cycles, temperature, and the plants and other creatures that influence the daily lives of your prospective pets. The learning process concerning such undertakings is ongoing and may lead you to the establishment of ever more complicated and fascinating habitats.

Aqua-terrariums

In the "Species Accounts" sections of this book (Chapters 7 and 10), you will find some discussion of creatures other than fish and the more traditionally kept invertebrates. Animals such as amphibians and freshwater insects are often well suited to aquariums that incorporate some areas of land in their design. You can easily create such setups using silicon and glass sheets to separate land and water areas. A number of aquariums that incorporate both land and water areas are also commercially available.

If you choose to establish an aqua-terrarium housing amphibians, be aware that frogs and salamanders are quite different creatures from fish. Although many species can be kept with fish, the sizes and temperaments of each must be carefully considered. Most fully aquatic amphibians, in contrast to their relatives, do not require live food but will feed upon commercially available pellets as well.

The amphibian most commonly kept with fish is the African clawed frog (*Xenopus laevis*), a fascinating creature with, unfortunately, a well-developed appetite for small fish. Related aquatic frogs of the genus Hymenochirus are generally quite harmless but require live food and may feed too slowly to compete with most fish.

Most amphibians produce waste in a highly toxic form, so your filtration system must be carefully considered. Also, amphibians such as newts must be given a way to easily climb out of the water. Many are not as effective swimmers as fish and cannot tolerate strong currents. Finally, nearly all amphibians climb well and so must be housed in well-covered enclosures.

Even if you do not intend to house amphibians, you may still find the aqua-terrarium to be of interest. The establishment of a mangrove community within an aquarium offers the opportunity to keep one of the world's most unique fish, the mudskipper. Living in close association with the semiterrestrial mudskipper is a variety of other interesting fish and invertebrates, including fiddler crabs and archerfish. See the chapter on brackish aquariums (Chapter 14) for a more complete discussion of this fascinating habitat.

Trout Holding Tanks

Trout holding tanks are large enclosures equipped with chillers and available from companies that supply trout farms and commercial fisheries. Although not specifically designed as aquariums per se, these enclosures can be quite useful to the serious hobbyist who has the space for a 4- to 6-foot tank. They are equipped with powerful pumps and allow for precise control of water temperature. Most are all plastic with a glass or acrylic front. Trout holding tanks are particularly useful for large, active fish, complicated aqua-terrariums, and for animals requiring cool temperatures.

Location of the Aquarium

An important but often overlooked point in deciding where to locate your aquarium is the strength of the floor upon which it will be placed. An aquarium filled with water and the associated gravel and rocks is an extremely heavy item. Be sure that the floor below your aquarium is suitably reinforced, and, if possible, place the aquarium stand over the support beams.

A 55-gallon aquarium filled with water and gravel will weigh in excess of 600 pounds. Always empty even small aquariums before moving them, because the shifting of the water will place great stress upon the tank.

Breakage and serious injuries commonly occur when water-filled tanks are moved.

The Aquarium Stand

The stand upon which the aquarium sits must be completely level. Even minor irregularities in the surface below the aquarium will cause areas of stress that may eventually fracture. This is especially true of glass aquariums. Ideally, the stand should have adjustable legs to compensate for an uneven floor. You should also place a sheet of cork or foam on top of the aquarium stand to further shield the tank from minor bumps in the stand's surface.

While your aquarium must be situated near a source of electricity, electrical sockets directly below the aquarium are a cause for concern due to water spillage. Try to place your aquarium off to the side of an outlet, and be sure to plan for future electrical needs that will arise if you decide to add equipment to your aquarium.

Water from a cracked aquarium can cause an incredible amount of damage to your home, or to the homes of people that may live below you. It is wise to consider purchasing flood insurance, especially if you keep large numbers of aquariums or tanks that contain a large volume of water.

It is also important to consider the space behind your tank, so you have room for various filters and other life-support systems that need to be installed. Again, it is better to err on the side of allowing extra space so that you can expand in the future.

Light, Vibrations, and Heat

Situating an aquarium near a window can assist in maintaining natural light cycles for locally occurring fish and invertebrates. Be aware, however, that the glass may raise the temperatures to unsafe levels in the summer, and that the additional light may spur the growth of algae. In most cases, it is simpler to use light timers to regulate day-night cycles.

Remember that fish and invertebrates are extremely sensitive to water-borne vibrations and thus will react unfavorably to televisions, stereos, or slamming doors within a room. Also, the sudden opening and closing of a door in close proximity to the tank will startle most animals. Be sure to locate your aquarium away from such sources of disturbance. Consider also that the noise from pumps and other equipment associated with your aquarium may disturb people in the same or the next room.

The room in which your aquarium is situated should, ideally, be equipped with lights that are controlled by dimmers. A light turned on suddenly in a darkened room will startle most aquatic animals, so dimmers should always be used when possible. As an alternative, you can set a timer on a small lamp to go on early in the morning, to allow the animals an adjustment period.

Plants and Coral—Live or Artificial?

Plants and coral are often considered to be mere decorative items by the aquarist, but both are actually living components of the habitat that you establish. Whether to use living or artificial plants and corals will depend upon a variety of factors, including the nature of the animals you have and your degree of experience in aquarium keeping.

Live Plants

Living plants are, of course, interesting in their own right, and their use can result in the establishment of stunning displays. They will also help keep the aquarium clean by utilizing the waste products of the animal inhabitants and will benefit the overall environment by producing oxygen and removing carbon dioxide. Plants can be arranged to fit specific needs within the aquarium, providing, for example, dense shelters for newly hatched fry or sight barriers for shy creatures. Plant roots prevent the gravel from becoming impacted and discourage the formation of potentially dangerous pockets of anaerobic bacteria.

Artificial Plants

Plants, of course, require nutrients and light of a specific wavelength. If you are keeping fish or invertebrates that are not particularly light sensitive, living plants will add additional complications to your aquarium setup. Plastic plants and marine algae are available in a variety of lifelike models. The utilization of artificial plants allows you to create specific effects with a degree of detail that may not be possible with live plants. Artificial plants will take on a more naturalistic appearance when interspersed with live plants, or if you allow green algae to grow on them.

ALERT!

Be sure to use only artificial plants that are specifically manufactured for use in aquariums. Plants designed for decorative use may have internal wire supports that will eventually rust and poison the water in your aquarium.

Live Coral

Coral, like plants, can be utilized in a living or nonliving form in the aquarium. However, the decision to use live coral must not be made lightly. Coral animals are living creatures that survive by filtering microscopic food particles from the water, and their maintenance in home aquariums is a science in and of itself. Most coral animals are extremely delicate and require excellent water quality and very specific types of food and light. In general, you should only consider keeping live coral if you are an experienced marine aquarist.

Coral Skeletons

Coral skeletons, on the other hand, may be used to great advantage in saltwater aquariums. However, many countries, including the United States and Australia, prohibit the collecting of any form of coral. People in Indonesia, the Solomon Islands, and other locations are now beginning to farm coral. The collection of coral and coral skeletons has caused environmental havoc in many parts of the world and should be strictly avoided. The fact that coral skeletons are offered for sale in a store or online does not guarantee that their ownership is legal. Be sure to research local laws concerning this. Also, be aware that coral legally purchased in another country will not necessarily be legal to possess in your own country.

The same considerations that have been mentioned regarding the use of plants may be applied to coral skeletons as well. They should be arranged to provide the creatures under your care with as natural an environment as possible. The unique shapes of coral skeletons render them particularly useful for creating caves, hideaways, and sight barriers. Coral also assists in maintaining the high pH required by many marine animals.

Coral skeletons must be carefully cleaned, as even pieces long removed from the ocean may harbor harmful organic materials deep within their structures. It is best to clean coral by allowing it to soak in a solution of 8 percent household bleach. The water in which the coral sits should be aerated throughout this period. After this process, the coral should be thoroughly rinsed and allowed to dry, preferably in the sun.

Artificial Coral

Extremely realistic coral replications, fashioned of various resins, are now readily available in the pet trade. When artificial coral is used in an aquarium that is planted with living macroalgae, they are virtually indistinguishable from the real thing, especially after they have acquired a covering of algae or sessile invertebrates. The wide variety of species and sizes available allows the aquarist to create virtually any habitat he or she may desire.

Decorating Your Aquarium

Establishing a marine or freshwater aquarium is far more complicated than merely setting up a display that is pleasing to the eye. Each item added to the aquarium will greatly impact the behavior and health of the animals that you seek to maintain.

Substrate and Rocks

Far from being simply a covering on the bottom of your aquarium, the substrate that you choose will affect both your water quality and the comfort of the animals that you keep. While some species are nondemanding in this regard, many, especially bottom dwellers, are very specific in their requirements. Stingrays and horseshoe crabs, for example, require sandy or muddy bottoms, while sessile invertebrates such as barnacles need hard substrates upon which to anchor.

FACT

The coral sand that accumulates in the vicinity of coral reefs is derived largely from the feeding activities of parrotfish and other species that actually chew living coral, and from the boring of worms and other invertebrates. Larger gravel is produced by the action of waves against the coral.

In marine aquariums, coral sand and coral gravel help to maintain an appropriately high pH. In freshwater systems, you have a greater degree of freedom in choosing a substrate. Depending upon the types of animals that you keep and the habitat that you are trying to establish, gravel, rocks, or even dead leaves and sand may be used.

Rocks

Rocks used in aquariums must be chosen from those types that are known to be safe. Some rocks contain metallic ores that can be released into the water, poisoning the animals inhabiting it. For marine aquariums, lava rock, live rock, and various types marketed as "ocean rocks" are safe. A greater variety of types may be used in freshwater aquariums, including sandstone, granite, and slate. Rocks with flourishing growths of plants and sessile invertebrates in either freshwater or saltwater habitats make interesting additions to the aquarium and will assist in maintaining water quality, but collecting rocks is a risky proposition. Even those rocks that are harmless in a large natural environment can cause problems within the confines of an aquarium.

As with coral and plants, rocks should be arranged with an eye toward the requirements of your pets and not merely treated as decorative items. Keep in mind the need for shelters such as caves, and remember that even actively swimming fish may retreat to such areas at night. Rocks should also be arranged so as to allow the tank's various inhabitants to stay out of sight of each other when necessary.

Building Your Display

One of the most important considerations to bear in mind when creating your display is that your pets will fare best when they are housed in a situation that approximates their natural habitat. In general, complex, well-planted exhibits will result in the display of more naturalistic behavior on the part of the animals that you keep.

Exhibiting Secretive Animals

In contrast to what might be expected, retiring species will actually show themselves more, not less, when they are given appropriate places to hide. In such situations, rather than staying out of sight, shy animals usually show themselves once they are confident that a secure retreat is nearby. In the process, they give you a peek into lives that generally pass unseen. If a fish or an invertebrate feels insecure and unable to hide itself, it will usually not behave normally and eventually will succumb to a stress-related disorder. Animals housed in a secure environment will provide you with a rewarding experience in terms of the behaviors that you will observe.

Place heavy rocks or driftwood directly on the bottom of the tank, not on the substrate. Rocks placed on the substrate are likely to become dislodged due to the burrowing and swimming activities of the tank's inhabitants over time, and may crush animals or glass when they shift.

The First Step

The first items to be placed in your aquarium should be the filters, heaters, and other life-support systems. By having these in place early on, you can arrange aquarium furnishings such as plants and rocks so as to hide these mechanical items from view. In doing so, be sure to allow yourself easy access to intake tubes, thermometer temperature controls, and the like.

If you are using a printed aquarium background to add interest and color to your tank, add a bead of silicone along the edges of your background to prevent discoloration due to water seepage. This precaution will add greatly to the overall appearance of your exhibit.

Substrates

In marine aquariums, the substrate should be kept to a level of an inch or so. Deeper substrates may allow for the development of harmful anaerobic bacteria, as oxygen will not penetrate these areas. If deeper substrates are needed—where, for example, you are keeping burrowing fish or invertebrates—consider the use of live sand. Live sand contains bacteria, microorganisms, and tiny crustaceans and worms and will remain aerated as long as these creatures survive. In freshwater aquariums, substrates can be deeper, provided that living plants are used, as their roots will help prevent impaction and allow for greater aeration of the gravel or sand.

With the exception of live sand, all materials used in the aquarium must be rinsed thoroughly to remove dust and organic material. Live sand and rock should be introduced to your aquarium in the same manner as are exhibit animals. Each contains hundreds of living organisms, which will perish if they are simply placed into water that differs greatly in chemistry from that in which they originated. Water added to the aquarium should be poured into a container that is placed on the substrate so as not to disturb it.

When your exhibit is completely set up and all life-support systems are running, it is time to begin the important process of testing for the functioning of the nitrogen cycle. It is vital that this is done before any animals are added to your aquarium. Review the section on cycling the aquarium in Chapter 2.

Chapter 6

Fish—Classification and Characteristics

Fish are the largest group of vertebrate animals, with over 25,000 species identified so far. While some species mature at barely ⅖ of an inch long, others, such as whale sharks, grow to a length of 40 feet or more. One type of fish or another has colonized nearly every aquatic habitat that can be imagined, from desert pools that reach temperatures of 104°F (40°C) to the frigid seas of Antarctica. You never quite know what to expect from these thoroughly captivating creatures.

Classification in General

The species is the basic unit in the classification of living organisms. In the most general terms, members of the same species can mate and produce viable offspring. Similar species are grouped into genera, and related genera comprise the next unit of classification, the family. Orders are larger classification units, made up of families of related animals or plants. Orders of similar organisms are grouped into a still larger unit, called a class. Organisms belonging to the various classes differ markedly in their evolutionary histories, and, usually, in their structures and in how they go about their lives. A phylum is composed of related classes of organisms. To further express relationships between living things, these groups are sometimes further divided into subfamilies, subclasses, and so forth.

FACT

Animals of different, but closely related, species can sometimes interbreed. A common example of this phenomenon is the mule, which is the offspring of two distinct species of animal, the horse and the donkey. Offspring born as the result of an interspecies mating are generally sterile. In natural situations, such hybridization rarely, if ever, occurs.

All of the organisms that have been scientifically identified and described are given a Latin name, consisting of two parts. The first part of the name represents the animal or plant's genus, while the second denotes its species. Unique or isolated populations within a species are sometimes designated as subspecies. In this case, a third Latin name will be added to the usual two. The current trend in taxonomy, however, is to eliminate the subspecies characterization and to classify such populations as species whenever possible.

Orders and Families of Fish

The approximately 25,000 species of fish are broadly placed into two main groups: elasmobranch (sharks, rays, and dogfish), which have cartilaginous skeletons; and teleost, or the bony fish. They are further subdivided into over 4,200 genera, 60 orders, and at least 485 families. The following is a list of several orders containing particularly unique or interesting fish. Hopefully this tiny peek at the marvelous diversity of this fascinating group of animals will inspire you to learn all that you can about them.

Jawless Fish (Orders Myxiniformes and Petromyzontiformes)

Truly testing the limits of what might be considered a "fish," the forty-three species of hagfish and forty species of lamprey are evolutionary throwbacks to a group of fish known as the Agnatha. These odd creatures arose in the Ordovician Period, over 500 million years ago, and modern surviving representatives have changed little since then.

Included among their unfishlike characteristics are a rasping, tongue-like structure known as the piston, lack of scales, and absence of paired fins. Both hagfish and lampreys possess eel-like bodies and are found in cold and temperate marine- and freshwaters throughout the world.

Lampreys pass through a distinct larval stage, which is spent buried in the substrate and may be up to three years. After a three-month metamorphosis, the adults take up life as parasites of other fish species. Most types of lamprey are anadromous, which means they reproduce in freshwater but spend the majority of their lives at sea.

Taxonomy, the science of classification, is a constantly evolving discipline. Today, advanced techniques in the science of genetics are enabling researchers to more accurately pinpoint the evolutionary relationships of fish. This, combined with improved collecting techniques, has resulted in identifying more species and families of fish.

Lampreys attach themselves to the bodies of other fish by way of a disk-shaped sucker and then use their tooth-lined tongue, or piston, to scrape through the body wall of the unfortunate host. Depending upon the species, lampreys may feed upon blood, muscle tissue, or both. Large, robust host fish may survive an attack, but a great many are killed.

Hagfish are bottom-dwelling scavengers of the deep sea. Unlike the rasping piston of the lamprey, that of the hagfish is extended into the flesh of the meal and then retracted, pulling off a chunk of meat in the process. Hagfish possess cartilaginous notochords as opposed to true backbones. These flexible structures allow the hagfish to literally tie themselves into knots. As the knot travels down the fish's body, it creates pressure that helps to tear flesh from the carcass upon which the hagfish is feeding. This unusual adaptation, combined with the production of copious amounts of mucus, can also be used as a means of escaping predators. Very little is known of the breeding habits of most hagfish species.

In a startling modification to their normal life history, a population of sea lampreys has become landlocked in the Great Lakes of the United States. This population has somehow been able to forgo the seagoing phase of its existence and now survives as a completely freshwater species. The adjustment has been so successful that the number of lampreys in the Great Lakes has skyrocketed, leading to the demise of several recreational and commercial fisheries.

Lizardfish and Relatives (Order Aulopiformes)

The over 200 mostly marine species of lizardfish and their relatives, ranging in size from 3 inches to 7 feet exhibit a unique combination of advanced and primitive features.

Many of the deep-sea forms are able to self-fertilize, perhaps an adaptation to a vast, featureless environment that renders finding a mate a highly unlikely prospect. The twenty-five or so species of true lizardfish are all elongated in body structure and possess large, toothy mouths to assist in capturing the fish and other marine life upon which they feed. The head truly is lizardlike in appearance, an impression furthered by the fish's habit of propping themselves up on their ventral fins as they scan the surrounding area for prey. Lizardfish are efficient, "sit and wait" predators, generally cryptically colored and able to bury themselves within the substrate, leaving their eyes protruding above.

The benthic-dwelling lancet fish (*Alepisaurus ferox*), the largest member of the group, has a high dorsal fin that runs from the head to the tail and a huge mouth filled with daggerlike teeth (a related species is commonly referred to as the "dagger tooth"). At 7 feet in length, lancet fish are among the longest of the deep-sea predators.

The closely related pearleyes are also fish of the ocean's abyss. They possess upward-facing eyes and binocular vision. Unique to these unusual animals is a white spot on the eye, known as the pearl gland, and also the existence of a second retina. It is speculated that the pearl gland functions to pick up what little light is available in this creature's deep-sea habitat and guide it to the eye's lens.

Flying Fish and Relatives (Order Beloniformes)

Flying fish are, in general, marine fish that dwell at the surface of many of the world's warmer waters. Nearly 200 species have been identified. True flying fish are equipped with pectoral fins that are uniquely modified into winglike structures. In several species, the pelvic fins also function in this manner, making them, in a sense, "four-winged" fish. All are surface-dwelling animals of the open seas. When preparing to glide above the surface of the water, these fish swim about rapidly to build up speed. The largest and most accomplished of the flying fish can attain a speed of nearly 40 miles per hour before leaving the water, and may soar up to 650 feet before returning to the sea.

Flying fish of all types are a prized food item in many countries, as is their roe. They are, however, difficult to catch on hooks, because most feed on plankton. Therefore, unique strategies have been devised to capture them, including taking advantage of the fish's attraction to light and also luring mating aggregations to floating rafts of vegetation (flying fish generally lay their eggs below floating debris or macroalgae).

Needlefish are closely related to flying fish and are instantly recognizable by their long, thin bodies and elongated, toothy jaws. Strangely, these seemingly benign animals have been implicated in several human fatalities. Attracted to the lights of small fishing boats operating at night, large needlefish leaping from the ocean have apparently impaled hapless fishermen in the eyes.

Oarfish and Relatives (Order Lampridiformes)

The oarfish (*Regalecus glesne*) is the longest of the bony fish and is exceeded in length only by the cartilaginous whale shark and basking shark. Measured at a length of 26 feet, estimates of oarfish observed but not captured indicate that they may possibly reach lengths of up to 56 feet, which would make them the longest of all fish. Sightings of these unusual creatures have, no doubt, given rise to many myths concerning sea serpents.

FACT

The larval phases of several members of the order to which oarfish belong are very unusual in appearance, so much so that they and their corresponding adult phases were once classified as separate species.

Almost all members of this order have unique body structures and shapes, such as long caudal filaments. Because these fish are not often encountered and are nearly impossible to keep in captivity, people know very little concerning the uses of these appendages or of the fish's natural histories in general.

The Senses

The wide range and variability of aquatic habitats colonized by the world's fish has given rise to an incredible array of sensory organs, structures, and adaptations. Different kinds of fish possess varied sensory strengths due to adaptations that have occurred over years of evolution. Each type of fish has sensory traits that allow it to best interact with and succeed within its environment.

Detecting Sound

Fish lack external ear openings, so you tend not to think of them as creatures that can hear sounds. Most species, however, have well-developed inner ears. These structures are very effective at sensing the waterborne pressure changes that accompany sound waves.

The connection between the inner ear and the swim bladder possessed by certain fish is known as the Weberian apparatus. It appears to be highly developed in carps and minnows, and it is speculated that these species rely on it for communication and predator detection.

In a further refinement of the inner ear, some species of fish possess a connection between this organ and the swim bladder. Gas in the swim bladder improves the fish's hearing acuity, because gas is very sensitive to the vibrations caused by sound waves. This results in an ability to decipher a wider range of frequencies and tones. It is believed that fish that possess advanced hearing abilities communicate extensively with one another using sound.

Lateral Line

The lateral line is a unique system of neuromasts, which are sensory organs that detect water disturbances caused by the movements of other animals or by the flow of water over objects. These organs are mainly comprised of jellylike substances called cupula that rest on sensory cells. The neuromasts are housed within lateral line canals that run along both sides of the bodies of most fish, although in some species, the organs are scattered about the surface of the head and body. The functioning of the lateral line system appears to be particularly effective and well developed in sightless species such as the blind cavefish.

Detection of Electricity

Many fish make good use of the fact that water is an excellent conductor of electricity. Electrical receptors in fish generally exist in the form of modified lateral line organs. These unique structures sense the electric currents generated by the muscular action of swimming fish or by the heartbeats of nearby animals. This ability seems to be particularly well developed among the sharks. It also appears that some fish can detect the earth's electromagnetic field and may use such to orient themselves during lengthy migrations.

Some fish can also produce electricity through the use of specialized cells in the swimming muscles. Most fish that can generate electricity, such as the knife fish, produce fairly weak currents that are used for communication and navigation. Several species, however, most notably the electric eel (actually a type of knife fish), the electric ray, and electric catfish, can produce currents of several hundred volts in strength, enabling them to stun prey and discourage would-be predators.

Swimming

Movement is, for fish, quite a challenge, because water is 800 times denser than air. The technical solution to this problem has, in general, been the development of a streamlined body and powerful swimming muscles known as myotomes. In the majority of fish species, such muscles account for over half of the body weight.

The most common mode of swimming among fish is through rapid movements of the tail and body. Certain species, however, have specially modified fins and utilize these in place of body and tail oscillations. In some, pectoral fins are oarlike in appearance and function; in others, such as the seahorses and pipefish, fluttering movements of the dorsal and anal fins propel the fish about.

A fish's buoyancy also affects its swimming ability. Many fish attain neutral buoyancy by virtue of their gas-filled swim bladders. Because the depth at which the fish is swimming affects buoyancy, those species with swim bladders must deflate or inflate the organ or produce gas when they ascend to the surface or dive. Bottom-dwelling fish are largely untroubled by questions of buoyancy and often do not possess swim bladders.

Respiration

Fish face a number of challenges in obtaining oxygen, because water is extremely oxygen deficient in comparison to air. Freshwater contains 95 percent less oxygen than does air, and saltwater has, in general, only 20 percent of the oxygen content found in freshwater.

Most fish have, therefore, had to develop an extremely efficient system for extracting oxygen from the water. In the majority of the species, water is drawn in through the mouth, whereupon it passes over the gills and out through the operculum, which are platelike structures that cover the gill cavity. Oxygen diffuses into the blood in the gills, and it is picked up by hemoglobin in the red blood cells (as it is in humans). The gills of most fish are so efficient that 80 percent of the water's oxygen content is removed. Carbon dioxide, a metabolic byproduct, diffuses out of the fish's body at the gills as well.

Some fish have evolved alternative methods for dealing with this problem and have bypassed the need for oxygen-bearing water altogether. The most well-known of these is the lungfish, which utilizes oxygen extracted directly from the air at the surface of the water.

Reproduction

In keeping with the remarkable diversity of species of fish extant today, and with the many habitats that they have colonized, reproductive methods are also extremely varied. Some fish, such as salmon and American eels, engage in massive breeding migrations, with millions of adults laying eggs simultaneously and then dying shortly thereafter. While the vast majority of fish lay eggs, up to 35 million in a season in some cases, a great many are live bearers that reproduce through internal fertilization. Many species merely scatter the eggs and leave them to take their chances, while others take great precautions in preparing nests, guarding the eggs, and caring for the young.

FACT

Adult tilapia protect their young by taking them into their capacious mouths at the slightest hint of danger, while male bullhead catfish accompany their offspring on feeding forays for several weeks. Perhaps most surprising of all, discus fish feed their fry with specialized skin secretions.

In one of the most unusual reproductive twists known in the animal world, female seahorses deposit their eggs in the pouches of the males. The "surrogate mothers" thereafter regulate the salinity content of the water in the pouch, brood the eggs, and bring forth the young. In yet another unusual strategy, certain species of fish all come into the world as females, with some becoming males at a later point in their lives (a phenomenon known as protogyny). Similarly, in a reproductive strategy known as protandry, the fish are all born as males and some later develop into females. Surgeonfish dispense with sexual differences altogether, existing only as females that reproduce by giving birth to clones of themselves. Several common aquarium fish use sex-changing strategies, including wrasses, which all begin their lives as females, and clownfish, which are all born as males.

Chapter 7

Fish—Species Accounts

Perhaps more than any other factor, it is the spectacular coloration and constant activity of many marine fish that beckons people to establish marine aquariums. Those who stay with the hobby for any length of time often discover that the fascination derived from observing the behavior of their pets outweighs the initial awe aroused by their beauty. In the following chapter, you will meet some of the more colorful and highly desirable species of fish that are commonly kept in marine aquariums and learn the pleasures and pitfalls of keeping them.

Angelfish (Family Pomacanthidae)

Angelfish, which might be termed "classic marine aquarium fish," are vibrantly colored, active, and alert (see color insert for photo). Some species also grow to be quite large, attaining a length of 24 inches or more. If you have an aquarium of 20 gallons or less, you might consider keeping one of the dwarf species of the genus Centropyge, several of which are fully grown at 4 inches or so.

Although some of the dwarf species such as the cherubfish (*Centropyge argi*) are fairly hardy, angelfish are not, as a rule, recommended for hobbyists without considerable experience in keeping marine fish. Nearly all of the approximately seventy-five species are, in general, intolerant of suboptimal water conditions. Many species are fairly specific in their food requirements as well, subsisting largely on sponges and corals in the wild, which makes them difficult to acclimate to captive diets.

Sponge- and coral-based foods are becoming easier to find, which makes your job of feeding them easier. Well-acclimated individual angelfish can actually become tame enough to take food from your fingers. In addition to sponge, coral, and algae type foods, angelfish should be offered a wide variety of live and dried foods, including brine shrimp, mysid shrimp, squid, prawn, and mollusks.

ALERT!

Be aware that large angelfish may not bother to eat so tiny a creature as live brine shrimp. In fact, the brine shrimp may be pulled into the fish's gills during respiration and will cause irritation and stress.

Despite their predilection for active swimming, all angelfish require rock work and coral where they can find shelter at night. Dwarf species in particular require a great deal of structure in the aquarium. Much of their time in the wild is spent swimming around similar structures. Deprived of secure hiding spots, most will languish and die.

Although captive breeding is an extremely rare event, several species of angelfish have successfully reproduced under captive conditions. All species, as far as we know, reproduce in pairs. Outwardly very similar, the sexes may sometimes be differentiated by the swollen abdomen of the pregnant female. Mated pairs of angelfish rise upward together, releasing eggs and sperm as they go. The tiny eggs float about among the plankton, and, after a time (which varies from species to species but averages approximately one month), the minuscule fry settle to the ocean's floor.

Flame Angelfish (Centropyge loriculus)

Vividly colored even for an angelfish, the flame angelfish has a brilliant red body with blue stripes, making it instantly recognizable to most aquarists. Inhabiting the South Atlantic Ocean from Mexico and Central America to Australia, the flame angelfish is by nature a grazer and should be provided with an ample amount of algae-based foods. The flame angelfish will also readily accept squid, chopped clams, brine shrimp, and other invertebrates. The flame angelfish matures at a length of approximately 4 inches and is a good choice for the hobbyist maintaining a smaller aquarium. It is fairly hardy but does require excellent water quality in order to thrive.

Queen Angelfish (Holacanthus ciliaris)

Well deserving of the title "queen," this attractive fish has a yellow-green body outlined in brilliant blue (see color insert for photo). Color varies a great deal among individuals, and it has been suggested that this species hybridizes with close relatives. The queen angelfish lives throughout the western Atlantic and Caribbean and is generally found in a mated pair situation. This large (28 inches) species requires a varied diet in which algae and sponge-based foods predominate. It will also relish such items as clams, prawn, and mussels. As with most angelfish, queen angels are intolerant of other individuals of their own or similar species and require a large, well-filtered aquarium with suitable hiding spots.

All angelfish appear to be extremely territorial and, with the exception of mated pairs, are largely intolerant of other fish of the same species. Many will also fight with similar species of angelfish and even with unrelated fish. Except for some of the dwarf species, a large tank does not necessarily guarantee harmony, as naturally sized territories are generally larger than can be provided for in the aquarium.

Why do the young of most species of angelfish vary so dramatically in coloration from the adults?
Young angelfish feed on external parasites of larger fish. It is likely that their patterns of coloration indicate this role to larger fish, which might otherwise eat them. This coloration may also inhibit aggression from territorial adults of their own species.

Angelfish can be distinguished from the superficially similar butterfly fish by the spine that all angelfish carry on the gill cover. Once classified with the angelfish, butterfly fish are more "compressed" in appearance than are angelfish.

Catfish (Family Plotosidae)

Included among this fascinating group of fish are several species that use their pectoral fins as "legs" to travel considerable distances over land. The most famous of these, the Southeast Asian walking catfish (*Clarias batrachus*) was introduced into Florida in the United States as an escapee from the aquarium trade. It is now well established in breeding populations and, in fact, is the most common freshwater fish in many areas of the southern part of that state. A voracious predator, the walking catfish often decimates populations of local fish and amphibians.

Freshwater Catfish

Although catfish are to be found in both freshwater and marine environments, it is in the realm of freshwater that these truly unique and often bizarre creatures come into their own. Worldwide in distribution, they have adapted to an amazing variety of lifestyles and diets, and in the variability of their appearances they are unrivaled. Members of this huge family, which numbers more than 2,500 species, are among both the largest and the smallest of the world's freshwater fish. While many, such as the minute *Corydoras pygmaeus*, mature at a body length of only ½ inch, the European wels, *Silurus glandis*, tops out at 16½ feet and may weigh up to 660 pounds.

Although catfish seem generally harmless. the tiny candiru catfish (*Vandellia cirrhosa*) is feared by many, even though it shares its South American habitat with creatures that appear far more formidable. Adapted to feeding on blood in the gills of larger fish, the candiru is for some reason also drawn to urine in the water. It follows the stream to its source, enters the unfortunate victim's urethra, and extends its spines. This, as one might imagine, results in excruciating pain and necessitates surgical removal.

All catfish possess from one to four pairs of whiskerlike barbells around their mouths, from which they derive their common name. These extremely sensitive organs are studded with taste buds, enabling their owner to find food in the murkiest of waters or on the darkest of nights. It is very interesting to watch the quick reaction of nearly any species of catfish to even the tiniest particle of food introduced into the aquarium. The dorsal and pectoral fins hide stout, pointed spines, which in some species can inject prey with a potent venom.

FACT

Although very different in appearance, catfish are closely related to knife fish, one of which is the electric eel (*Electrophorus electricus*), which reaches a length of 7 feet and is famed for the powerful electrical discharges it can produce. At least one species of the catfish, the electric catfish, also makes use of electricity while hunting or defending itself.

In contrast to most other fish, the catfish's body is covered by a type of skin as opposed to scales. In some species, however, a scalelike plate has evolved to provide additional protection from attack.

Nearly all species of catfish engage in some form of parental care, and many take this to the extreme, with the fry following the male about and deriving protection from him for several weeks. Some types incubate the eggs in the mouth, and one African species (*Synodontis punctatus*) has added a unique twist to this already unusual form of reproduction. This enterprising fish takes advantage of the overly protective nature of certain mouth-brooding cichlids that share its habitat. Pairs of the catfish release their eggs in close proximity to spawning cichlids. The "foster parents" inhale the catfish eggs along with their own, thus relieving the catfish of the burden of protecting their young!

When medicating catfish, be aware that their skin allows for a greater absorption rate than do the scales of typical fish. Some fish medications have specific doses for catfish (and for other scale-less fish such as eels) or may state that the medication is not suitable for such fish. In the absence of such instructions, start with half the recommended dose and monitor your pet's reactions carefully.

Corydoras *spp.*

Many species of these squat, peaceful catfish, all very similar in shape but varying widely in pattern, are available to the aquarist. They are extremely engaging little creatures, constantly in motion as their vacuumlike mouths sweep substrate for food. Their ability to extract uneaten bits of food from the smallest of crevices, along with their prodigious appetites, render them nearly essential to most aquariums. They should not, however, be left to survive on leftovers alone. True, they are scavengers, but they require quite a bit of food and a balanced diet if they are to thrive. In aquariums housing active surface-feeding fish, be sure that flake food reaches the bottom of the aquarium, and also that pellet food is provided for bottom-dwelling fish such as *Corydoras*.

This is also one of the few catfish species to travel about in schools, and they will pair up with related species when doing so. Although they hail from the warm waters of Central and South America, most are quite adaptable in regard to temperature and, if adjusted slowly, will thrive in unheated aquariums. Many species breed readily in the aquarium.

Walking Catfish (Clarias batrachus)

The eel-like body, large size (up to 22 inches), and unique habits of this catfish endear it to those with an interest in unusual aquarium animals. Native to southeast Asia and India, walking catfish have established colonies in the southeastern United States since their introduction there as escaped pets in the 1960s. Because they are quite destructive to native aquatic animals, many places now prohibit their importation.

Olive green in color in the wild, captive strains of walking catfish are now available in albino and ones with gold and black flecks. They possess a well-developed auxiliary breathing organ and can thus survive for extended periods out of water. This, combined with their ability to "walk" upon their stout pectoral spines, enables this aptly named fish to travel over land when conditions deteriorate in the home environment. This ability has also thwarted efforts to control introduced populations in the United States; when poison is added to the pond, the catfish simply walk to another!

ALERT!

Like all catfish, walking catfish possess sharp pectoral and dorsal spines. In this species the venom injected by the spines produces a very painful wound. Handle only with a heavy-duty net.

Walking catfish are voracious feeders and soon become quite bold and willing to feed from the hand (watch your fingers!). Their appetites know no bounds, and they fare quite well on all manner of frozen, pelleted, and live foods. It is quite impossible to house any fish smaller than walking catfish in the same tank as walking catfish. A heavy hood on your aquarium is an absolute necessity, unless you want them walking about the house at night.

Saltwater Catfish (Plotosus lineatus)

This species, or a closely related family member, is the most commonly encountered marine catfish in the aquarium trade. Approximately one-third of the thirty or so species of its family inhabits marine or estuarine environments.

The saltwater catfish carries spines that inject a potent venom. These are located in front of the pectoral and dorsal fins. For this reason, these fish are best left to the care of professionals. The large (12 inches) adults can inflict a potentially deadly wound with their spines.

Saltwater catfish are one among several species of marine animals that can administer dangerous wounds with their venomous spines. The trade in most of these species is largely unregulated, so it is left to the hobbyist to use sound judgment with regard to such animals. With so many thousands of harmless species available, it really makes no sense to keep such animals in the home. They are included here as a matter of general interest, and for the reference of professionals.

The boldly striped young of the saltwater catfish travel about in schools and form a tight, writhing clump when disturbed. This behavior may deny potential predators a specific target, or it may confer upon the young the appearance of a much larger creature. The adults are fairly solitary and lose much of the juvenile coloration.

Saltwater catfish will accept a wide variety of animal-based foods and are especially fond of shellfish such as clams, mussels, and scallops. Spawning in the aquarium has, of yet, not been observed. Freshwater members of the family lay their eggs in a gravel nest that is guarded by the male, but it is not known if marine species exhibit this behavior as well.

Butterfly Fish (Family Chaetodontidae).

Approximately 120 species of butterfly fish inhabit the world's warmer oceans, with the vast majority being found in the Indo-Pacific region. Superficially similar to the angelfish, with which they were once classified, butterfly fish may be distinguished by the lack of a spine on the gill cover and by the more laterally compressed body. Unlike angelfish, several species of butterfly fish are fairly tolerant of company, but this should be determined by observing them in the aquarium before purchase. Butterfly fish range in size from 3½ to 12 inches.

ESSENTIAL

Despite their gorgeous coloration and often robust appearance, butterfly fish should not be purchased without careful thought. Most are quite specific in their dietary requirements. Be sure to observe your potential pet eating in the store before you decide to take it home.

Many types of butterfly fish display a false eye spot near the tail, a tactic likely designed to divert the attacks of predators away from the real eye. The true eyes are often camouflaged by a black stripe, patch, or other marking. Jaw shape varies greatly among the butterfly fish, from short and blunt in those species that feed upon coral polyps to very elongated in those that pick tiny invertebrates from among the coral heads.

Butterfly fish reproduce in pairs or small groups, with the male of some species having been observed to nudge the females in an apparent attempt to induce egg laying. Spawning in captivity has been recorded, but efforts to rear the young have largely been unsuccessful. In the wild, the free-floating planktonic stage of the fry is thought to last for up to two months, nearly twice as long as in the closely related angelfish.

Butterfly fish are not, as a rule, pets to be kept by inexperienced hobbyists. Their apparent vitality belies a delicate constitution. This is particularly true of the many types that rely upon coral polyps, sponges, and algae as their principal foods. Such animals are often extremely difficult to maintain on an artificial diet. If you attempt to keep butterfly fish at all, only young specimens should be selected, as adults are extremely difficult to acclimate to captive diets.

One occasionally successful technique to induce finicky butterfly fish to eat has been to offer tiny worms, such as black worms, tubifex worms, or white worms. These are particularly well accepted by those long-nosed species that, in the wild, consume tiny invertebrates living within coral heads. Be aware that these worms are freshwater rather than marine animals, and uneaten ones will quickly perish in your aquarium where, if not removed, they will foul the water.

The laterally compressed body form of butterfly fish is a clue to their preferred habitat. Most species and individuals will become extremely stressed if housed in a bare aquarium, so be sure to provide ample retreats. Aquarists commonly worry that providing their animals with adequate hiding spots will allow them to remain constantly out of sight and thus lessen the joy inherent in keeping them. Actually, however, the opposite is usually true. Once acclimated to captive conditions, these gorgeous creatures will, if provided with a proper environment, attain the confidence to explore their new home and exhibit natural behaviors.

ALERT!

Do not attempt to house butterfly fish with living coral, sponges, or sea anemones. These creatures are the natural prey of most species of butterfly fish, and will quickly be consumed.

Sunburst Butterfly Fish (Chaetodon kleini)

Although not by any means an easy fish to keep, the sunburst butterfly fish is, when compared to other members of its family, reasonably hearty. The most difficult time will be the acclimatization period, when the fish must learn to accept its new diet. Once past this stage, the sunburst butterfly fish will do well if given excellent water quality and a diet structured around tiny worms. Although not as vibrantly colored as some, its subdued hues of blue and gray fading to yellow are quite attractive. As with all butterfly fish, the sunburst will do best if given access to a variety of coral hideaways.

Copperband Butterfly Fish (Chelmon rostratus)

In the copperband butterfly fish we see the epitome of mouth specialization. The long, pointed jaw allows this fish to pluck tiny invertebrates from even the most secure of retreats among the coral. Unfortunately, however, its preferred diet is difficult to duplicate in captivity, and this species is also extremely sensitive to water quality. Despite these drawbacks, the copperband butterfly fish's uniquely shaped mouth and brilliant coloration—blue and gold stripes on a silver background, with a black false eye spot—renders it a perennial favorite among fish keepers. (See color insert for photo.) Some success has been had with the diets high in black worms, white worms, and algae. Sadly, however, this gorgeous creature remains a very difficult species to maintain for any length of time in the home aquarium.

Damselfish and Clownfish (Family Pomacentridae)

Individuals of the more than 325 species that comprise this large family of fish are among the most numerous and conspicuous fish on many coral reefs. Members of this family are found throughout the world's tropical and semitropical seas, with the greatest diversity occurring in Australian waters and the lowest in the Atlantic and East Pacific oceans. They occupy a startling variety of habitats, with many species restricted to specific depths or specific areas of wave action.

Anemone fish, or clownfish, are well-known for living in close association with marine invertebrates known as sea anemones (see color insert for photo). Usually home to just one pair of clownfish, the host anemone forms the basis of their territory, and they rarely stray far from it. Long thought to be immune to the anemone's stinging tentacles, the clownfish is now known to secrete mucus that mimics that covering the tentacles of the anemone. This mucus inhibits the tentacles from stinging one another and, in essence, prevents the anemone from recognizing the clownfish as prey. The clownfish thus derives protection from the anemone and returns the favor by chasing off fish that might prey on its host.

QUESTION?

Why do many species of damselfish so zealously guard their territory?
One explanation is that they are protecting their food source, algae. The thick mats of this favorite food often grow within well-guarded territories but they are absent outside these territories due to a large number of other animals that eat algae.

Damselfish are generally small, brilliantly colored, and in almost constant motion. These characteristics render them quite popular with aquarists. The speed at which they move and their eagerness to feed allows them to survive in aquariums with much larger fish. Be aware, however, that they can be quite aggressive toward their own and similar species.

Percula Clown (Amphiprion ocellaris)

A true darling of the aquarium world, the percula is one of the most widely recognized marine fish in the world. Its brilliant coloration and "comic" mode of swimming endears it to all. Hailing from the Indo-Pacific region, this clown-fish reaches a length of 3.2 inches. The percula is quite protective of the anemone in which it lives, and generally only one pair per tank can be maintained. It accepts a wide variety of dried and frozen foods. If you are considering a percula clownfish, be sure to select a captive-bred animal, which is readily available. Also, remember that they are best displayed with a living anemone, and that the keeping of anemones is a separate discipline. Carefully read the section on anemones in Chapter 10 before deciding to purchase one.

The relationship between the clownfish and their hosts might best be described as "commensal," in that they seem to derive benefit from living in close association with each other, but are not strictly limited to that situation. The vast majority of anemones live without clownfish. Clownfish, however, seem more dependent upon the relationship. While they will live well alone in the aquarium, experiments in the wild have shown that clownfish without anemone hosts are quickly eaten by larger fish.

Jawfish (Family Opistognathidae)

Jawfish sport large eyes and mouths on a blunt head that, to many, evokes the image of a bulldog. The body tapers quickly behind this and is quite graceful in appearance. These characteristics suit jawfish well to their burrowing lifestyle. The strong jaws and head are used to hollow out their subterranean retreats, while the tapered body allows the fish to slip in and out quickly at the slightest sign of danger. Once the burrow is established, most jawfish rarely stray far from it. These unique creatures cover the entrance of their homes with a pebble at night, and the males incubate the eggs within their mouths.

Yellow-headed Jawfish (Opistognathus aurifrons)

A group of these beautiful fish in established burrows makes a delightful exhibit. Their bright yellow heads constantly appear and disappear as the jawfish survey their territories for food or foes. They slip tail-first into their homes with amazing speed and pop out just as quickly.

ALERT!

Because jawfish rarely leave the immediate area of their burrows, we tend to think of them as "bottom fish." However, for reasons as yet unexplained, jawfish often jump out of poorly covered tanks at night. Be sure that your aquarium cover or hood fits securely, especially around filter tubes and other equipment.

In contrast to many other fish that establish a regular home base, jawfish are relatively inoffensive toward one another. Growing to a length of 5 inches, these interesting animals are delicately colored in yellow and pale blue. They require a fairly soft substrate in which to burrow, so be sure to mix in some sand if you use crushed coral or similar material in your aquarium. Jawfish readily feed on all manner of animal-based foods, but be aware that many individuals will not venture far from their burrow. Therefore, be sure that a suitable amount of food is placed within easy reach.

Cichlids (Family Cichlidae)

Among the cichlids are found some of the most interesting and highly desirable of the freshwater aquarium fish. With well over 1,500 species, and many as yet undescribed, this family is one of the largest. Members range in size from 1 to 36 inches and exhibit an incredible range of body forms, behaviors, and dietary preferences. One nearly universal trait among the family is an amazing degree of parental care of the young. Included among various species are those that take the young into the mouth during times of danger and others that feed the young with specially produced mucus. In nearly all cases, both the parents tend to the young—cleaning both them and the nest site and driving off potential predators.

Cichlids have a pair of pharyngeal jaws in the throat for processing food. This feature has freed the primary jaws to develop an amazing array of adaptations to deal with specific and unusual food items. Included among this family are fish that feed upon bacteria, other fish, hard-shelled mollusks, and those that graze upon algae. It is speculated that such adaptations have allowed cichlids to become the dominant fish family in many of the ecosystems in which they occur.

Freshwater Angelfish (Pterophyllum scalare)

One of the most universally recognizable and beloved of aquarium fish, the angelfish hails from the Amazon and Negro river systems of South America. A second species, the deep angelfish (*P. altrum*) is limited in range to the Orinoco River system of Venezuela and is rarely found in the pet trade. This fish has a combination of interesting behavior and incredible beauty. Long, trailing fins accentuate the height and graceful appearance of the laterally compressed body. The body form and dark lateral bands of the wild, or naturally occurring, color phase of this fish are adapted for life in the reed beds that form its natural habitat. Through selective breeding, a large number of color varieties are now available. A number of unrelated marine fish are also commonly referred to as "angelfish." While similar in body form to the freshwater angelfish, they are quite different animals and are discussed in Chapter 7.

ESSENTIAL

Angelfish sometimes inexplicably stop eating. Often a change in the foods offered will stimulate them to begin to eat again. This is particularly true of live food—try adding black worms, brine shrimp, or guppies to the diet. Possible reasons behind the problem should be investigated, such as water quality and temperature.

Angelfish prefer slightly acidic water (pH 6.8) and are carnivorous in nature. Although very adaptable, they are most at ease in heavily planted tanks, where their grace in swimming about the foliage can best be seen. They will accept a wide variety of live, frozen, and flake food, the size of which should be geared for their relatively small mouths.

Angelfish will spawn readily if given the proper environment. Adults should be preconditioned with live food of various types, and, of course, they should be in a secure environment without competing fish. They prefer to lay eggs upon plant leaves but will also use flat pieces of slate. Even among adults, the sexes are very difficult to distinguish. Well-experienced aquarists are able to discern that the line of the body between the "feeler" and anal fin is longer and straighter in the female. The most reliable method of determining sex, however, is to maintain a small group and allow them to pair off naturally. Once the pairs are established, the excess fish can be removed to other aquariums. The adults will clean off the spawning site and guard the eggs.

Upon hatching, the young have an adhesive-producing gland on their heads, which allows them to stick to the plant's surface. The adults may be seen frequently taking the fry into their mouths and spitting them back out, apparently cleaning them. Any that miss the plant and float to the bottom are quickly rescued and returned to the nursery area.

Oscar or Velvet Cichlid (Astronotus ocellatus)

Appearing to be clothed in velvet as opposed to scales, this large (12 inches) South American cichlid is quite popular in the pet trade, despite certain drawbacks. It can be acutely pugnacious and will likely consume or attack any and all tank mates. It is, however, a fairly hardy and incredibly interesting animal. Nearly all individuals become quite tame, anticipating food upon sighting their owner and readily feeding from the hand.

The dark and rust-colored markings of the wild oscar are quite spectacular, and a variety of captive-bred color variants have also been established, including the very popular red oscar. Oscars are very attentive parents but will tolerate no other fish within the aquarium during the breeding season (and only rarely at other times). If you have the space to accommodate them—for example, a 55- to 100-gallon aquarium—maintaining and breeding a pair of oscars as they raise their numerous fry (up to 3,000) is an undertaking you are not likely to forget. As they are always in great demand in the pet trade, any young produced will likely be snapped up by other hobbyists or pet stores.

Why do the young of some cichlid species cling to their parents skin?

Among those species popular in the aquarium trade, this phenomenon can most easily be seen in the discus (*Symphysodon aequifasciata*). A native of the Amazon basin in South America, this gorgeous fish feeds its young with a modified mucus secreted from the skin.

Oscars are, unfortunately, among the many species of fish that have been introduced into foreign environments, much to the detriment of the local ecology. In the southern part of the United States, especially in the Everglades National Park in Florida, huge populations of oscars released from the pet trade are decimating populations of local species. Many of these animals have been released by owners who were not prepared to care for their oscars as they grew into adulthood. Be sure to carefully consider the full size of the fish that you purchase, and never release your pet into a foreign environment.

African Rift Lake Cichlids

In Lake Victoria and other rift lakes in Africa lives a variety of cichlids that have, apparently, all evolved from a very small number of "parent species." About 90 percent of these species are endemic to the lakes in which they are found, and this process seems to have occurred in the relatively short time (in terms of evolution) of perhaps 1 million years or so. Up to 200 closely related species, often termed flocks, can be found in one lake. They have developed an amazing array of body forms and adaptations for feeding upon all of the food resources of the particular lake in which they occur. Unfortunately, Nile perch (*Lates niloticus*) were introduced into Lake Victoria and others in the 1960s to provide a food resource and economic boost for communities in the surrounding area. This large, predatory fish has eliminated nearly all other species in the lake and is now itself disappearing as it runs out of food.

Rift lake cichlids prefer, in general, hard water. Many are denizens of rocky habitats and do best when given a variety of secure retreats. Almost all are extremely active, and the colors of some rival those of marine fish. Many species require a good deal of vegetable material in the diet, but there are exceptions, so be sure to research the fish that interest you before deciding upon a species.

Carp and Relatives (Family Cyprinidae)

The 2,000 or so members of the family Cyprinidae are related to carps and goldfish, and include many staples of the aquarium trade, such as barbs, rasboras, and danios. They range throughout the temperate and tropical waters of Eurasia, North America, and Africa and have been introduced to South America and Australia. All are egg layers, with most scattering the eggs about and leaving them to fend for themselves. The notable exception is the bitterling (*Rhodeus sericeus*). With the assistance of a long ovipositor, the female deposits her eggs inside a mantle cavity of a freshwater mussel. The male sheds sperm into the water directly above the mussel, relying on the mollusk's breathing process to draw the water into the mantle, whereupon the eggs are fertilized. In return for this favor, the parasitic larvae of the mussel sometimes attach to the female's ovipositor, to be carried away to new homes. Oddly, the bitterling has been introduced into the Bronx River in New York City, where it has apparently found a new host species of mussel in which to breed.

Although cyprinids lack teeth within the jaw, all possess pharyngeal teeth in the throat. These occur at a variety of shapes and sizes and enable members of the cyprinid's family to feed on all manner of foods, ranging from algae to snails.

Native to China, the grass carp (*Ctenopharyngodon idella*) possesses a voracious appetite and has been introduced into many parts of the world to control evasive aquatic plants. In the United States, trade in this species is limited to sterilized animals that are not capable of reproduction, to avoid the establishment of breeding populations.

Many cyprinids make use of a unique early warning system to avoid danger. When the skin of a cyprinid is broken, during an attack by a predator for example, a powerful chemical is released. School members or fish in the neighboring area flee upon sensing this chemical and thus avoid becoming a meal themselves.

FACT

Cyprinids possess an organ known as the Weberian apparatus. This structure of modified vertebrae transmits sound waves to the fish's inner ear. The entry point for the sound waves is the swim bladder. It is believed that some members of this family have a fairly sophisticated sense of hearing.

Red-Tailed Black Shark (Labeo bicolor)

As it relentlessly patrols the aquarium, the body shape and high, angular dorsal fin of this beautiful fish does indeed evoke a sharklike appearance. It is, however, fairly nonaggressive and generally quarrels with members of its own species only if suitable hiding places are lacking. The jet-black body set off by the bright red tail renders it an aquarium favorite.

Growing to a length of 6 inches, the red-tailed black shark prefers water that is slightly alkaline (pH 7.1 to 7.3). It is, by nature, a vegetarian and prefers to eat growing algae, but it will also accept algae-based pellets and spinach and other vegetables that have been soaked in hot water. It is native to Thailand and other parts of south Asia. The black shark and other close relatives are also to be found in the pet trade and can be cared for a similar manner.

Gouramis and Other Anabantids (Family Anabantidae)

Numbering approximately seventy species, gouramis and their relatives are found throughout Africa and South Asia. Most members of the family are adapted for survival in oxygen-depleted waters. They are assisted in this by the presence of a "labyrinth organ"—an accessory breathing apparatus above the gill chamber that stores and utilizes oxygen from bubbles that are gulped at the surface. This adaptation allows anabantids to live in environments that are lethal to fish that must breathe oxygen dissolved in water. This ability is carried to the extreme in the Siamese fighting fish (*Betta splendens*) a beautiful species (although aggressive to its own kind) that is commonly raised in small glass jars without any aeration whatsoever.

Anabantids build floating bubble nests created by the male. The male does this by gulping bubbles from the surface and coating them with saliva. During spawning, the male envelops the female in a circular embrace with his body and pushes the eggs into the nest with his mouth. Once egg laying is completed, he drives off the female. In a small aquarium, he might kill her, so it is important to remove her to a separate tank to be on the safe side. The male makes an attendant father, replacing burst air bubbles with fresh ones (a glass cover over the aquarium will reduce the amount of bubbles that burst, thereby lessening his workload).

Dwarf Gourami (Colisa lalia)

The dwarf gourami is an ideal choice for nearly any aquarium, combining the interesting characteristics of his larger relatives with a peaceful disposition and small size (2 inches). Native to India and other parts of south Asia, this fish's silvery gray body is brilliantly marked with red and blue stripes. This color deepens in breeding males, which are spectacular to behold.

Like most of its relatives, the dwarf gourami possesses long, threadlike fins equipped with taste cells. Located at the front of the body, below the pectoral fins, they assist the fish in locating food. Breeding is as described for the family in general, and the bubble nest is sometimes reinforced with bits of plant material. This species is quite undemanding in it's dietary requirements, taking nearly all aquarium foods and relishing, as do many fish, the occasional meal of live invertebrates.

Piranhas, Tetras, and Relatives (Family Characidae)

Characins are members of the order Characiformes, an extremely diverse group of fish containing well over 1,500 species. Ranging in size from the

²/₃-inch pygmy blue characin (*Xenurobrycon polyancistirus*) to the 4½-foot tigerfish (*Hydrocynus goliath*), characins are found throughout Africa and in Central and South America.

Many species of characins are important to people as a food source and as popular aquarium fish. Within this group are found the tetras, many species of which are among the most popular and commonly kept freshwater aquarium fish. Also numbered among the members of this group is the infamous piranha, much feared throughout South America as a voracious man-eater. As usual, the truth is far less dramatic, with the well-publicized piranha "feeding frenzies" occurring far less regularly than people may think. The species most associated with this phenomenon is the red-bellied piranha (*Pygocentrus nattereri*). (See color insert for photo.) The razor-sharp teeth of this predator and its habit of hunting in large schools does render it dangerous under certain conditions, particularly during the dry season when the water levels drop, crowding the fish and diminishing food supplies. Blood in the water can trigger a mass attack, and reportedly, fairly large animals can be stripped of flesh in a relatively short time. It is also said that piranhas that live in the vicinity of wading bird rookeries are more prone to aggressive behavior, accustomed as they are to feeding on nesting birds that fall into the water.

QUESTION?

Can piranhas be legally kept in captivity?
It depends on where you live. The fact that an animal is offered for sale at a pet store does not guarantee its legality. Many countries prohibit or carefully regulate the sale of potentially dangerous creatures such as piranhas.

Although famous for their meat-eating tendencies, in actuality, most members of the subfamily to which piranhas belong are peaceful vegetarians. One, the Amazonian tambaqui (*Colossoma macropomum*) is an important source of food throughout its range. Another, the silver dollar (*Metynnis argenteus*), is a well-known and fairly peaceable aquarium fish.

Blind Cave Fish (Astyanax fasciatus mexicanus)

Fascinating in appearance, habits, and life history, the blind cave fish does not get nearly the attention it warrants. Native to only one stream near the town of San Lois Potosi in Mexico, individuals that had been swept into a cave by the stream's current have undergone a remarkable series of adaptations to their new environment. All those just outside the cave entrance appear quite normal in all respects, but the fish isolated within the cave are white in color and lack eyes. Deprived of light and, therefore, the need for eyesight, eyes have degenerated and become covered with skin, and the body color has been lost as well. They navigate entirely by the use of the lateral line organs, and it is quite amazing to see how well they get around objects and how alert they are to the presence of food, despite not be able to see. Blind cave fish are actually fairly good community tank members, despite their unique habitat. Growing to a length of 5 inches, this fish does best in hard water but is somewhat adaptable in that regard. They will consume all matter of aquarium fish foods and compete well at feeding time with their sighted relatives. The young are born with what appear to be fully functional eyes, but they degenerate rapidly and are soon covered by a fatty pad of skin.

Marbled Hatchetfish (Camegiella strigata)

This and the other ten or so species of hatchetfish might well be dubbed "freshwater flying fish." Although they lack the advanced aerial abilities of their saltwater namesakes, hatchetfish are specifically adapted to gliding above the water surface for short distances to escape predators. This feat is accomplished through the use of powerful muscles that propel the long pectoral fins. The unique, very thin body form also appears to lessen water resistance as the fish breaks the water's surface.

Hatchetfish range throughout the area from Panama to Paraguay in Central and South America. Most have silver coloring, with the marbled hatchetfish possessing a very attractive black pattern as well. They are specifically adapted to feeding upon surface-dwelling insects and flying insects that fall into the water. The uniquely upturned mouth suits the hatchetfish well in this regard and allows it to exploit a food source denied to fish with more generalized mouthparts.

Hatchetfish will take a variety of floating aquarium foods but should be offered small insects whenever possible. Their reaction to crickets placed on the water's surface is fascinating to behold—they go into immediate action and really do seem to enjoy it.

Chapter 8

Understanding Fish Behavior

The study of fish behavior is a fascinating endeavor in its own right and will also lead to much greater success in keeping your pets healthy and in predicting how they may react to different circumstances. In considering behavior, it is important to bear in mind that the amazing diversity of fish species and lifestyles is mirrored by a nearly unbelievable variety of behavioral adaptations. In this chapter, we will examine fish behavior in general and see how it relates to aquarium keeping.

General Patterns of Activity

The overriding influence on the behavior of any creature (with people as notable but not complete exceptions) is the need to survive. Biologists are examining the phenomenon of play—that is, behaviors engaged in seemingly for enjoyment alone, among birds and mammals, but our fish and invertebrate friends seem to have a definite reason for everything that they do.

Motivations for Behavior

These reasons, or motivations, for behavior, generally exist to assist the animal in finding a suitable environment, obtaining food, avoiding predators, and reproducing. Armed with this knowledge, the wise aquarium keeper will analyze what is observed in the aquarium and will use what is learned to better care for his or her pets. Of course, many fish, will, of necessity, modify their behaviors in captivity. In some cases, the adjustments will be so drastic that the actual purpose or function of what the fish are doing will be lost on us. However, as you gain experience, you will generally be able to see the relation that the captive behavior has to its natural counterpart.

Knowledge of the meaning behind a pet's behavior will allow you to modify captive conditions so that the animal might feel more at ease. Also, this may allow us to adjust the care that we are giving to our pets, so that their modified behavior might work to their advantage in captivity.

It is, as always, very important that we know as much as we can about the natural histories of the fish that we keep in captivity. Knowing, for example, whether a particular species is an active hunter or a sessile ambush predator will enable us not only to provide adequate care but also to recognize problems when they arise.

Diurnal and Nocturnal Fish

When selecting fish for your aquarium, it is important to consider whether they are normally active by day or night. This will affect not only your enjoyment of your pets, but also the choice of tank mates that you might wish to include in the aquarium.

General Considerations

Nocturnal fish such as freshwater eels need a place to hide during the daytime. If denied this, they may become stressed and will languish in captivity. However, eels and other such species change radically at night, and their level of activity will surprise you. Most catfish, for example, spend the night swimming about looking for food. These nighttime wanderings may disturb shy, diurnal fish and prevent them from resting properly, thereby impairing their health. Many fish that are innocuous by day morph into quite aggressive predators as night falls. Be sure that you are aware of and understand all such predatory propensities before deciding which species to keep. For example, small octopus and moray eels are usually quite content to spend the day secluded in a favorite retreat. If this is the only time that you observe them, you might mistakenly believe such animals to be compatible with your other fish. However, at nighttime they undergo quite a change and will quickly devour smaller neighbors.

Resting and Eating

Be sure that diurnal fish have appropriate retreats, as many species use them at nighttime. Certain fish, such as a parrotfish, do not use shelters by day, when they swim about quite like most other fish. However, at night, they habitually secret themselves within caves and crevices, and they may become stressed if prevented from doing so in captivity.

Bear in mind that many nocturnal fish will not feed during the day. Some, as is pointed out in the various species accounts (Chapter 7 and Chapter 10), will forego their nocturnal habits once they adjust to captivity. Bullhead catfish, moray eels, and, occasionally, octopus fall within this category. Many fish, are, however, strictly nocturnal and must be fed during those times when they are normally active if they are to do well in the aquarium.

Keep in mind that the cautions that have been mentioned concerning housing nocturnal fish with diurnal species apply to active and sessile fish as well. For example, most typical "sit and wait predators," such as anglerfish, will be greatly disturbed if forced to remain in close proximity to vigorous, actively swimming fish and will usually not obtain enough food when aggressive feeders are present.

Feeding Behavior

Both freshwater and marine fish have evolved an astounding array of methods of obtaining food. One species or another is able to utilize as food nearly any plant or animal to be found in the world's aquatic habitats.

Fish That Feed "on Land"

Many fish are able to exploit food resources that arise in terrestrial habitats. The most common example of this is when fish consume insects that fall upon the water's surface, or scavenge animals that have drowned. In certain areas of South America, numerous fish species invade the rainforest during the rainy season, thereby gaining access to a rich source of land-based foods that are unavailable during the dry season. Some fish, moreover, are specifically adapted for consuming nonaquatic foods. Mudskippers leave the water to chase crabs across mudflats, while arowanas—active, elongated fish of Central and South America—are well suited for leaping and plucking insects and other small creatures from overhanging branches. Pacu, the large, vegetarian relatives of the infamous piranha, are equipped with jaws that make short work of the thick husks of the various seeds and fruits that grow along their native South American streams and rivers.

Strange Hunting Methods

It is impossible to even begin to describe the lengths to which some fish have gone, concerning unique specializations, to exploit unusual food sources. While most species are limited to swallowing food items that will fit within their mouths, some fish use a remarkable behavior that enables them to eat pieces of large food items that would otherwise be denied them. Certain types of piranha, for example, rush at larger fish and clip off a piece of their fin for a meal. Cookie-cutter sharks have uniquely structured mouths that allow them to grasp onto the sides of larger fish and twist off a hunk of flesh.

FACT

Cavities below the eye of the flashlight fish (*Photoblepharon palpebratus*) contain bioluminescent bacteria that light up during the fish's nighttime forays. These lights lure the zooplankton upon which the flashlight fish feeds. Flashlight fish regulate the light using muscle control, thereby allowing them to communicate and to confuse predators.

Some fish, such as barracuda, actively search for their prey, while others, such as the anglerfish, remain sedentary while manipulating a wormlike lure designed to draw prey to within striking range. From fish that stalk their prey to those that shock it with electricity or are carried to food sources after attaching themselves to larger animals, the array of the feeding behaviors utilized by these remarkable creatures seems to stretch the limits of what is possible for animals.

Unusual Food Sources

The actual food sources utilized by fish are also interesting and, often, improbable. Strangely, many of the largest species, such as basking sharks, whale sharks, and manta rays, feed upon plankton, the tiniest of the ocean's numerous food items. At the other end of the scale, large ocean-going predators, such as great white sharks, are quite capable of consuming large marine mammals such as sea lions and, on rare occasions, people. As you will read in more detail in the various species accounts, there are, among countless other interesting feeding techniques, fish that create and protect gardens of algae, species that have evolved long, thin snouts to reach coral polyps, and others that can crush coral with their powerful jaws.

Defensive Behaviors

Of course, the unique feeding strategies that predatory fish have developed have resulted in a number of adaptations by prey species seeking to avoid becoming a meal. An extremely common form of predator avoidance is the forming of schools. Over half of all the known fish species form schools when young, and a great many retain this habit into adulthood. It is believed that schooling confuses predators by denying them a specific victim upon which to focus their attention. Large schools of fish may also appear to be one large organism and might therefore be avoided by predators as being dangerous or too large to consume.

Every species of fish has its own unique way of avoiding predators, from the mucus coating of parrotfish that disguises their outline and scent as they sleep to the toxic cloud of chemicals emitted by the Australian prowlfish. In some cases, the protection is structural in nature, such as the rigid, boxlike skin of the cowfish or the sharp spines and inflatable body of the porcupine fish. Specific methods of predator avoidance will be discussed further in the accounts of the various fish species.

Territoriality

Many types of fish are quite territorial and will not tolerate others of their own species or, in some cases, of other species, in close proximity. This is important for you to understand from the start so that you can be aware of potential aggressive behavior or conflicts when choosing animals for your collection.

Peaceful Coexistence?

Viewing aquatic environments in nature or on television may give you the false impression that a large variety of creatures can easily coexist in an aquarium. While it is possible to create complex community aquariums, such an undertaking requires a good deal of experience. Oftentimes, species that might coexist quite well in nature will not do so within the confines of an aquarium.

Understanding Aggression

As always, it is important to learn as much as you can about your pets if you are to be successful in keeping them. Understanding a fish's natural behaviors and habitat will help you to determine whether or not it will coexist with others. In many cases, territorial behavior is engaged in to protect a favorite food source. This phenomenon may easily be observed by those keeping marine damselfish. These tiny yet aggressive beasts tend and protect small patches of their favorite algae. Despite their small size, they will make life miserable for even much larger fish that dare intrude.

ALERT!

Aggressive territorial behavior may be inhibited in aquariums that are too small for the establishment of territories. Keep in mind that if the fish are moved to a larger aquarium, or if the size of the available territory is increased as a result of the death of a tank mate, aggression may develop among fish that had previously cohabited peacefully.

Other common reasons for aggressive behavior among fish are the protection of a nest site or competition for mates. It is important to bear in mind that normally peaceable fish may undergo an overnight transformation in behavior once they enter breeding condition or upon the introduction of a member of the opposite sex. Review the section on mating strategies in Chapter 20 to learn more about the effects of breeding behavior upon overall lifestyle.

Eliciting Natural Behavior in the Aquarium

Once a fish's behavior is studied and understood, you can set about creating a habitat that will allow the fish to thrive and, perhaps, to exhibit a range of its behaviors. An aquarium of appropriate size and furnished in a close approximation of the natural habitat of the fish is the first prerequisite.

Basic Requirements

The proper temperature, light cycle, pH level, and careful attention to all other environmental parameters are all essential if your fish are to feel at home. For many species, normal behavior will be exhibited only when day length and temperature are alternated in an approximation of a natural cycle. Your fish must also be given the opportunity to engage in their normal behaviors. For example, sticklebacks must be provided upright twigs and properly sized bits of grass and other materials if they are to construct their incredible little nests.

Contrary to popular belief, providing numerous hiding places to shy aquarium fish will not result in their remaining hidden from view. Rather, such will provide a sense of security and they may become quite visible. You will then be able to view a number of interesting behaviors that would not be exhibited were the animals kept in unnatural conditions.

Providing Natural Prey

An interesting and easily manipulated facet of fish behavior is the obtaining of food. Providing natural foods whenever possible will result not only in healthier animals but also in your ability to see a number of fascinating activities. Allow your pets to forage whenever possible. This is most easily accomplished with predatory species by introducing food items that will live in the aquarium. In freshwater aquariums, for example, black worms might be allowed to burrow into the substrate, while small hardy food fish such as mummichogs might be introduced into marine aquariums. It is important to allow the food animals to adjust to the aquarium water, just as you would were you introducing a new pet fish, so that they themselves will thrive. This type of feeding technique might best be used as an adjunct to your normal feeding schedule, as it may be difficult to ascertain if your animals are getting enough to eat when live prey is the main source of food.

Other Natural Feeding Opportunities

Putting whole greens into the tanks of herbivorous species or encouraging the growth of algae in such tanks are excellent ways to observe a number of unique feeding behaviors. Another interesting option is to crack a whole clam or mussel and drop it into a community aquarium. You will be quite surprised and amused at the lengths that various fish will go to to obtain this welcome treat.

Interpreting Fish Behavior

Once you have learned to recognize and understand what your fish are doing, you may be able to interpret the forces driving the behavior that you observe. This will eventually lead to an improvement in your ability to provide better care for your pets, and to predict the effects of various changes or additions that you may introduce into the aquarium.

It is extremely important that you are able to recognize environmental problems that your fish's behavior might indicate. Many types of disease or harmful changes to your aquarium's environment will incite specific behaviors on the part of your fish. For example, constant swimming by a normally sessile species, such as the flounder (see color insert for photo), might indicate a water quality problem or that the animal is being harassed by a tank mate. Seahorses that are constantly in motion and swimming about are probably stressed for some reason. Similarly, bottom-dwelling fish rising to the surface might indicate a deficiency in oxygen, while color changes or listless behavior could presage disease or an environmental problem. Any unusual or atypical behavior on the part of your pets should send out a warning signal to you. The cessation of normal activities may also indicate a problem. Likewise, the refusal to feed may indicate that a female is gravid or that the animal is ill.

Chapter 9

Invertebrates— Classification and Characteristics

Invertebrates comprise 95 to 97 percent of the approximately 2 million species of animals that have thus far been identified. Despite the large number of species of which we are aware, we do not yet have any idea of their total numbers. In terms of diversity of species and lifestyles, invertebrates are unrivaled by any other animal group. Ranging in size from microscopic organisms to 66–foot-long giant squids, invertebrates of one kind or another are to be found in every habitat imaginable.

An Overview of the Invertebrates

In the most general terms, invertebrates are creatures that lack a backbone and internal skeleton. That being said, there exists within this immense group of animals a mind-boggling number of variations on that general theme.

In contrast to other types of organisms, invertebrates appear to be as numerous in the freezing seas of Antarctica as they are in the warm tropics. Colonies of bizarre sponges, clams, giant tubeworms, and other unique invertebrates have even colonized the hot, mineral laden waters in the proximity of deep sea vents. These animals form the only communities known to exist in the complete absence of sunlight, using chemical reactions as opposed to photosynthesis as the basis of the food chain. The incredible diversity of lifestyles found among invertebrates precludes any attempt at generalizations concerning their senses, reproduction, behavior, or modes of living. Instead, such details are covered during discussions of the phyla, or in the various species' accounts.

Sponges and Relatives (Phylum Porifera)

The approximately 10,000 species of animals commonly known as sponges are largely ocean dwellers, with all but 150 or so species inhabiting freshwater. Sponges are among the simplest of the invertebrates, being comprised of aggregations of cells and lacking true organs. These sessile creatures are important components of their environments, and many species are hosts to communities of other animals such as shrimp and fish. Identification of individual species is complicated by the fact that many take the shape of the objects upon which they have attached, or assume different forms depending upon the rapidity of the water currents in which they live. Although the bright colors of many advertise their toxicity, a variety of marine animals such as turtles, fish, and sea slugs do manage to consume sponges regularly. Sponges have amazing powers of regeneration.

Living sponges are given their texture and shape by a material known as spongin, which supports the rest of the body's cells. Movement of water into the sponge is accomplished by the action of hairlike flagellum. Water enters and waste products exit the animal through a single opening, with microscopic organic material being removed to nourish the sponge in the process. Sponges reproduce by releasing eggs and sperm into the surrounding water. The newly hatched young become part of the plankton and float around for a period until attaching to the substrate, a rock, or a similar surface, where they spend the rest of their lives as sessile organisms.

QUESTION?

How are sponges transformed for use in human bathing?
Several species of sponges, commonly known as bath sponges, have been harvested from the Mediterranean Sea since the time of the Roman Empire. The part of the animal used for washing is a fibrous material called spongin. The animals' softer body parts are removed by drying the sponge in the sun.

Jellyfish, Sea Anemones, Sea Fans, and Corals (Phylum Cnidaria)

This phylum contains an odd assemblage of seemingly very dissimilar creatures. Numbering at least 10,000 species, and likely many more, the jellyfish, sea anemones, sea fans, and corals are, despite their very different appearances and lifestyles, actually quite closely related.

The basic body plan of all the cnidarians is a saclike structure with a single opening that serves as a mouth and exit port for waste products. All creatures within this phylum possess stinging cells, known as the nematocysts, whose needlelike barbs readily pierce the skin of both predators and prey. The various species within this group exist in two forms, as polyps attached to the substrate or as swimming animals known as medusas. In some groups, such as the jellyfish, the animal passes through both stages at different points in its life.

Jellyfish (Class Scyphozoa)

Comprised of at least 95 percent water, the jellyfish are quite appropriately named. Rarely exhibited until fairly recently, public aquariums are currently making great strides in their captive husbandry. Most species are, however, very delicate, and not suitable for home aquariums. All are carnivorous, feeding on a range of tiny creatures, and, in some cases, small fish that are overcome by the stinging tentacles.

ALERT!

Many species of jellyfish, especially those from tropical waters, are quite toxic to humans, and their venoms have been little studied. Even temperate species should be avoided or handled with extreme care, as their stings may cause a severe allergic reaction in people sensitive to their particular venom.

Sea Anemones and Corals (Class Anthozoa)

It is among the sea anemones and corals that we find many of the cnidarians most sought after by aquarists. Approximately 6,500 species inhabit the world's temperate and tropical seas, with many species of sea anemones being found in quite cold waters as well. The majority of these animals are filter feeders, and many rely on commensally living single-celled algae known as zooxanthella for a large portion of their food supply. The host animals apparently utilize carbohydrates and oxygen produced by the algae, and the algae may derive some benefit from the invertebrates' waste products. Proper lighting is essential if the algae, and therefore their host animals, are to thrive in the aquarium. Larger species of sea anemones will consume small animals and, in the aquarium, thrive on bits of shrimp and fish.

Soft corals are not often kept by aquarists but are actually fairly hardy, as corals go. Usually sold as pulse corals or leather corals, they require good water quality and an ample supply of tiny food items. Hard corals possess a calcareous exoskeleton and are responsible for the formation of coral reefs. The animal itself is somewhat similar to a sea anemone in its body plan and sits in a calcium-based cup. Individual coral animals range in size from 0.2 inches to 20 inches across. Most hard corals offered for sale today require the presence of thriving colonies of zooxanthella and water with high pH and calcium levels.

FACT

Coral reefs build up very gradually in tropical seas as living animals colonize the exoskeletons of deceased corals. The world's largest coral reef is the Great Barrier Reef of Australia, which is 1,250 miles in length.

Corals reproduce by releasing sperm and eggs into the sea. A number of species have evolved the reproductive strategy of simultaneous spawning, with all of the animals in a given area releasing gametes at the same time. Even in ecosystems as large as the Great Barrier Reef, the individual coral animals are somehow synchronized to reproduce at a specific time.

Segmented Worms (Phylum Annelida)

The segmented worms differ from most other invertebrates in that they lack a true exoskeleton. In place of the tough outer covering that protects the other creatures to which they are related, segmented worms have developed fluid-filled bodies for rigidity of form. Although given only scant consideration by most people, including aquarists, this phylum contains creatures of immense importance to hobbyists and nonhobbyists alike. Earthworms, for example, are vital to the functioning of most temperate ecosystems and are important food sources for a variety of wild and captive animals. Other relatives such as marine worms and leeches are also vital links in ecosystems in which they live, and many are fascinating subjects for home aquariums.

Leeches, segmented worms of the class Hirudinea, are familiar to most of us as blood-sucking parasites. The majority are, however, predatory. The next time you purchase black worms as food for your fish, look closely for a small type of leech that usually lives with them—their ability to quickly suck down black worms is quite interesting. One family of leeches lives in the sea and consumes the blood of marine fish.

Bristle Worms (Class Polychaeta)

Among the class of segmented worms known as bristle worms are a number of creatures of interest to marine aquarists, both as exhibit animals and as somewhat noxious pests. Many of the marine species are gorgeously colored, but, unfortunately, we know little of their husbandry. The sea mouse, which actually resembles its namesake far more that it does a worm, is occasionally offered for sale but should only be purchased by serious hobbyists with experience in keeping similar creatures. The bristles, or chaetae, of the sea mouse form a furlike covering over the plump body and lend this odd creature its common name. These bristles are actually quite sharp to the touch and render the sea mouse unpalatable to most predators.

ALERT!

The bristles of the fire worm take the form of long hairs that easily pierce skin to inject a venom that causes great pain. These hairs are shed at the slightest disturbance. Bristle worms generally arrive in marine aquariums as uninvited intruders hidden within coral or live rock. They are voracious predators of sea anemones, corals, and other sessile invertebrates.

The tubeworms, or fan worms, are the Polychaetes of greatest current interest to marine aquarists. These worms live within winding calcareous tubes that are attached to rocks, docks, or the shells of snails, horseshoe crabs, and other invertebrates. The worms extend a stiff ring of tentacles from the tube's end, appearing, at first glance, to be brightly colored underwater flowers. These tentacles serve both as gills and as food-gathering organs, trapping organic material from the surrounding water.

Tubeworms occur in a great variety of colors, including blue, red, orange, green, and purple. In contrast to the general rule that animals dwelling in temperate regions are more somberly colored than are their tropical relatives, tubeworms from the northern parts of their range are often quite brilliant.

Where it is legal, tubeworms are easily collected from rocks, dock pilings, and even from the shells of other invertebrates. Tubeworms retreat with an amazing rapidity into their shelters at the slightest disturbance, but they are quick to reappear and resume their feeding. Most tubeworms are quite easy to maintain if provided with good water quality and an ample supply of food. Food is most easily provided in the form of commercial pastes formulated for filter-feeding invertebrates.

Horseshoe Crabs and Relatives (Phylum Chelicerata)

It may come as a surprise to learn that the familiar horseshoe crab is not a crab at all but rather a member of a huge group of animals that includes spiders, mites, and ticks. Certain mites and bizarre creatures known as sea spiders are, along with the horseshoe crab, the only marine members of this phylum.

The horseshoe crab and related creatures possess a chitinous exoskeleton that is shed as the animal grows. Members of this phylum have a body that is divided into two distinct parts: the cephalothorax, which contains the head and the legs; and the abdomen. The jaws, or chelicera, take the form of stabbing or grinding mouth parts and lend the phylum its common name.

QUESTION?

Why are horseshoe crabs sometimes referred to as "living fossils"?
The four living species of horseshoe crab are among the oldest known surviving creatures on the planet. They have remained essentially unchanged for over 300 million years.

The smooth texture and domed shape of the horseshoe crab's exoskeleton allows it to easily burrow through the sand and mud substrates that it favors. The shell itself is quite interesting to behold, as it usually is colonized by a fascinating array of marine algae, tubeworms, barnacles, sea anemones, and other organisms. Horseshoe crabs are quite active creatures, and both in the wild and in the aquarium they appear to be perpetually searching for the worms, soft-shelled clams, and other creatures that make up their diet.

The horseshoe crab's long tail, more properly termed the telson, is believed by many people to function as a weapon of defense. Actually, these creatures are quite harmless, with the telson's only function being to assist the animal in righting itself after a wave has deposited it on its back. Among this odd animal's other unusual characteristics are its book lungs, unique in the animal world and used for swimming as well as respiration. Horseshoe crabs engage in massive breeding migrations. See the individual species accounts in Chapter 13 for a description of this amazing natural phenomenon.

Crabs, Shrimp, and Relatives (Phylum Crustacea)

This enormous phylum of animals contains at least 50,000 species, with many more undoubtedly waiting to be discovered. Although the vast majority dwell in marine waters, there are numerous freshwater species and many that are completely terrestrial. The diversity of these creatures is truly amazing, in terms of lifestyles and appearances. Many are microscopic, while the largest, the giant spider crab of Japan, has legs that span a distance of over 10 feet. A large number are of great interest to both freshwater and marine hobbyists.

Like most invertebrates, crustaceans are housed in a protective exoskeleton that is composed of various calcium salts and is shed as the animal grows. The tail, or telson, of crayfish, lobsters, and shrimp is hinged and serves as an escape mechanism. When threatened, the tail is thrust forward, creating a powerful current of water that propels the animal backwards, in the opposite direction that the predator might expect it to go.

The hard exoskeleton of crustaceans protects them from many predators, but it must be periodically shed. Immediately after shedding, the animal is very soft to the touch and vulnerable to attack. Shedding generally occurs at night, and hardening time varies. Be sure to provide your crustaceans with secure hiding spots and water of an appropriately high pH.

Brine Shrimp and Relatives (Class Brachiopoda)

The brachiopods are considered to be the most primitive of the crustaceans. Their members include animals such as daphnia, brine shrimp, and copepods, all of which are extremely valuable food sources for captive and free living fish. Despite their classification as the least advanced of the crustaceans, most of these tiny creatures are quite successful and have colonized in a wide variety of extremely inhospitable environments. Brine shrimp, for example, thrive in highly saline waters that few other creatures can tolerate. Their tiny eggs survive in dried form for years and are shipped all over the world to be hatched by aquarists and used as food for tiny fish fry.

FACT

Krill are small, shrimplike crustaceans that float about in uncountable billions in the open seas. They are the primary food for a number of large creatures, including certain whales, basking sharks, and manta rays, and form the basis of the food chain in many of the world's oceans.

Crabs, Lobsters, Crayfish, and Shrimp (Order Decapoda)

It is among the decapods that you find the crustaceans most of interest to both freshwater and marine hobbyists, as well as some of the world's most commercially important food animals. Decapods have much to recommend them as aquarium subjects, including the fact that they are active by day, have easily satisfied appetites, display spectacular coloration, and have fascinating habits. Many are, however, quite aggressive toward their own kind and are efficient predators of a number of other invertebrates and fish.

A vast array of shrimp is suitable for marine and freshwater aquariums. Many have evolved quite unique lifestyles, such as living commensally with sea anemones and other sessile invertebrates. Other species clean parasites and debris from the scales and even from within the mouths of fish that unhesitatingly consume other species of shrimp of the same size as the "cleaners."

Among the lobsters and crabs is an enormous range of creatures suitable for maintenance in aquariums. They too have evolved a nearly unbelievable range of appearances and lifestyles. Crabs are to be found living in association with the sea vents 1.7 miles below the surface of the ocean, as well as in completely terrestrial habitats. Some species camouflage themselves with debris from their environments, while others store food on their carapaces or in empty mollusk shells, which they use as homes. One species, commonly known as the coconut crab, grows to a massive size and is reputed to be capable of opening coconuts with its powerful claws.

Many crab and lobster species engage in extensive migrations and complicated mating displays. Some release sperm and eggs into the sea and leave the young to their fates, while in other species the females hold the eggs below the telson and protect them during their development.

ESSENTIAL

The larvae of most crabs and lobsters are free swimming and undergo several distinct developmental stages before reaching the familiar adult form. So bizarre and different in appearance from the adults are immature crabs that many were formerly classified as entirely different species.

Crayfish, the freshwater relatives of the crabs (one family of which also dwells in freshwater) and lobsters, have successfully colonized in an extremely wide variety of habitats. Some species build extensive tunnel systems in wet meadows, while others grow quite large and are formidable predators within their aquatic habitats. A number of species are farmed commercially for food. Escapees from farms and bait buckets (crayfish are widely used as fishing bait) have established feral populations in several countries, much to the detriment of local plants and small animals.

Snails, Clams, Squid, and Relatives (Phylum Mollusca)

With over 100,000 species having been described, and with untold numbers likely as yet unseen by scientists, the mollusks are among the earth's most successful creatures. Inhabiting freshwater, marine, and terrestrial environments, many mollusk species are commercially important as food animals and are also much in demand as aquarium subjects.

The mollusks form an unlikely group of animals, whose members seem, in many cases, to possess no similarities to each other whatsoever. They are, however, united in the possession of a shell comprised mainly of conchiolin and calcium carbonate, although this has been lost in the octopus and the squid. This phylum numbers among its members creatures that are vastly dissimilar, from the basically sedentary clam to the highly intelligent and active octopus.

FACT

The irregularly spaced lines that occur on the shells of mollusks are actually growth rings. Much like the more familiar growth rings on trees, these markings can, in some cases, be used to age the animal. This is especially true for temperate species, most of which appear to create one ring per year.

Individual mollusk species may reproduce utilizing separate sexes or may be hermaphroditic. Most simply release eggs and sperm into the water, but squid and octopus practice internal fertilization. Many species begin life as planktonic larvae and are important components of the food chains in which they occur. Marine larvae may drift for hundreds of miles before settling down and maturing into the adult form.

Snails, Slugs, and Relatives (Class Gastropoda)

Although people may tend to think of snails and slugs as somewhat simple, inactive creatures, the over 70,000 members of this group actually follow quite a diverse number of lifestyles. Individual species may be scavengers, carnivores, or herbivores. Some are surprisingly active predators. Marine snails known as whelks feed upon bivalves (two-shelled creatures such as clams) by prying open their shells or by boring holes through them. Other sea-dwelling snails known as cone shells impale their prey on retractable tongues, or radula. The venom thus injected paralyzes their victims and can be fatal to humans.

Sea slugs, or nudibranchs, are brilliantly colored, free-swimming animals that appear, unfortunately, to be difficult to maintain for any length of time in captivity. All species of this group dwell in saltwater and seem to be fairly specialized feeders upon sea anemones, sponges, and corals (a fact that does little to simplify their care in captivity). Those species that feed upon sea anemones incorporate the anemones' stinging cells, or nematocysts, into their own gill tufts as a form of protection.

Clams, Oysters, Mussels, Scallops, and Relatives (Class Bivalvia)

Numbering over 6,000 species, the bivalves form the second-largest group of mollusks after the gastropods. Many are extremely important commercially as human food items, and a number are adaptable to life in the aquarium.

Bivalves are unique in that they have gills that function not only as organs of respiration but also as a means of acquiring food. All species studied thus far have been found to be filter feeders, most of which trap plankton in the sticky mucus that covers the gills.

At weights in excess of 220 pounds the giant clam (*Tridacna gigas*) is the world's largest mollusk. Native to Australia's Great Barrier Reef and surrounding areas, this huge creature relies upon zooxanthellae (commensal algae) for a good deal of its food. Although pearls are usually associated with oysters, the world's largest pearl actually originated in a giant clam and is 14 pounds in weight.

Shipworms are, despite their appearance, not worms at all. These commercially important pests in the dock-building and shipping industry are actually bivalves that have retained only a vestige of shell. The animal pushes this shell through water-logged wood, boring a hole as it moves along and feeding on the resulting wood shavings.

Although basically sedentary creatures, bivalves in the aquarium often surprise their caretakers with their degree of movement. Particularly unusual are several species of scallop, which can rapidly open and close their shells, expelling water in the process and propelling themselves quickly.

Squid, Octopus, Chambered Nautilus, and Cuttlefish (Class Cephalopoda)

The squids and their relatives comprise a group of nearly 700 species of extremely active and intelligent invertebrates. Their lifestyles and appearances render them distinctly unlike the rest of their mollusk relatives. The shell is much reduced or completely absent, with only the chambered nautilus retaining what appears to be a full shell. Even in this species, however, the animal lives in a small portion of the shell, with the rest being devoted to gas-filled chambers that control the animal's buoyancy. In the cuttlefish and squid, the shell has been internalized. The familiar cuttlebone that pet keepers feed to birds is actually the remnants of the cuttlefish's shell.

The eight tentacles of the various cephalopods are extremely effective organs of touch and taste. Octopus and squid are equipped with sharp, parrotlike beaks, which they use to help overcome their prey. All cephalopods are predators, feeding upon crabs, fish, shrimp, and other marine creatures. They move by crawling on the substrate or by actively swimming using the force of water expelled from the mantle. Several species of squid are actually able to soar above the surface of the ocean using this form of jet propulsion.

FACT

The giant squid is the largest known mollusk, and the largest invertebrate. Growing to a length of at least 66 feet, this deep-sea predator has been the subject of legend for centuries. Formerly known only from beached corpses, it was not until the year 2005 that Japanese scientists finally captured a living giant squid on film.

Those cephalopods that have been studied have been found to be extremely intelligent and capable of learning simple tasks. Octopus seem especially quick to make various associations and to remember those that result in a food reward. And, as anyone who has kept these fascinating creatures can attest, their ability to escape seemingly secure enclosures seems to evince a degree of mental acuity. Octopuses are capable of rapid and quite startling color changes, which they use as a form of communication, camouflage, and defense. At least one species of octopus changes the actual form of its body to mimic creatures as diverse as sea snakes and flounders, in an effort to escape or threaten predators.

Many cephalopods are equipped with an inklike substance known as sepia, which can be released as a "smokescreen," apparently to divert the attention of would-be predators so that the animal can escape unnoticed.

Cephalopods reproduce by internal fertilization. The males of most octopus species insert a sperm packet into the mantle of the female. In what appears to be a quite unique and unusual fertilization technique, male squid of certain species seem somehow to thrust a sharply pointed sperm packet deep into the arms of the females. Female octopuses guard their eggs and often die shortly after they hatch.

Until recently, it was believed that female squid of all species released their eggs into the ocean without further parental involvement. Photographs taken in the year 2005, however, revealed a species of squid that carries its eggs wrapped in the arms and actively aerates them as well. Amazingly, this shallow-water species descends to great depths during the egg-brooding process.

Sea Stars, Sea Urchins, and Relatives (Phylum Echinodermata)

All members of this large (over 6,500 species) phylum live in marine waters. As with nearly all groups of invertebrates, there is, among the echinoderms, a great deal of variation in terms of appearance and lifestyle.

Echinoderms are unique among all animals in possessing a highly specialized water vascularization system. Canals originating from the many hundreds of tube feet transport water through a series of valves that, when opened or closed, allow the animal to move. The pressure that can be achieved using this system can be surprisingly high, allowing sea stars for example, to pry open the shells of the clams and oysters upon which they feed.

QUESTION?

What purposes do tube feet serve?
The tube feet of the echinoderms are unique in the animal world. In addition to locomotion, they function as respiratory organs and assist in feeding and in sensory perception.

Among the other unique organs possessed by echinoderms such as sea stars and sea urchins are the tiny, pincherlike pedicellariae. Thousands of these "living forceps" are to be found all over the exoskeleton. In some species they are thought to remove sand and other debris from the animal's surface, while in others they appear to be connected to poison glands. Echinoderms are bottom dwellers that do not actually swim but are, nevertheless, fairly active in many cases. Various species obtain their food by predation, scavenging, or by filtering it from the water. The eggs and sperm are simultaneously shed into the surrounding ocean, and the wormlike larvae swim or float about for a time before maturing into the adult form.

Sea stars are among the most popular of the echinoderms in the aquarium trade. Many species are extremely colorful and grow to quite large sizes. Most sea stars are adapted to opening bivalves such as clams and oysters via the water pressure built up through the vascularization system. Their actual method of feeding is equally unique, with the stomach being everted through the mouth and into the open clam or oyster shell.

Sea urchins are also quite popular with marine aquarists, despite the fact that they possess spines that can inflict painful wounds. Sea urchins move about on tube feet in much the same manner as sea stars.

Brittle and basket stars are extremely unusual. The brittle stars have long, sinuous arms and lie about motionless until they detect the presence of food in the water. At that time the arms begin to snake about rapidly and the animals unerringly head toward the origin of the food's scent. These interesting scavengers do quite well in the aquarium when fed bits of clam, shrimp, and fish. The equally strange basket stars hold their many-branched arms out to form a type of net to snare small food items from the surrounding water.

ALERT!

Sea cucumbers are sessile echinoderms that are occasionally offered for sale or collected from tide pools by hobbyists. When disturbed, they have the unsettling habit of discharging their stomach through the anus. Amazingly, the stomach can be regenerated, but handle these creatures very carefully so as to avoid eliciting this bizarre form of defense in the first place.

Sea lilies look just the way their common name suggests. These filter feeders are rarely kept in aquariums. They have existed in their present form for nearly 500 million years.

Animals with Backbones (Phylum Chordata)

This phylum is mentioned in a discussion of animals without backbones only because of the existence of what appears to be a unique "missing link" between the invertebrates and the vertebrates. This unassuming animal, known commonly as the sea squirt, possesses a stiffened rod known as the notochord. This unique structure is thought to be the precursor of the vertebrate backbone. Both the notochord and its associated dorsal nerve cord appear only in larval sea squirts and are, for reasons as yet unknown, lost during the transformation to adulthood.

Sea squirts are marine animals that usually arrive in the aquarium accidentally, attached to coral, rocks, or other such animals or materials. The approximately 1,000 species are all sessile filter feeders and most are relatively small, although several types may grow to 20 inches in height.

Chapter 10

Invertebrates— Species Accounts

The vast majority of all living creatures are invertebrates. We do not yet even know the magnitude of their numbers, but research suggests that it is incredible. For example, in Panama, 100 new species of beetle have been discovered in a single tree! Aquarists with an interest in invertebrates have before them a lifetime of fascinating observations and discoveries. From the sessile corals to the intelligent, active cuttlefish, the surprises and opportunities are endless.

Octopus

An alert, active hunter, the octopus exhibits a good deal of intelligence and is quite adept at solving simple problems. Research has shown it able to distinguish and associate various shapes with a food reward, and many individuals learn to unscrew glass jars and go through other manipulations to obtain food. All too frequently, it turns these amazing abilities to the problem of escape, and it is thus one of the hardest creatures to keep contained. The body can slip through amazingly small crevices, and the muscular arms are quite able to dislodge coverings from the aquarium. Therefore, be sure your aquarium lid is not only tight fitting but also weighed down or otherwise secured.

ALERT!

All octopus possess a hard, sharp beak and they are capable of inflicting a painful bite. The blue-ringed octopus (*Hapalochlaena maculosa*) possesses one of the world's deadliest known venoms and can kill a human with one bite. Amazingly, it is sometimes offered for sale in the pet trade. Learn to recognize this species and avoid it at all costs.

Octopus are, in general, solitary animals, and mixing individuals in the same aquarium is nearly impossible, no matter what their sex. Fertilization is internal, with many species gluing the eggs to the rooftop of a cave or other retreat, where they are guarded by the female. Octopus are capable of incredible color changes, and even changes to the texture of the skin, to help camouflage themselves or, possibly, to communicate with other individuals (see color insert for photo).

Several species of small octopus are occasionally imported into the pet trade, most typically the common tropical octopus (*Octopus cyaneus*). Growing to a maximum length of 12 inches, this creature is fairly hardy if given excellent water quality and a number of secure retreats in which to hide. This and other octopus are extremely intolerant of disturbance, although once acclimated many individuals will anticipate feedings and leave their homes for food, even with the lights on. They should be handled with care, however, during their initial entry into the aquarium, and the lights should be left off for the first few days. It is also important not to suddenly turn the light on in a dark room, to avoid startling the animal. If greatly disturbed, this sensitive creature will release a dark-colored ink into the aquarium, which will necessitate a water change, and further disturbance of the animal.

All octopus are carnivorous, and the common tropical octopus will thrive on fish, crabs, clams, snails, scallops, and the like. While it will coexist with corals, sponges, and tubeworms, most other tank mates will quickly be consumed.

Corals, Jellyfish, and Sea Anemones

Although they vary dramatically from one another in appearance, these animals are all members of the phylum Cnidaria and are thus closely related. Until recently, corals were considered by most as nearly impossible to keep and, indeed, they still present problems. Water quality is exceedingly important, as is the wavelength and intensity of lighting. Many coral species obtain a good deal of their food via the action of symbiotic algae, which live within them. Without proper lighting the algae perish, and no amount of additional food provided thereafter can keep the coral alive. Most corals feed upon plankton-sized food items, and although commercially prepared diets are now available, many are still difficult to maintain. One exception is the tooth coral. Now routinely available in the trade, this species eats large food items, such as pieces of shrimp, and is thus fairly easy to feed.

FACT

Until recently, collection of coral for commercial aquariums was a leading cause of coral reef destruction. Reef ecosystems are extremely delicate and very slow to recover from injury. Although collection is now outlawed in many areas, be sure that any coral you purchase is commercially cultured and not collected from reefs.

Jellyfish (see color insert for photo) are increasingly exhibited in public aquariums but are, as yet, too delicate for most home aquarists to maintain. Indeed, very few are offered for sale. One possible exception is the upside-down jellyfish (*Cassiopeia andromeda*). In contrast to nearly all of its relatives, this jellyfish spends its life resting on the substrate with its tentacles trailing in the water currents above. Much of its food is produced by a symbiotic algae, so intense lighting is absolutely necessary. This jellyfish will also feed upon newly hatched brine shrimp, but it cannot compete with faster-moving invertebrates or fish and so must be housed accordingly. It is, at present, the only species regularly offered for sale.

Sea anemones are among the heartiest of the cnidarians, although even they will perish quickly if kept in suboptimal water quality. Most also require a fairly steady current of water flowing over them at all times. A very commonly available species is the Caribbean anemone (*Condylactis gigantea*). Varying in color from white to brown or pink, this species is quite hearty, but unfortunately it is rarely adopted as a home by clownfish, which often find shelter in the appendages of anemone. More attractive to these popular fish is the purple-based anemone (*Heteractis magnifica*). This is a very active species that quite frequently travels about the aquarium. All anemones will thrive on infrequent (once or twice a week) meals of shrimp, clam, fish, and similar foods.

All species of anemone, coral, and jellyfish possess stinging cells that are capable of causing painful rashes, and none should be handled with bare hands.

Hermit Crabs, Arrow Crabs, and Boxing Crabs

"Delightful" is perhaps the best way to describe an aquarium housing a colony of hermit crabs. These inquisitive, active creatures are constantly in motion—squabbling over bits of food, settling territorial disputes, and, in general, exploring their environment. Hermit crabs lack a hard exoskeleton on the rear of their bodies, but they make up for this shortcoming by sheltering in the empty shells of other creatures, such as snails. Hermit crabs carry these appropriated homes around, exchanging them for larger "models" as the crab increases in size. Investigating empty shells and trying to dislodge tenants from occupied ones takes up a good deal of their time.

The appetite of the typical hermit crab knows no bounds, and they make excellent scavengers. These crabs can coexist well with all but the largest of fish, protected as they are by their hard shells, and they are one of the few species of crab that can be kept in colonies. Be sure to include plenty of extra empty shells of various sizes, so that the animals can relocate as they grow.

Many species are commercially available, for example the long-clawed hermit crab (*Pagurus longicarpus*). They are also easily collected along shores and in tidal pools, where doing so is lawful. A particularly interesting member of the family is the anemone hermit crab (*Pagurus prideauxi*). This species often places a stinging sea anemone on its shell as a deterrent to predators, carefully relocating its protector when the time comes to change shells. The anemone, it seems, benefits from the arrangement as well by gaining access to bits of leftovers from the crab's meals.

QUESTION?

Can I keep tiny individuals of the various swimming crab species in a community tank?

"Swimming crabs," identified by their paddlelike rear legs, are incredibly aggressive predators. Even the tiniest of specimens will seek out and attack any creature that can be overcome. They are very interesting animals in their own right but must be housed separately.

The arrow crab (*Sterorhynchus seticornis*) is a particularly amiable fellow. Except for particularly large individuals, it rarely disturbs other aquarium inhabitants. Thinly built, with long, spindly legs that give it its alternative name of spider crab, this species makes an unusual and interesting addition to the marine aquarium that lacks aggressive predators. Amazingly, the arrow crab will impale extra pieces of food upon its pointy carapace, to be consumed at its leisure or in times of need. Like many of its relatives, the arrow crab is usually intolerant of company, and individuals confined together will usually fight to the death.

The boxer crab (*Lybia tessellata*) has a fascinating habit of carrying small sea anemones in its claws as a deterrent against predators. When threatened, this tiny (1.2 inches) crab will rear up on its hind legs and wave its "weapons" at the interloper. Due to their small size, boxing crabs will mix well with many species of fish, but be aware that, like all crabs, they will consume animals smaller than themselves.

The exoskeleton of all crabs and other crustaceans is very soft for several hours after the animal sheds. Animals in this state are extremely vulnerable and will be sought out and consumed by fish and invertebrate neighbors. Be sure that there are adequate numbers of secure retreats and substrates suitable for burrowing.

Mantis Shrimp, Banded Coral Shrimp, and Other Shrimp

Mantis shrimp (*Odontodactylus* spp.) are interesting and voracious predators found throughout the world's tropical and temperate seas. Although their bizarre appearance and often bright colors suggest creatures of tropical origin, one species actually ranges into the temperate waters of the eastern United States, as far north as the state of New Jersey.

Much like the terrestrial insect for which they are named, mantis shrimp lie in wait for prey to approach, then grasp the hapless victim with a lightning quick thrust of its hooked forelimbs. Nearly any small animal is fair game, and, indeed, they're happy to consume smaller members of their own kind. In fact, even males and females are difficult to keep together, so these interesting beasts are best kept singly.

ALERT!

Large mantis shrimp are capable of opening a nasty cut with their powerful forelegs and thus should be handled only with a net. Be careful when servicing their aquarium, because they are attracted to movement and may strike out at your fingers in anticipation of a meal.

Despite their rather ferocious nature, mantis shrimp require a secure hiding spot if they are to thrive. Some species evacuate their own burrows, while others prefer to shelter within small caves or under abandoned shells. Although they prefer living prey such as shrimp, small fish, and worms, many individuals can be induced to strike at small bits of clam or fish dangled on a straw in front of them.

Banded coral shrimp (*Stenopus hispidus*) are among the most colorful of the shrimp commonly available to aquarists. Their long legs, red and white "candy cane" colors and habit of foraging about in the daytime endear them to all. Inoffensive to most other creatures, banded coral shrimp will fight among themselves and will definitely be attacked by large fish. Like many of their relatives, these shrimp have an easily pleased appetite and will consume pelleted and flake foods, algae, and small bits of clam and other shellfish.

Interestingly, these unique creatures seemed to form long-term pair bonds, and males have been observed sharing food with pregnant females. Developing eggs are glued to the female's swimmerets, below her abdomen. There they are aerated by constant movement and, perhaps, derive some protection from the mother. Once the young hatch, her maternal instincts vanish, and any offspring that choose to remain close by are quickly consumed. For this reason, tanks containing mated pairs should be provided with a good deal of cover in the form of coral and live or artificial plants, so that the young may escape the attention of their formally attentive parents.

The world's seas and shorelines contain a nearly limitless variety of shrimp that are suitable to keep in home aquariums. Only a very small percentage of these have been maintained in captivity, so the field is wide open for those with the interest and experience to experiment. Particularly hardy are various species of grass shrimp (genus Palaemonetes) and sand shrimp (genus Crago). Mostly very small in size, these fascinating creatures are constantly in motion, darting about the aquarium and foraging through the substrate for anything they might consume. They live quite well in large groups, and you will be fascinated by their interactions. Many breed quite readily. They are, however, delicate and will not survive with aggressive tank mates. While there are, of course, specialists in the shrimp world, most species are useful scavengers and will quite happily feed up flake and pelleted foods, as well as whatever bits of meat escape the attentions of their tank mates.

Starfish, Brittle Stars, and Sea Urchins

Starfish are perhaps the most familiar of the echinoderms, and many adapt well to aquarium life. Most people are quite surprised to realize that they are active, interesting predators, fully capable of exhibiting a wide variety of behaviors in the aquarium. Many are quite useful scavengers, but all are predatory in nature and will consume mollusks, coral polyps, and other sedentary invertebrates.

Red-Knobbed Starfish (Protoreaster linckii)

When a picturing a starfish, most people think of the simple reddish orange animal so often seen as a dried curio in beachfront shops. However, many starfish are fantastic in appearance and coloration. The red-knobbed starfish typifies these—it has brick red dorsal spines, set off brilliantly against a white background. Native to the Indo-Pacific region, this perennial favorite reaches a length of 12 inches and is capable of consuming large mollusks. It is best fed by placing a piece of clam, scallop, or muscle directly below the animal, although it is quite active and capable of finding food on its own.

FACT

Although starfish are quite adept at sensing and finding food, they do, in general, respond slower than do most fish and therefore will be outcompeted unless care is taken to see that food is placed directly below each animal.

Brittle Stars

Brittle Stars bring the word "bizarre" to mind instantly, even to those well acquainted with the sea's curiosities. They react very quickly to the scent of food, and their long, slender arms thrash wildly about as they begin to explore. It is quite a sight to see a tank housing several of these normally sessile creatures suddenly come to life. The animals quickly move across the substrate, unerringly toward the source of the odor that has aroused them.

Brittle stars are harmless to most other creatures and are extremely valuable scavengers in that their very thin arms can get into the tiniest of crevices between coral heads and other places where bits of uneaten food might go unnoticed.

Sea Urchins

These spine-covered, slow-moving invertebrates are often collected in tide pools and are worldwide in distribution. The spines of all sea urchins are potent weapons, and many secrete venoms whose chemistries are not well studied. Hot-water baths seem to assist in alleviating the sting caused by most species.

Many unusual species are commercially available, including the long-spined sea urchin (*Diadem* spp.) and the pencil urchin (*Heterocentrotus* spp). Both feed mainly on algae but will also consume meaty foods. The former has extremely sharp spines (much to the chagrin of bathers in tropical waters), and the latter has a reduced number of spines that are very thick and blunt in shape.

QUESTION?

Why do sea urchins seem to orient their spines toward a shadow that passes overhead?
Sea urchins respond to overhead shadows or objects as though they were predators and direct all the spines to face the possible threat. Although some fish are adept at clipping off the spines or turning the urchins over to expose the softer parts of the body, the defense is, in general, foolproof.

Despite their slow-moving ways, sea urchins are quite active and adept at getting in to all nooks and crannies of the aquarium. Be sure to check that they do not wedge themselves too tightly into small corners, or tumble backwards into coral and become stuck.

Crayfish

Looking exactly like freshwater lobsters, crayfish of one type or another are found throughout the world but are, strangely, missing from Africa. They range in size from minute forums to the giant Tasmanian crayfish (*Astacophis franklini*), which, at a body weight of over 7 pounds, is the world's largest species. Several types of crayfish are important food animals, and crayfish farms exist in many parts of the world, including the southeastern United States.

The first three leg pairs of the crayfish end in tiny claws, and with these the crayfish constantly probes about the substrate for food. The larger main claws are used to capture or dismantle large prey or are used in defense. The "tail" is hinged and, in times of danger, is thrust forward, creating a current of water that propels the crayfish backwards and out of harm's way. Crayfish are found in a wide variety of colors, with bright blue specimens occasionally available in the pet trade.

You will need to experiment to see which types of crayfish can be kept with other animals—some species do not spend much time chasing prey, preferring to scavenge, while others are acutely efficient predators and will also decimate aquarium plants. The appetites of most are quite easy to please, and all manner of plant and animal foods, including pelleted foods, flake foods, table scraps, and live foods are readily accepted. Crayfish are particularly efficient at removing food and black worms embedded in the substrate and are thus of great service as scavengers in the aquarium.

FACT

Several species of crayfish in the United States, generally referred to as chimney crayfish, live in wet fields and meadows and evacuate burrows that reach down to the water table. In some instances, these burrows can be over 10 feet long.

Crayfish make fascinating pets and allow us to view almost all of the activities that might normally occur in nature. All species are quite active and quickly lose their tendency to hide during the day. Many types, especially those with flattened bodies that dwell in rocky streams, are quite adept at rearranging their homes to their liking, and they will move surprising amounts of stones, gravel, and small rocks in their quest to create the perfect home. Their one drawback is their tendency to be aggressive toward each other, so be sure that they have plenty of room to avoid one another and that they have hideaways in which to retreat at shedding time. Like all crustaceans, their bodies will be soft for several hours after this process, leaving them unable to defend themselves against the attentions of their ever-hungry tank mates.

If you do choose to keep crayfish as pets, do not release any into areas to which they are not native. Introduced crayfish have become a serious problem in several parts of the United States and Europe. Breeding populations that result from the release of pets purchased as fishing bait, as well as escapees from crayfish farms, have depleted populations of native fish, crayfish, and aquatic plants.

Red Swamp Crayfish, or Edible Crayfish (Procambarus clarkii)

Raised as food animals on crayfish farms in the southeastern part of the United States, especially in the state of Louisiana, this large (averaging 3 inches) crayfish makes a fascinating, if aggressive, aquarium pet. It becomes quite bold in captivity and will feed from the hand, but it cannot be trusted with aquatic plants or smaller animals. Some specimens are a brilliant red color and are quite attractive, and blue specimens are occasionally available as well. They breed quite readily in captivity, and the female carries the eggs attached to the swimmerets at the lower part of her body. Sweeping motions of these tiny organs serve to aerate the eggs. Newly hatched crayfish are replicas of their parents and after a time will leave the swimmerets to forage and then will return. At a certain point—and this seems to vary from individual to individual—the female will tire of her responsibilities and abruptly begin to consume the young that she has so aggressively defended. The best way to prevent this is to keep her in an aquarium stocked with rocky crevices and other shelters into which the young can retreat. You can also remove her once you see the young spending a good deal of time on their own—it is usually safe to dislodge the few crayfish that remain on her swimmerets at the time of her removal. You can raise the young together only if they are provided with a fairly large aquarium containing many hiding places, as they are cannibalistic.

Small fish bowls and other containers lacking filtration may be aerated by hand. To do this, scoop out some water and pour it back into the tank from a height of about 12 inches above the water's surface. Of course, this works only for hardy animals with low oxygen requirements, such as some species of crayfish and snails.

Single crayfish make ideal inhabitants for unaerated goldfish bowls or other small containers. If kept in shallow water with access to the surface, they will get along quite well without aeration. In deeper bowls, the water should be changed every two or three days or aerated to provide oxygen.

Aquatic Insects

In terms of numbers of the species, insects are the earth's most successful animals, and we lack a true picture of their actual numbers. Of the insects, the beetles are the most numerous, and among them, the weevils form the world's largest family of animals. Although much maligned and rarely kept as aquarium animals, aquatic insects can provide a lifetime of fascination to those willing to look closely. One advantage in keeping such creatures is that they can be collected almost anywhere. And, indeed, this is half the fun of keeping them. Each new trip to even the tiniest of temporary ponds will yield new discoveries. Another reason to keep aquatic insects in an aquarium is the fact that you can usually observe all their behaviors, including reproduction, within the confines of a relatively small aquarium.

Giant Water Bug (Family Belostomatidae)

A true terror in its world, the giant water bug is a voracious predator. The first pair of legs have developed into large, piercing hooks, which can grasp and hold sizable prey. Species from temperate regions grow to be over 2 inches long, and tropical types can be twice that large. The rear legs have become adapted as effective swimming paddles, and the body terminates in a breathing tube, which can be thrust above the surface of the water.

Giant water bugs of all species are quite hardy in the aquarium and extremely interesting to observe. In some species the female glues her eggs to water plants at the water line, but in many she deposits them on the male's back, where they are quite safe from all but the largest predators. Giant water bugs can be maintained in an unfiltered bowl or a filtered aquarium. Be sure to provide upright sticks upon which they can rest and adequate space for them to move about, because they are quite active. In the wild, they feed upon all manner of insects, tadpoles, and even small fish and frogs. In captivity they are content with crickets or other insects, and they take quite readily to feeding upon bits of raw meat.

ALERT!

Be aware that giant water bugs and nearly all other species of aquatic insects can deliver a quite painful bite with their piercing mouth parts. If you must handle them, do so only with nets or gloves, and watch your fingers!

It is quite impossible to even touch upon the great variety of aquatic insects that are suitable for maintenance in the aquarium. Go out and explore, and experiment with the animals that you find. Maintenance for each must be tailored to the individual species, but some generalizations are possible.

Backswimmers (Family Notonectidae)

Backswimmers and the closely related water boatman are quite comical to watch as they row madly (and, often, upside down) through the water with their greatly enlarged, hair-lined rear legs. They require aquatic plants or sticks on which to anchor themselves when they are not swimming and will feed on smaller insects and pieces of meat. Water scorpions are amazingly well camouflaged as waterlogged sticks. They lie in wait attached to aquatic plants, usually at the water's surface with their breathing tubes extending into the air, to snare small invertebrates.

Whirligig Beetle (Family Gyrinidae)

One of the most entertaining insects that you can keep in the aquarium is the whirligig beetle. Possessing eyes that see simultaneously above and below the water's surface, these active beetles occur in large groups, remaining fairly motionless until they are disturbed or detect food. At that time they begin to spin madly about in circles (the source of their common name), and it is quite impossible to keep your eye on any one individual. They are extremely sensitive to the presence of food in the water; a bit of tropical fish flake food tapped into their aquarium will set them stirring. They also enjoy feeding upon other insects and will attack a cricket that is put onto the water's surface, tearing out bits of flesh with their well-developed mouth parts. They are quite easy to maintain on a diet consisting of other insects and tropical fish food.

Water Scavenger Beetles (Family Hydrophidae)

Water scavenger beetles are, as their name suggests, useful scavengers in the invertebrate aquarium. They feed on all manner of decaying plants and animals and readily accept pelleted and flake fish food. One of the more interesting aquatic insects to observe is the larvae, or nymphs, of dragonflies. They stalk about the bottom of the fish tank in the manner of a hunting cat, pausing when they observe a possible meal. They slowly move toward their victim and, when about a body length away, rapidly extend the lower lip. This unique organ is hinged and tipped by a small cup with several grasping hooks. This implement snares the meal and pulls it to the mouth. Dragonfly nymphs seem to require live food, or at least the stimulation of movement to induce them to feed. They are quite easily raised on black worms and brine shrimp, and the largest species will also eat other insects, tadpoles, and even small fish. Be sure to provide some sticks that extend up above the surface of the water in the dragonfly larvae's tank. When it is time to transform into an adult, they will climb up out of the water, split their exoskeleton and unfurl their transparent wings. This generally occurs that night, and the adults will usually be found still on their sticks, hardening the wings, in the morning. If this occurs while you are not at home, the adults will usually fly toward the nearest widow, whereupon they can be released to perform their important task of feeding upon noxious insects such as mosquitoes.

Freshwater Snails (Family Gastropoda)

Aquatic snails are to be found in a wide array of sizes and shapes. Although usually relegated to the role of scavenger in the aquarium, and paid little heed, they are extremely interesting animals that deserve close attention. Larger species, especially, need supplemental food and cannot survive solely on the leftovers of others.

Snails of many types may easily be collected in most aquatic habitats. Be sure to slowly adjust them to the water in which they are to be kept, as it is likely very different from their home pond. Many species are tolerant of varying water chemistries if the introduction is made slowly.

When keeping snails with fish or other animals, be sure that the snails get enough to eat. This is particularly true of items such as algae tablets, which fish will consume before the snails can feed. One way around this is to feed the snails a food that your other animals do not favor, such as vegetables or greens.

Most snails breed readily in the aquarium. Individuals contain both male and female organs, but they do need to mate to produce viable eggs. The eggs can be left to fend for themselves—although fish and other snails will consume the eggs, some young will survive. Apple snails and their relatives deposit their eggs just above the water line, usually on the aquarium glass. These egg masses are enclosed in a sort of hard cocoon and should be sprayed daily with water. The hatchlings will fall into the aquarium and begin to forage immediately upon emergence.

While food preferences vary from species to species, most snails are fairly undemanding in their requirements. Nearly all will accept algae tablets, greens that have been soaked in hot water, tropical fish flake food, and bits of fish. Any animal that dies in the aquarium will quickly attract their attention. Although many, especially the smaller types, will eat only decaying vegetation, some do favor living plants. Those that do can eat an astonishing amount in a short time, so keep an eye on any new species that you introduce. Most snails also scrape algae from the glass and will appreciate an algae-covered stone on which to feed. A bit of cuttlebone or plaster of Paris will provide necessary calcium in the diet. Despite their overall hardiness, most snails require clean water and will congregate at the surface when water quality deteriorates.

Apple Snails

Several related species called apple snails are occasionally offered for sale in the pet trade. Growing to the size of a child's fist, a fully extended apple snail is impressive to behold. Golden and white morphs are now available as well. The apple snail is one of the species that consumes live aquatic plants, and it will feed on the items listed in the previous section as well. As mentioned earlier, the egg mass is attached to the aquarium glass above the water line and should be sprayed with a fine mist of water daily.

Freshwater Shrimp

With few exceptions, freshwater shrimp are only rarely offered for sale, although their marine counterparts are quite commonly available. This is a shame, for while they are not, as a rule, very colorful, many types make delightful and undemanding aquarium subjects.

Most types of shrimp get along quite well and can be exhibited in large groups. They are nearly always busy, foraging about in a constant search for food. Pregnant females carry their eggs on the swimmerets, as has been described for crayfish and marine shrimp. Unfortunately, the smaller types of freshwater shrimp lack much in the way of defense from larger animals, and so can only be housed with peaceful tank mates such as snails or surface-dwelling aquatic insects. Although the more common temperate species are generally bland in coloration, tropical freshwater shrimp grow quite large, and some exhibit fantastically long legs and claws.

Nigerian Sweeper Shrimp

Various related species are sometimes sold under the name of Nigerian sweeper shrimp or bamboo shrimp. This is one of the few freshwater shrimp that is commercially available. The first pair of legs of these interesting little creatures is equipped with filamentous hairs, which seem to assist in trapping the tiny food particles upon which they feed. Although they will feed in more usual shrimp fashion by foraging about the bottom and consuming whatever they might find, sweeper shrimp really are quite specialized to strain food from the water column. It is very interesting to watch—even in a large aquarium, they will gravitate toward the filter outflow and position themselves in the water current with the front legs held outstretched. They can occasionally be seen to bring these legs toward the mouth, apparently consuming the small food particles trapped therein. Sweeper or bamboo shrimp are tropical in origin and fare best in waters from 74° to 80°F.

Leeches

Though they are not exactly what comes to mind when you imagine the ideal aquatic pet, leeches are nonetheless fascinating creatures, especially for those people who lean toward the unusual in their interests. Although their habit of feeding upon the blood of living creatures is well known, most species are actually predatory by nature and feed upon other invertebrates. All leeches are equipped with two suckers, one at the head and one at the rear of the body, by which they move about and attach themselves to their victims. Closely related to earthworms, leeches are best known as aquatic animals, but, in fact, several species are terrestrial. These types inhabit tropical rainforests and find hosts by anchoring themselves on plants along trails used by other creatures.

FACT

Leeches were used in earlier times to remove the "bad blood" that was thought to make people ill. You may be surprised to learn that thousands are still used in modern medical practice to prevent blood from coagulating in certain types of microsurgery.

Leeches are quite undemanding as pets, having relatively low oxygen and food requirements. The needs of most can be met with a small piece of meat or earthworm provided once every two weeks. Leeches have been said to have survived in sealed glass jars of water with no food or supplementary oxygen for periods of up to one year (don't try this with your own leeches!). Despite their rather "simple" appearance, leeches are quite alert to the presence of food. The tiniest bit of meat or blood placed into the water will induce an immediate and frantic search for the source. They unerringly arrive at the food item in a very short time. An interesting experiment is to rub your finger along the bottom of their aquarium. Heads raised, the leeches will crawl around until they reach the spot where your finger was, and where the scent is the strongest, whereupon they will search for its source. Hungry leeches will also respond to a shadow passing overhead, rousing themselves to search for the "fish" that produced the shadow.

One species of leech often arrives in aquariums mixed in with black worms that are fed to fish. This type favors black worms as food, sucking them down with gusto. Once established in an aquarium, they are quite difficult to remove. Their hard egg cases are nearly impregnable to attack by fish or other animals. They generally burrow below the gravel and, in fact, do a great service by being excellent scavengers. They especially favor fish, and any fish that dies in the tank will be reduced to bones by morning.

Chapter 11

Oddities for the Aquarium

The creatures in this chapter are among the most fascinating that you can keep in captivity and therein lies a dilemma. They are, in a sense, too attractive to collectors, and this quality can cloud your judgment. Do not rush into keeping an animal that, while immensely interesting, may require a degree of care that you are unable to provide.

Seahorses (Family Syngnathidae)

As if being armor plated and having a tail that can grasp things, along with independently moving eyes and fins that flutter like wings (see color insert for photo), is not unusual enough, the seahorse adds to these characteristics the phenomenon of "pregnant males." While the male seahorse does not actually give birth, he does incubate the eggs in a pouch and adjusts the salinity of the water therein as needed. Add to this the fact that seahorses change color and can grow and, apparently discard, filamentous appendages to assist in camouflage, and you will have some idea of the uniqueness of these fascinating fish. All of the 120–130 species are, however, strict live-food specialists and rarely thrive on the most easily provided food item, brine shrimp. Read the section on live foods (Chapter 17) and see if you are capable of providing these delicate creatures with a varied diet before trying your hand at keeping them.

ALERT!

Untold millions of seahorses are collected for use in traditional medicines, and the curio and pet trade. Many more perish due to habitat loss and as "bycatch" in commercial fishing operations. Be sure to purchase only commercially bred seahorses.

The two species highlighted here are the most likely to survive on a diet that is within the means of most aquarists. Do not be tempted to try other species until you are well experienced with the following animals.

Dwarf Seahorse (Hippocampus zosterae)

"Seapony" might be a more appropriate name for this diminutive creature, which matures at a length of only 0.9 inches. Ranging from the eel grass beds off of Florida to the Bahamas, the dwarf seahorse may be white, yellow, green, or black in color.

In sharp contrast to larger fish, dwarf seahorses offer the aquarist the opportunity to observe nearly all of their natural behavior in captivity. As a consequence, their captive husbandry is well understood, and many specimens in the trade are commercially produced. In the United States, interest in this charming creature peaked in the 1960s and early 70s, when they were advertised for sale in the back of magazines and comic books.

Dwarf seahorses are one of the only species of seahorse that will thrive on a diet consisting solely of enriched brine shrimp (see Chapter 17 for enrichment techniques), although they will appreciate the addition of tiny, wild-caught invertebrates. As with all seahorses, they require calm water and suitable "hitching posts" upon which to wrap their tails.

Atlantic Seahorse (Hippocampus erectus)

Most people seem to consider seahorses to be tropical in origin and may be surprised to learn the Atlantic seahorse ranges as far north as Nova Scotia, the waters of which are decidedly untropical. Found from the shoreline to depths of over 230 feet (70 meters), this species somehow survives areas of strong tidal activity.

FACT

The Pygmy Seahorse, *Hippocampus bargibanti*, first described in 1970, seems to live on only two 2 species of soft coral. It so closely resembles the coral's polyps that the seahorse was not discovered until it was seen on a coral that had been placed in an aquarium days earlier! At 0.8 inches, it is the smallest known seahorse.

Its rather large size (up to 7.3 inches) allows it to take a wide variety of prey, such as small shrimp, black worms, and fish fry. This, coupled with the fact that many individuals can be tempted to eat frozen foods moved about in front of them, makes it an ideal, but still delicate, candidate for the aquarium. Hailing as they do from temperate waters, Atlantic seahorses should be kept in unheated aquaria. Breeding will be more likely if they are provided with natural fluctuations in day length and temperature.

Moray Eels (Family Muraenidae)

More than 200 species of moray eels are found throughout the world's tropical and subtropical seas. Ranging in size from the red faced eel, Monopenchelys acuta, which grows to only 8 inches in length to the giant moray, *Strophidon* spp. (12.5 feet), all share a similar body pattern and habits. The latterly flattened body allows them access to the narrow caves and crevices that form their home base. Indeed, many spend their entire lives within close proximity to their cave, leaving only to mate and to forage nearby.

All moray eels are carnivorous, and will readily accept fresh and frozen meat based foods such as crustaceans and mollusks. Well-fed animals will coexist with smaller fish, but there is always the possibility of predation. On the other hand, morays are not quick feeders, and indeed can be rather shy about this, so you must take care that they are getting enough food if they are housed with large, aggressive fish. Moray eels, like all eels in general, are master escape artists. Although they can withstand a good deal of time out of water, great care should be taken that they do not escape. If this does happen, be sure to move the animal back and forth in the aquarium once it is replaced, so that water is forced through the gills, and it begins to breathe regularly.

ALERT!

Even small moray eels are equipped with needle sharp teeth, and they are not shy about using them in defense or if they mistake your finger for food. The resulting wound almost always becomes infected, and large animals can cause permanent damage. These are definitely not animals for homes with children.

Brilliantly patterned in black and white, the small snowflake moray, *Echnida nebulosa* (40 inches) is an ideal first choice if you are considering keeping moray eels. Many individuals become quite tame, extending their bodies from their lairs to accept food offered on forceps. They are, like other members of their family, slow feeders, and so are best individually fed if kept in a community aquarium. Be sure, however, to employ forceps or a feeding tube, as, despite their small size, they can give a nasty bite. Snowflakes will readily accept all manner of frozen or fresh foods such as shrimp, mollusks, and fish. See color insert for a photo of a green moray eel.

Boxfish, Trunkfish, and Cowfish (Family Ostraciidae)

With their rigid bodies propelled "helicopter fashion" by tiny, rapidly moving fins, these fish are an amusing sight as they motor about the aquarium. Their appeal is heightened by an "alert" face, and, in many species, horn-like projections at the head and rear of the body (see color insert for photo).

Although immune from attack by most large predators due to their hard covering of bony plates, box- and cowfish are slow moving and their rapidly undulating fins seem to draw attacks from smaller fish. The skin over the rigid plates is, strangely, quite sensitive and also suffers from the attentions of aggressive tank mates.

Cowfish (Lactoria cornuta)

A brilliant yellow body highlighted with blue spots and set off by "horns" at the head and rear renders this droll fish instantly recognizable. Slow feeding and peaceful, they do best with similar species and are one of the few fish that will coexist with seahorses. They are quite entertaining as they cruise about, hovering as they examine their homes for their favorite foods, algae and crustaceans.

ESSENTIAL

Many species of cow-, box-, and trunkfish are, despite their apparent calmness, quite excitable. Frightened fish will release a chemical into the water that is toxic to most other fish. Establish them in the aquarium before you add other fish, and in a dark room, turn room lights on before switching on the aquarium lights.

Hovercraft Boxfish (Tetrosomus gibbosus)

This species' mode of swimming truly fits its name, with only the fins fluttering, propeller-like, to move the rigid body along. They are extremely inquisitive, seeming to notice and examine all happenings in, and even outside of, their aquarium. Growing to only 4 inches in length, hovercrafts do best when kept with nonaggressive fish. Because they are often slow to feed, their condition should be monitored closely—thin animals rapidly develop a sunken stomach area.

Anglerfish (Order Lophiiformes)

Found throughout the world's temperate and tropical oceans, the 300 or so species of anglerfish have attained the epitome of specialization in capturing prey. The first 2–3 rays of the dorsal fin are separated from the rest and have evolved into movable "fishing baits" that lure other fish near enough to be swallowed. Most anglerfish can also change color and grow a variety of filamentous projections, adding to their effectiveness as hunters.

Small specimens of the genus Antennarius are occasionally available to aquarists. These fish are best kept alone, considering their specialized dietary requirements. Also, be aware that they can swallow fish equal to their own size. Most have a remarkable ability to change their color in accordance with their backgrounds, allowing you to have a green fish one day and a red one the next!

Males of deep sea dwelling species of anglerfish solve the problem of finding a mate in the inky blackness in which they live by attaching themselves, using their mouths, to the first female they encounter. Thereafter, their internal organs degenerate, and they remain attached to the female for life, nourished by her blood and providing sperm to fertilize her eggs when needed.

Anglerfish all are confirmed live-food specialists and will rarely if ever accept dead food that is moved in a lifelike manner before them. Be sure to acclimate food fish to the aquarium so that they will show interest in the angler's lure. If this is not possible, gently "herd" the fish toward the angler —they will be captured if they venture close enough, even if they show no interest in the lure.

Sargassum Fish (Histrio spp.)

A Sargassum fish floating among marine algae is virtually indistinguishable from its surroundings. This amazing camouflage really must be seen to be believed. Basically, this fish is a "sit and wait predator," but it can become quite tame in captivity and will leave its protective covering to seek food throughout the aquarium. Generally, they float slowly toward their prey, engulfing it with a "gulp and suck" motion when they get close. Most prey remains unaware of the Sargassum fish's approach until it is too late.

The calm, slow movements and mild manners of the Sargassum fish belie its predatory instincts. The stomach has an amazing ability to expand, allowing this fish to swallow prey nearly as large as itself. Bear this in mind when selecting tank mates. Although they are confirmed to be live-food specialists, Sargassum fish can be tricked into accepting small dead fish waved about before them on forceps.

Snakehead (Channidae)

Forty to fifty species of these large, predatory fish inhabit the fresh waters of Asia and central Africa. They are aptly named, as the elongated body and the shape of the head do evoke images of a snake. Snakeheads possess auxiliary respiratory organs that allow them to breathe air and to survive in waters that few other fish can tolerate. Important food fish wherever they occur, snakeheads are routinely shipped from Asia to food markets in the United States wrapped in wet burlap. They almost always arrive feisty and ready to snap at their captors!

Although some species can reach lengths in excess of 3 feet (1 meter), most commonly imported species, such as the Asian snakehead, *Channa asiatica*, are mature at about half that size. However, large or small, all are voracious predators with gigantic mouths and appetites to match. They will accept all manner of animal based foods, including fish, earthworms, and crustaceans. In the wild they are said to take small mammals, and pet store owners have reported that these fish have even swallowed escaped parakeets that unwittingly fall into their aquarium.

ALERT!

Do not be misled by the snakehead's ability to survive in adverse conditions. Water quality should be monitored carefully, especially given the copious amounts of waste these large fish produce.

Snakeheads make interesting pets for those able to provide them with the space they need. Captive reproduction is not common. Males of some species evacuate nests while others leave the eggs to fend for themselves.

Snakeheads must be housed in large, well-covered aquariums. They generally uproot most plants, so their homes are best decorated with rocks and driftwood. Be sure to check the legality of keeping these fish before deciding to purchase one. Snakeheads have been much in the news in the United States lately, after free living populations were found in Virginia and, of all places, New York City (although it is unlikely that they would survive the winter there). Given their aggressive ways, these fish could cause environmental havoc if established outside their natural range, and for this reason their importation is banned in many areas.

Frog Mouth Catfish (Chaca bankanensis)

If ever a freshwater fish were to be qualified to be included in a chapter concerning aquarium oddities, it is certainly this bizarre fellow. This flattened fish really does seem to combine both fish like and amphibian like characteristics in its appearance, its walking rather than swimming motions, and its ability to vocalize. It is a squat, mainly brownish fish, possessing a huge mouth that gives the head a square shape. The tiny eyes are nearly invisible, and from the wide head the body tapers sharply. Cutaneous flaps of skin help to break up the body's outline and add to the camouflage effect as the fish lies on the river bottom waiting for prey. Native to India, Myanmar, Malaysia, Sumatra, and Borneo, the frog mouth catfish is only rarely available in the pet trade. It is, however, well worth searching for.

Although not an active fish, the frog mouth catfish does require quite a bit of room, as it reaches nearly 1 foot in length. It spends most of its time hunkered down on the bottom of the aquarium, preferably under cover of some sort, and even at night it does not actively hunt for food. The frog mouth catfish is best kept alone, as it can swallow prey nearly half its own length. Also, it is very prone to stress and does not do well in aquariums housing actively swimming fish. The water should be a bit on the acidic side, and the tank should be dimly lit, as this fish naturally inhabits muddy waters and is uncomfortable in bright light. In fact, some aquarists have had much success by staining the water with commercial products available for that purpose. In nature, the frog mouth catfish hides itself within the muck at the bottom of the rivers and lakes that it inhabits. A thick bed of leaves (be sure to check that the water does not become too acidic) will allow it to do this in the aquarium as well, or you can provide shelters such as driftwood caves. This catfish is most comfortable at temperatures of approximately 77°F (25°C).

You should be aware that the spine next to the dorsal fin can inflict a painful wound.

QUESTION?

Is it true that a frog mouth catfish "fishes" for its prey in the manner of the marine anglerfish?
It has been reported that the frog mouth catfish wiggles the barbells near its mouth to lure fish within striking range. Documenting this would be an interesting project for the aquarist fortunate enough to acquire one of these fascinating animals.

Adding to the frog mouth catfish's list of unusual characteristics is its propensity to vocalize when removed from the water. The sound it makes, "chaca-chaca," has given rise to its scientific name. The frog mouth seems to be a fish specialist in terms of diet, although it has been reported to feed upon earthworms and tadpoles as well.

Lungfish (Lepidosireniformes)

Six species of these unique "living fossils" dwell in Africa, South America, and Australia. Remaining virtually unchanged since ancient times, lungfish are important in the study of the evolutionary development of fish and amphibians. The largest species, the East African lungfish is, at 6½ feet (2 meters), a truly impressive beast, but even the smaller ones are quite unusual. Elongated and eel-like in appearance, lungfish possess unique, threadlike pectoral and anal fins (the one Australian species has lobed, paddlelike fins), with which they can pull themselves around.

The swim bladder of the lungfish has evolved into a highly efficient lung, allowing them to dwell in oxygen poor waters and to survive periods of drought. This organ is most highly developed in the four African species, with some being able to survive periods of up to four years without food or water. The dry period is spent within a cocoon made from mucus secreted by the lungfish. The fish breathes air through a small hole at the top of the cocoon.

The Australian lungfish, *Neoceratodus forsteri*, is the most primitive of the group and offers a peek into the evolutionary history of vertebrates. Unfortunately, its continued survival is severely threatened by development around its tiny range in southeastern Australia. This lungfish is now protected by the Australian government, and recovery projects are being considered.

FACT

Lungfish are related to the Coelacanth, a true "dinosaur" that, until the accidental capture of one in 1938, was believed to have become extinct 65 million years ago. This ocean-dwelling fish lives at depths of 2,300 feet (700 meters) and is not well studied.

Lungfish are voracious feeders, adapted as they are to environments where the food and water supply fluctuates wildly. Carnivorous in nature, they will take all types of fish, insects, earthworms, and frozen meat based foods. Lungfish do best in aquariums with soft substrates into which they can burrow. Despite their propensity to hide, once acclimated to the aquarium lungfish will readily leave their retreats at feeding time. Their aquarium should be well covered lest they escape during their nocturnal wanderings. Most species fare best at temperatures of 77°F (25°C) or so, but they are remarkably tolerant in this regard, due, again, to the ever changing environments to which they are adapted. They should not, however, be subjected to rapid temperature changes. Captive breeding is not common. The male constructs a nest or breeding burrow and steadfastly guards the eggs from predators.

Bichirs and Reedfish (Polypteridae)

The dorsal fin of these elongated fish rises and falls in a series of humps, giving them the appearance of miniature dragons. The pectoral fins are rimmed with fleshy lobes and are paddlelike in shape and function. These fish swim in short bursts, but mainly they scull along the bottom. Confined to tropical Africa and the Nile River system, the eleven species of bichir and the reedfish are not well studied in captivity and much can be learned by the patient aquarist. Most species are a greenish brown in color. The largest can reach 3 ½ feet (1 meter) in length, but those commonly imported are considerably smaller.

The only member of the family that is commonly available in the pet trade is the reedfish, *Erpetoichelys calabaricus*. It is generally sold under the name of "ropefish"—quite apt considering its eel-like body and brown color. The reedfish is quite unlike the typical bichirs in appearance and habits, living at or under the substrate and emerging at night to feed upon insects and worms. It can reach a length of 3½ feet (1 meter) but rarely attains that in captivity. Bichirs and reedfish prefer live food in the form of other fish, insects, earthworms, and black worms and do well at a temperature of 77°F (25°C) or so.

African Clawed Frog (Xenopus laevis)

Possessing claws and lacking a tongue, this unique amphibian is often sold in aquarium stores as an "underwater frog." It is completely aquatic, being flattened in shape and unable to "sit up" like other frogs can. A very hardy and entertaining pet, the clawed frog becomes quite responsive to its owner, feeding from the hand and living in excess of twenty years. The clawed frog is nearly always in motion, driven, in part, by a near insatiable appetite (be careful, they become obese quite easily in captivity). The body is lined with sensory glands in the manner of the lateral line of fish, and, in contrast to other frogs, they also locate food by scent.

African clawed frogs were used to detect pregnancy in the Hogben Test. Hormones in the urine of pregnant women cause the frogs to lay eggs within a matter of hours after being injected with the woman's urine. Millions were imported into the United States for this purpose in the 1950s.

African clawed frogs thrive in a wide range of water temperatures and conditions but do best at temperatures suited for tropical fish in general (77°F, 25°C). This adaptability has led to the establishment of feral populations in many countries, including the United States. They rapidly decimate local fish and amphibian populations and thus should never be released into foreign habitats. They have even been found, apparently healthy and content, in underground cisterns in English castles, where water temperatures do not rise above 59°F (15°C) and in pools sprayed by saltwater along the coast of England!

That being said, these frogs do require clean water, or they will be killed by ammonia poisoning. Due to their large appetites, the tank must be well filtered or given frequent water changes.

African clawed frogs will eat nearly any form of animal based foods and should be given a varied diet. The basis of the diet can consist of the commercially available food pellets formulated specifically for them (it is one of the few frog species to accept nonliving food). To this should be added crickets and other insects, earthworms, fish, and black worms. They can coexist with nonaggressive fish that are too large to be swallowed (they may try anyway, but they seem to learn their lesson quickly!). Allowing the water level to drop and then adding water 10 degrees cooler than that in which they are normally housed will often stimulate reproduction. The eggs are fertilized externally, and the parents should be removed because they favor nothing so much as frog eggs for dinner. The tadpoles are filter feeders. Commercially prepared diets are available through biological supply houses, or the tadpoles can be reared on cool nettle tea. These frogs are amazingly good at finding even the tiniest spaces to escape from, so be particularly careful and tape up the areas around external filter tubes.

Two related frog species that are sometimes offered for sale are the dwarf African frog, *Hymenochirus* spp., and the Surinam toad, *Pipa pipa*. The dwarf African frog grows to only 1.3 inches in length. Charming and active by day, it is a slow feeder that usually consumes live food only and will quickly starve in an aquarium housing active fish. However, kept in a well planted tank and fed on black worms and brine shrimp, a group of these amphibians will provide limitless entertainment. Be careful not to confuse them with baby African clawed frogs, as their care is very different. Dwarf frogs can be distinguished by their more flattened bodies, pointed heads and the webbed toes on the front feet.

ALERT!

African clawed frogs are often sold as auxiliary animals to be placed in fish tanks and expected to thrive on fish flakes as a diet. While they can be kept with certain fish, they have specific requirements that must be met if they are to thrive. Be aware that females reach 5½ inches in length and can consume fish nearly that long.

The Surinam toad is a live-food specialist that prefers fish and earthworms. The eggs are incubated on the males' back, covered with skin that breaks down when the newly developed frogs are ready to emerge (the entire tadpole stage is passed within the skin of the male's back). Breeding for these and dwarf frogs is similar to that described for African clawed frogs. Surinam toads require a deep tank if they are to reproduce, as the egg laying process involves a circular swimming motion that positions the male below the falling eggs.

Chapter 12

Selecting Fish and Invertebrates

Careful research, as well as your own personal interests, should be your guide in deciding the types of aquatic animals that you buy for your aquarium. Unfortunately, modern collecting methods and modes of transportation have made readily available scores of species that are completely unsuitable as captives. All too often, these animals perish relatively quickly in captivity, without having reproduced. Yet the demand remains unabated, and so continued collection pushes the species ever closer to the brink of extinction.

Selecting a Species

Your first consideration in selecting a species should be whether or not you are qualified to maintain that animal in a healthy condition for the balance of its life. More and more, environmental ethics also require that you consider whether or not you can successfully breed certain species in captivity, especially those that are collected from the wild or that face an uncertain future there.

Navigating Regulations

You must also carefully research the legality of your proposed acquisition. The fact that an animal is offered for sale in a pet store, at a trade show, or on the Internet is not an indication that you can legally keep that animal in your home. Increasingly, governments and regulatory agencies around the world are moving to protect the animals and plants under their jurisdictions. In the United States, an extremely complicated maze of city, state, county, federal, and international regulations is in place to assure that endangered species and those of special concern are not brought into the marketplace. These rules and regulations change frequently, so it is virtually impossible for the average person to keep abreast of the situation. In the United States, if you are a prospective purchaser of an animal that seems of questionable legality, you should call your state's Department of Environmental Conservation, and also the regional office of the United States Fish and Wildlife Service. The staff at both of these agencies will be immensely helpful in advising you concerning the laws or regulations that may be in place regarding that particular species.

Other Considerations

Once you have determined that you are competent to care for the animal that interests you and that the species is legal to purchase, several other factors should be considered. You may wish to choose animals that are of interest to you because of their behavior or natural history, as opposed to those that are merely attractive in appearance. By focusing on such creatures, you will be assured of maintaining your long-term interest and, hopefully, of learning more about the animals as time goes on.

A variety of practical considerations are also important to bear in mind. While heating an aquarium is a fairly straightforward and simple matter, the same cannot be said for cooling them. Although aquarium chillers are commercially available, most are expensive to purchase and operate and they are often designed for rather large systems. Therefore, it may be difficult or at least extremely impractical to keep temperate or cold-water species if you live in an area with a very warm climate.

You should also calculate not only the overall expenses involved in pursuing the hobby in general but also those connected with the species of particular interest to you. Animals that require complicated life-support systems or diets that are difficult to procure may place an inordinate strain upon your budget. Similarly, time constraints should figure into your decision-making process. Animal species whose care places a heavy burden upon your time will soon rob you of any enjoyment inherent in keeping them and most likely will cause your interest to wane.

Paying Attention to Feeding Habits

Certain species of invertebrates and fish are extremely specialized feeders. Those that require a varied diet of live food may be difficult to maintain unless you live in close proximity to a habitat where you can collect their natural food items. Seahorses, for example, are particularly sought after favorites by many marine aquarists. However, these animals are confirmed live-food specialists, and the most readily available diet offered to them—brine shrimp—is unsuitable as a sole diet for all except, possibly, the dwarf seahorse (*Hippocampus zosterae*). If you plan to acquire these and similar creatures, such as pipefish, you really do need to live in an area where you can collect a variety of small marine organisms for them to feed on. In the alternative, you would need to establish thriving colonies of several species of such organisms, such as mysid shrimp, grass shrimp, and amphipods.

Although some animals that feed upon live food in the wild, including certain individual seahorses, can be trained to accept nonliving food items, most require a close approximation of their natural diet if they are to survive. Despite the increased availability of a variety of live food animals to hobbyists, and advances in their culture in captivity, most live-food specialists require far more dietary variety than can be supplied by the average hobbyist.

If you decide to keep delicate animals such as seahorses, you would be well advised to keep species that are native to your local area. In this way, free-living food sources may be collected and natural temperature and light cycles will be easier to duplicate.

If you do decide to keep delicate creatures, whether freshwater or marine, focus on those whose habits are well understood and where others have had some success in their husbandry. It is also important that you have access to hobbyists or professionals who will share with you the secrets of their successes. You may wish to maintain the slightly larger species of a group of animals that is delicate in general, as their more generously sized mouths may allow them to accommodate a wider variety of food items. Tiny animals that specialize in unique diets are particularly difficult to maintain in captivity.

Acquiring Animals Bred in Captivity

Always strive to acquire fish and invertebrates that that have been bred in captivity, as opposed to those that are collected from the wild. It is often a fairly simple matter to ascertain this, especially if you choose to purchase from private dealers who maintain breeding colonies of animals within their homes or shops. Magazines, the Internet, aquarium societies, and public aquariums are also valuable sources of information as to which animals are being bred in captivity.

The purchase of captive bred animals is not only an environmentally sound way to approach your hobby, but it is also a favorable decision from a practical point of view. Captive bred individuals, even those of species that are notoriously difficult to keep in captivity, always adjust more easily to life in the aquarium. They also present the best prospects for the hobbyist if he or she is to maintain the animals for long periods of time, learn about their life cycles, and, possibly, to have them reproduce successfully. An additional benefit of this route is that the breeder from whom you purchase your animals will be able to give you a wealth of information that may be unavailable elsewhere, and will increase your likelihood of success.

Selecting an Individual

The process of selecting an individual invertebrate or fish should begin with firsthand observation of the animal for as long a period as is possible. It is very important that you observe their feeding habits, especially of those with which you are unfamiliar. Of course this is not always possible within the confines of a pet store or dealer's facility, and certain individuals may be newly acquired and not yet well settled (in which case you should refrain from purchasing them until they have had a chance to acclimate to their new surroundings). It should, however, be taken as a bad sign if the seller refuses to allow your reasonable requests in this regard. It is particularly important that you assure yourself that delicate creatures, especially marine or freshwater fish that consume live food only, are well acclimated to captivity and feeding prior to purchasing them. Consider placing a deposit on a specimen of particular interest to you and returning at later dates to observe its progress if you are not satisfied at your first visit.

FACT

Seahorses are notoriously selective feeders and their body condition is difficult to assess. The skin between the hard body ridges of well-fed individuals will not be indented, but rather will be even with or slightly bulging above the ridges.

When choosing animals for your aquarium, bear in mind that behaviors that indicate a problem in one species may be normal in another. For example, clamped fins, a sign of poor health in most freshwater fish, are usual for many marine species. Most eels breathe by rapidly gulping water, a behavior that would indicate distress in many other types of fish.

Assessing Body Weight

Animals that you select should show evidence that they are in normal body weight range. This is nearly impossible concerning invertebrates, due to their hard exoskeletons, but with some practice, you can become adept at determining whether or not most fish have been feeding. Even species that are normally elongated or thin in body shape, such as loaches and eels, will display pinched stomachs if they are in poor condition. Fish that are encased in bony coverings, such as seahorses and cowfish, will nonetheless exhibit an indented stomach if they have not been feeding regularly.

Recognizing Normal Behavior

It is important that you understand and recognize the normal behavior of the species that interests you, because typical behaviors can provide clues as to the animal's overall health. For example, flounders generally do not swim about much, and their doing so may indicate a problem. Well-adjusted individuals will be found partially buried in sandy substrates or just above it. Sessile invertebrates should be firmly anchored to a substrate and the shells, where present, and should not be gaping widely or loosely attached to each other. There are innumerable considerations to be aware of, and those concerning each species are different. The point is that you must go shopping well armed with a detailed understanding of and knowledge about the creatures that you intend to purchase.

You should know, for example, that activity is not necessarily a sign of good health. Many fish become agitated when stressed by disease, parasites, or the lack of oxygen. Invertebrates such as crabs and crayfish should, in general, be hiding unless they are foraging for food. Those scuttling madly about the aquarium, outside of feeding time, are not exhibiting normal behavior.

The eyes of most fish should be clear and the animals should be alert within the confines of their normal behavior. Search carefully for signs of fungus, which may appear as dark or light films on the body, and for parasitic infections in the form of small swellings or discolored areas on the scales. Of course, you should take note of obvious injuries such as wounds and frayed or missing fins. Most fish can regrow torn fins, and invertebrates often replace lost legs at their next shedding, but such may indicate that the animals have been improperly transported or housed by the seller.

QUESTION?

Should I purchase an animal that is obviously in distress to pro-vide it with a better home in my aquarium?
Such a notion, while noble, is usually not a good idea. Animals in poor condition have generally been through a long period of unfavorable transport and husbandry and are likely to die, and they may infect your collection with disease or parasites in the process. Report the offending seller or store to an appropriate local authority.

Avoid fish that are constantly rubbing up against substrates or rocks, because this may indicate that they are attempting to remove external parasites from their scales. You should be completely familiar with the normal coloration of the fish or invertebrates that you plan to purchase. Individual and regional variation will come into play, but avoid those that are dull or lackluster in appearance (unless, of course, this is their normal coloration). Be aware also of the species' usual rate of respiration, as bad water quality or other stress factors may cause fish to respire at an abnormally high rate.

Assessing the Health of Invertebrates

The overall health and condition of invertebrates is much more difficult to assess than that of fish. The rigid exoskeletons of most give little clue as to whether or not they are in good weight, and their movements may not be of much diagnostic value either. Sessile invertebrates are particularly difficult to evaluate, but you should check that they are attached to a substrate, and that any visible tissues are intact and free of fungus or unusual marks. Soft-bodied invertebrates such as sponges and sea cucumbers should be checked for wounds or other injuries and for discolored areas on their bodies. The spines of sea urchins and missing legs of crayfish, lobsters, and sea stars will regrow, but the process places an additional strain on the animal's bodily functions.

Aquarium Conditions

Be especially aware of the condition of the aquariums in which the animals that you intend to purchase are kept, and of the state of repair and cleanliness of the store or dealer's facilities in general. Of course, animals offered for sale in commercial establishments cannot be housed in complicated, well-decorated aquariums due to the constraints imposed by large-scale operations. However, the animals' basic requirements should be met. Here, again, you will need to know a good deal about the animals themselves if you are to be able to make an accurate assessment of commercial facilities. Although the tanks in most pet stores and dealers will, of necessity, be fairly barren in terms of decorations and plants, aquatic organisms that are particularly delicate or have very specific needs should be housed with such considerations in mind. Moray eels, for example, will be extremely stressed unless they are able to hide in a secure retreat. Housing such creatures in a bare aquarium will almost guarantee that they become ill from a stress-related disorder. A seller who lacks a basic understanding of or concern for his charges is likely to make mistakes that jeopardize the overall health of the stock.

Especially for animals that are difficult to acclimate to captivity, you should request details as to how the animal has been maintained and what it has been eating. Particularly important are parameters such as temperature and pH and, for marine animals, specific gravity.

ALERT!

Many animals, including aquatic organisms, quickly become fixated on one food item and will eat it to the exclusion of all others. This may impair the creature's future health and will complicate the process of adjusting the specimen to your own aquarium. Always ask for complete details as to the diet of your prospective purchase.

For animals of special concern, especially those that are rare in captivity and/or in nature, you should also attempt to obtain background information as to the place of origin. Species with large natural ranges may experience extreme differences in climate, behaviors, and food preferences over the expanse of that range. You will need to adjust for such factors if you are to successfully meet the husbandry challenges that such creatures present. This is especially important if you are concerned, as you should be when dealing with such animals, with captive reproduction. Many invertebrates and fish are stimulated to breed by fluctuations in day length and temperature. Animals originating in the more northerly parts of their ranges will experience significantly different seasonal fluctuations than will those from the south.

You should make every effort to determine the origin of any particularly rare animal that you maintain. If at all possible, the breeding of such creatures should occur only with other individuals from the same home range, so as to preserve any genetic differences that may exist between local populations of the same species.

Introducing Fish and Invertebrates to Your Aquarium

As mentioned previously, you should ask the seller details about of how your prospective pet has been maintained. Knowing as much as you can about factors like the temperature and salinity to which the animal has been exposed will greatly increase your chances of successfully acclimatizing it to your own aquarium. Of course, only purchase specimens that have been kept under the environmental conditions that are required for optimal health. If the water quality parameters of the store or dealer are acceptable, but vary somewhat from your own, ask the seller for an extra quantity of water so that you can very slowly adjust the animal to the changes that it will need to face.

Fish and invertebrates are generally transported in plastic bags. Approximately two-thirds of the bag should be filled with air (many stores and dealers now keep oxygen tanks on hand for this purpose) and one-third with water from the aquarium in which the organism has been kept. If the fish or invertebrate is to be kept in the bag for a considerable amount of time, ask the seller to use a large bag and, if possible, to fill it with oxygen. If the animal will be exposed to extremely hot or cold temperatures during transit, be sure to bring along an insulated box of Styrofoam or a similar material to help offset the temperature. You may also wish to consider a hot-water bottle or a cold pack as well.

In all cases, the animal that you purchase should be kept in the dark on its journey to your home. Of course, take precautions not to shake or drop the shipping container, and to shield it from strong vibrations such as those that might be experienced in a car traveling over a rough road surface.

FACT

Hand warmers, available at most sporting goods stores, are quite useful in raising the temperatures within transport boxes housing aquatic creatures. If you are unfamiliar with their use, be sure to purchase one ahead of time and experiment before using it with living animals.

The actual introduction of the animal into the aquarium is best done in a dimly lit room to reduce the animal's stress levels. You may also wish to feed the current aquarium inhabitants prior to introducing a new creature, to lessen their aggression toward or interest in their new tank mate. The plastic bag in which your animal has been transported should be floated in the aquarium for fifteen to twenty minutes to allow the temperature within the bag to equalize with that in your aquarium. To avoid the shock associated with changes in pH, specific gravity, or other water parameters, you should add a bit of water from your tank to the bag every five minutes or so.

When dealing with particularly delicate creatures, or with any animals that have been housed in water that differs considerably in makeup from your own, you should use a drip system of acclimatization. This process may require more water than is typically sent home with the creature, so be sure to ask the retailer for extra water if you anticipate such a need. To do this, place the animals, with their original water, in a plastic bucket. Run a length of airline tubing from your aquarium to the bucket and allow the water to drip into it slowly. The rate of flow from the aquarium into the holding container can be easily adjusted via the use of plastic valves, available at most pet stores, or even with simple paper clips or binder clips. Be sure to take occasional readings of the various water quality parameters and adjust the flow of water from the tank into the holding bucket accordingly.

Remember that plants, like fish, invertebrates, and live rock and sand, are living organisms and will suffer the effects of drastic changes in water quality parameters. This is especially true for marine algae.

Newly introduced fish and invertebrates should not be exposed to bright lights for the first few hours after their introduction into your aquarium. They need not be kept in total darkness, but it is best to leave the main aquarium light off and instead utilize the room light at this stage. Your new pets should, of course, be observed carefully for their first few days in their new home. Be especially careful to see that they are eating and that they are getting along well with the other animals in your aquarium.

As has been mentioned previously, it may be prudent to quarantine certain new animals, especially those that are particularly rare or delicate, or those that are to be introduced into a collection housing such creatures. Again, you must weigh the value of such a quarantine period against the disadvantage in exposing the fish or invertebrate to two separate acclimatization periods. A quarantine tank that is maintained with environmental conditions that are essentially the same as in the main aquarium will go a long way toward easing the adjustment of new creatures to your collection.

Avoid the temptation to add large numbers of fish or invertebrates to your aquarium at one time. Animals should, ideally, be introduced one at a time, and the introduction process should spread over as long a time as is possible. This will allow your filtration system to adjust to the new load on its capacity and will ease the stress on the animals already living in the aquarium.

Purchasing Fish and Invertebrates

In most cases, it is prudent to purchase all of your aquatic animals from the same dealer. Maintaining a good relationship with this person will assure you of the highest-quality stock, and it will also enable you to trace any problems that arise back to their original source. Reputable dealers, especially small-scale private breeders, are usually quite willing to share their expertise with customers and alert those with specific interests as to the availability of unique creatures.

Retail pet stores vary widely in the degree of expertise of their staff and in the quality of the animals that they supply. If you are fortunate enough to have a high-quality store nearby, use it to purchase the majority of your animals and supplies. Purchasing animals from a number of different sources will complicate the process of tracking down the origin of a disease and will make it less likely that individual suppliers will cooperate in helping you with such problems.

Public aquariums, aquarium societies, and aquarium trade magazines are all excellent sources to check when attempting to locate responsible fish and invertebrate importers and breeders. An additional benefit of using such organizations is that you may obtain access to the expertise of serious hobbyists and professional aquarists.

ALERT!

If you purchase animals from other countries via the Internet, bear in mind that species legally exportable from their country of origin may nonetheless be illegal to import into your own country. The liability in such cases will rest with you as the buyer and not with the seller.

The Internet has opened to hobbyists vast new sources of freshwater and marine organisms. In many cases, the range of species available can be overwhelming. It is, in some ways, "too easy" to buy aquatic creatures today. The ease of ordering all manner of creatures without leaving your home can lead to problems that are not faced when you must go out and locate an animal. Animals purchased sight unseen and shipped to your home present a number of risks that were not faced in earlier times. Remember that it is essential that you exercise control when shopping on the Internet and that you remain mindful of all of the cautions that were outlined concerning purchasing animals firsthand.

Collecting Fish and Invertebrates

There is little that can compare, in terms of adventure and satisfaction, with collecting your own aquatic animals and successfully establishing them in captivity. Opportunities for collecting are, quite correctly, becoming ever more limited as time goes on. However, where legal and environmentally sustainable, collecting your own fish and invertebrates is a fascinating prospect. The subject of collecting is more thoroughly explored in Appendix A.

One way to combine a passion for collecting with important scientific work is to become associated with projects sponsored by professional aquariums or governmental agencies. Funding restrictions on research activities often dictate that such entities must rely on the cooperation of interested volunteers. (Refer to Chapter 1 for more on this topic.)

Chapter 13

Cold Water Aquariums

Many aquarists are misled into thinking that exotic and interesting creatures are to be found only in far-off tropical places, but this is not true. Wherever you live, you need only to look at the nearest shoreline or ocean to find animals of unimaginable variety and interest. One great advantage to keeping animals native to where you live is that you can collect them yourself, and can provide a natural environment for them. In this chapter are a variety of animals rarely sold in pet stores that can supply endless hours of fascination.

Basic Considerations

If you live near a body of water, you are in the enviable position of being able to observe firsthand the environments and habits of a variety of aquatic creatures. You're also free to do a good deal of experimentation, in terms of different species. You should consider modeling your aquarium after a particular habitat—for example, a rocky pool, a bog, or an eel grass bed. You might even consider using local substrates, rocks, and other natural items in your tanks. Pay particular attention to the light and temperature cycles of the area in which you live. By duplicating these in captivity, you will be able to provide a healthier environment for your pets, and you will also encourage breeding.

QUESTION?

Why do the colors of temperate species of fish seem more subdued than those of tropical fish?
Although some temperate fish species do rival the colors of tropical fish, it is true that the most spectacularly colored animals are found in the warmer parts of the world. This is possibly because there is more diversity of species in the tropics, and the bright colors help males and females of the same species recognize each other.

Although the basics of maintaining a cold-water aquarium are similar to those of tropical aquariums, you do have to consider the effects of heat. Many animals from temperate regions are very sensitive to rising water temperatures and have various ways of escaping these temperatures in the summertime. In the close confines of an aquarium, your pets will be denied the option of seeking deeper water to cool off. You may, therefore, need to install a chiller to moderate the temperatures during the summertime. Fortunately a wide variety of small models are now marketed for use in home aquariums.

Oyster Toadfish (Opsanus tau)

This unusual beast fits the bill for anyone seeking a pet that seems to cross the line between fish and amphibian. Although quite capable of swimming, they generally "walk" across the bottom of the aquarium, and, indeed, some Asian species are known to leave the water and cross mud flats for considerable distances. They're also quite vocal, and many of their sounds are audible above the water.

The male oyster toadfish can reach a length of 14 inches and a weight of up to 1 pound. Although the colors are a muted brown, green, and gold, they are quite attractive and serve to camouflage the animal very well. Fleshy tassels also help break up the animal's outline and help it to ambush unwary prey. The oyster toadfish ranges from Maine to North Carolina, along the eastern coast of the United States, and is also found sporadically as far south as Cuba.

Oyster toadfish will become quite bold, and even tame in captivity, but they do feel stressed without a shelter. In the wild, they often live inside discarded cans, shoes, and the like. If denied a shelter in captivity, they will attempt to dig into the substrate until they find themselves a suitably hidden spot. If you have a large enough aquarium, perhaps 55 gallons or so, you can embark on no more interesting project than that of attempting to breed oyster toadfish. Males guard the eggs, which are laid in their caves or shelters, until hatching. During this time, they eat only what food happens to come near to the entrance of their shelter, and they have been known to stay with nests that are exposed at low tide.

E ALERT!

Oyster toadfish have large powerful jaws and sharp teeth and will bite when handled. They also have spines that can inflict painful wounds. The spines of several South and Central American species are connected to venom glands.

Oyster toadfish have been known to survive in captivity for up to fifteen years, and have extremely large and easily pleased appetites. They especially enjoy foods such as small fish, shrimp, and clams, but will also take sinking pellets. Well acclimated individuals will leave a shelter to feed from forceps, and they seemed to anticipate feeding when their owner approaches, leaving their shelters and swimming back and forth along the glass.

Atlantic Spider Crab (Libinia emarginata)

Very common in many areas, the spider crab reveals itself to be a fascinating animal to those who take the time to know it. These interesting crustaceans are members of a family containing over 600 species, the largest of which, the Japanese spider crab, reaches a leg span of 8 feet.

The Atlantic spider crab is a scavenger and uses its tiny, pointed claws to probe into nooks and crannies below seashells and aquarium decorations, performing therein a valuable service. Younger animals have the endearing habit of jamming algae, vegetation, and whatever else they can find into the crevices of their shells. Animals so decorated appear to be walking plants and, once they settle down, the camouflage effect is readily apparent. They will also "harvest" from this portable garden, nibbling at it when they are hungry. For some reason, spider crabs seem to forgo this habit when they reach a carapace size of about 3 inches.

In general, crabs that possess flattened paddles on the rear legs, an adaptation for swimming, are extremely aggressive and are difficult to keep with any other animals. "Walking" crabs, on the other hand, such as spider crabs, are generally much less aggressive and more easily assimilated into a community tank.

Spider crabs make inoffensive aquarium inhabitants, and consume all sorts of foods, including flakes, pellets, black worms, and frozen food. They also enjoy algae and all sorts of green leafy vegetables. Be aware that terrestrial plants have a more rigid structure than do aquatic plants. To increase the digestibility of foods such as kale and spinach, soak the leaves in very hot water for a few minutes before feeding them to your pets.

Spider crabs are extremely slow moving, and may be easily collected in tidal pools and eelgrass beds. Although they get along fairly well with each other, care must be taken that they have a place to hide when the shell is molted, because at that time they are soft and vulnerable to attack by other animals. Spider crabs seem to possess a suicidal impulse to leave the aquarium at night, so be sure that your tank is well covered.

American Eel (Anguilla rostrata)

Although not normally considered an aquarium fish by most, the American eel makes a fascinating and long-lived pet. A member of family containing over 700 species of fish, including the decidedly uneel-like Tarpon, all American eels apparently spawn in the Sargasso Sea, near Bermuda, at a depth of 23,000 feet. The fry grow slowly and, over a period of two years, migrate back to the streams and rivers from which their parents departed earlier (the parents apparently die after spawning). Most males remain in the vicinity of saltwater until breeding time, while the females take up a freshwater existence in rivers, lakes, and ponds, often far from the sea.

FACT

Young eels were long believed to spontaneously generate from the mud, or to arise from horse hairs. It wasn't until the early 1900s that Danish naturalist Johannas Schmidt somehow traced the larva back to the Sargasso Sea, and began unraveling the fantastic mystery of their reproductive behavior.

In captivity, American eels quickly give up their nocturnal habits and show themselves well in the day, especially around feeding time. They should, however, be provided with shelters in which to retire, or a deep substrate into which they can bury themselves. They are both scavengers and predators, and will consume nearly any sort of animal matter and even table scraps. Certain individuals do, however, develop food preferences, but in general, all will readily feed upon small fish, earthworms, insects, and a variety of pellets and frozen foods. They can be kept with fish larger than themselves but will quickly consume any smaller aquarium inhabitants. All eels are extremely adept at escaping, and even the smallest spaces around filter tubes must be tightly sealed. They can survive a good deal of time on land, so if your pet is found in this condition return it to the water right away and move it through the aquarium by hand so that water is forced into the gills. American eels can live for over twenty years in captivity.

Fifteen Spined Stickleback (Spinachia spinachia)

Sticklebacks are found throughout the temperate regions of the Northern Hemisphere, mainly in freshwater. Their breeding habits are fascinating—so much so, in fact, that they are credited with inspiring the development of the aquarium hobby in Europe in the 1700s. The males construct tiny nests consisting of plant material held together by secretions from the kidneys. Males then display for the females, who lay their eggs within the nests. The expectant father then guards the nest from any and all intruders, exhibiting aggression far out of proportion to his size.

The fifteen spined stickleback is one of the few marine dwelling members of the family. Native to the northeastern Atlantic Ocean, it attains a length of 8 inches and is quite hardy in the aquarium. This curious fish does, however, prefer live food in the form of brine shrimp and tiny worms. Sticklebacks in general seem to require quite a bit of food and will lose condition rapidly if not fed adequately. Although quite territorial, small groups can be maintained in aquariums, if enough nest sites are available. Be sure to provide widely spaced groups of sticks and plants so that nesting pairs may have the privacy they require. Watching them go through their reproductive behavior and display to each other is a treat rarely afforded those who study marine fish.

Carefully consider tank mates to keep with sticklebacks. On the one hand, they are live-food specialists, and fairly slow feeders will be out competed by larger fish. On the other, they are quite aggressive and prone to "fin nipping" less agile neighbors. They get along quite well with spider crabs, pipefish, and seahorses.

Horseshoe Crab (Limulus polyphemus)

This "living fossil" is actually not a crab, but a member of the spider family, and is more closely related to them and to scorpions and ticks than it is to crabs. The Atlantic horseshoe crab dwells on sandy and muddy bottoms along the eastern coast of North America. Millions emerge from the sea at the spring high tide to lay their eggs in the mud. Several species of shorebird time their migrations to coincide with this event, so as to take advantage of the rich food source provided by untold billions of eggs. Animal interest groups and natural history societies sponsor field trips to observe this amazing spectacle.

A chemical in the blood of the horseshoe crab is used to test for any impurities in drugs produced by companies in the United States. Millions yearly are collected and released after providing a blood sample for this purpose, especially in the Chesapeake Bay area.

A confirmed scavenger, this animal's constant foraging and digging about renders it a valuable addition to the aquarium. In doing so, it not only uncovers uneaten food but also helps prevent pockets of anaerobic bacteria from developing.

Small horseshoe crabs are extremely entertaining—always on the move and perpetually hungry. If flipped upon their backs they use the long spike-like tail to flip themselves back over. Although many people are afraid of this animal, assuming it to be able to sting, it is actually quite harmless. Large specimens (they can grow to be 20 inches) are best observed in the wild, as they require quite a lot of space and also seem to lack the ability to go around any object in their path, preferring instead to knock it over.

Horseshoe crabs readily accept small bits of clam, prawn or fish, and also appreciate an occasional meal of live black worms or other such creatures. They require a fairly deep, soft substrate in which to burrow but are by no means shy about exposing themselves once adjusted to captivity.

Sunfish (Centrarchidae)

Thirty species of sunfish are found in the freshwaters of Canada, the United States, and Central America. Although quite popular among European aquarists, sunfish have been, for some reason, neglected in American aquaculture. This is a shame, as all are very colorful, active, interesting fish that, for the most part, adjust well to aquarium life. From the tiny black banded sunfish, *Enneacanthus chaetodon,* to the very aggressive, largemouth bass, *Micropterus salmoides*, which, at 39 inches in length, is the largest of the sunfish, there is something for everyone. Although rarely offered in the pet trade, many species are easily collected, where this is legal, through the use of a seine net. Young sunfish will school together, but adults generally become quite territorial and each pair may require a tank to itself.

Pumpkinseed (Lepomis gibbosus)

Oval in shape, and with a golden brown background color mottled with iridescent blue and green spots, this alert fish is the rival of any tropical species in terms of beauty. The spotted pattern gives way to lines of blue-green around the head, and there is a bright red edge to the "ear flap" on the gill cover. Males in particular become quite brilliant during the breeding season.

FACT

The pygmy sunfish, *Elassoma* spp., a highly desirable species in the European aquarium trade, has recently been reclassified in a family separate from the sunfish. It is a delightful aquarium subject, combining all of the sunfish's desirable traits with a small body size and a less aggressive disposition.

Found throughout the eastern half of the United States and Canada, pumpkinseeds grow to be 9 inches in length. They are extremely active and inquisitive fish, seeming to take notice of everything that occurs around their aquarium. Adults, however, become quite aggressive toward each other and are thus best kept as a pair.

As with all sunfish, the male pumpkinseed evacuates a circular nest in the substrate and stands guard over the developing eggs. During this time, he can be seen cleaning the nest and the eggs and aerating them with his pectoral fins. Breeding is most likely to occur in large, well planted aquariums that have been subjected to natural temperature and light fluctuations. The male seems not to venture far from the nest at this time, so be sure to feed him close to this area. Try not to disturb him, for he is quite high strung, even to the point of attacking any hands placed in the aquarium.

Pumpkinseeds are, like other sunfish, carnivorous and prefer to feed upon live foods such as insects, worms, and small fish. They can, however, often be induced to accept frozen meat based foods and freeze-dried items such as prawn.

Brown Bullhead Catfish (Ictalurus nebulosus)

One of the most common catfish to be found in the fresh waters of the United States, the brown bullhead is relatively unknown as an aquarium specimen. It makes, however, a fascinating and long-living captive. Like most catfish it is covered with a highly sensitive skin as opposed to scales. Taste buds are located within this skin, as well as along the four pairs of barbells around the mouth. The bullhead's reaction to the presence of even a small amount of food in the aquarium is rapid and very interesting to behold. It is quite hardy, thriving in waters with a low oxygen content and able to pass short droughts buried in mud.

Young bullheads will get along with each other quite well, but adults tend to become territorial. These fish to grow quite large (to 18 inches) and thus require spacious aquariums. There is evidence that they recognize one another by scent, this being a useful ability to a largely nocturnal creature that often lives in mud bottomed water bodies. In captivity, however, bullheads quickly give up their nocturnal ways and become active whenever they sense the presence of food. They are, interestingly, able to hear airborne sounds and can, through the use of food rewards, be taught to leave their shelters upon hearing a sound such as a whistle or tuning fork.

As with all temperate fish, breeding is more likely to occur if the bullhead is subjected to seasonal fluctuations in temperature and day length. Both sexes participate in nest building, cleaning the eggs, and in driving off potential predators. Upon hatching the fry school together and follow the male about for some time. It is thought that he might lead them to food sources, but this has not been documented.

Madtoms (Noturus spp.)

Madtoms appear to be miniature bullheads and are actually closely related to them. Most species are less than 5 inches long. Their similarity to bullheads ends, however, with their appearance. Unlike their larger cousins, madtoms are, in general, creatures of clear, flowing streams. As such, they are intolerant of bad water quality and also require a good deal of aeration in their aquarium. They are also more strictly nocturnal than are bullheads but when well-adjusted will explode from their hiding places during the day at feeding time. They really are extremely frantic while feeding. They get along together much better thanbullheads, and so they may be kept in groups. Where legal, madtoms may be collected with a net in their daytime retreats (usually below stones) or in baited minnow traps.

Weatherfish (Misgurnis fossilis)

Weatherfish are temperate, freshwater representatives of the largely tropical family of fish known as loaches (Cobitidae). The body is long and eel-like, and the mouth is surrounded by sensory barbells. The color varies depending upon location but is generally brown mottled with black, gray, and gold. The weatherfish grows to about 8 inches in length.

A related Japanese species, which also inhabits temperate waters, is occasionally offered for sale. Many of the tropical species of loach are brightly colored and are popular aquarium fish. The weatherfish owes its common name to its unique habit of becoming very active during air pressure changes. This activity apparently results from the effects of barometric pressure upon the swim bladder, and medieval peasants in Europe were said to keep the fish for its weather predicting abilities.

Although they prefer to feed upon insects and small worms, weatherfish make excellent scavengers. They can tolerate a wide range of water temperatures. Most of their time is spent below the substrate with just the head exposed. As soon as food is scented by the barbels, the fish explodes from the substrate and swims wildly about, stopping occasionally to thrust the barbels into the gravel or sand. It is quite a hearty creature, and captive longevities of over twenty years have been reported. Weatherfish fare well on a varied diet consisting of black worms, crickets, flake food, and pelleted tropical fish foods.

Bullfrog (Rana catesbeiana)

Reaching a length of 8 inches, the bullfrog is the largest frog in North America. It is native to the eastern half of the United States but has been introduced throughout the country and also in many other places, such as Japan and England. The bullfrog's large meaty legs are a delicacy in many places, and escapees from frog farms are largely responsible for the introduced populations.

Tadpoles

Tadpoles of the bullfrog are also quite large, growing to a length of 4 inches. This renders it very easy to observe the transfer from tadpole to frog, and their overall hardiness makes these tadpoles ideal subjects for classroom study. Unlike most temperate frog species, bullfrog tadpoles take a relatively long time to transform. Especially in the northern parts of their range, the tadpole stage can last for up to two years (they hibernate during the winter).

Tadpoles may be housed with nonaggressive fish, but be aware that they are extremely slow feeders and will not be able to compete with fish for food such as fish flakes. If kept with fish, tadpoles should be fed greens or other items that the fish do not favor.

Bullfrog tadpoles can be kept in an aquarium at normal room temperatures. They do not favor fast currents, so filtration should be mild. They are ravenous eaters and should be fed daily. They will accept commercial fish food flakes, algae tablets, and various greens, such as kale, that have been soaked in hot water to render them more digestible. The front legs will develop first, followed by the rear. Once the fourth leg has appeared, the tadpoles generally stop feeding until the tail has nearly disappeared. At that time, they should be provided with an easy method of exiting from the water. Although they will crawl out onto cork bark floats in relatively deep water, it is safer to transfer them into a tank with a lower water level with easy access to floating plants, rocks, and other dry areas. Or they can be provided with a tilted aquarium, so that one-side is left dry (this area should be provided with some cover, as they are fairly shy animals).

Feeding and Care

The young frogs make ideal pets, but they do require live food in the form of insects, small fish, and earthworms. Be aware if one frog does outgrow the others, their prodigious appetites include a taste for frog meat as well! Adults are voracious predators and will take anything that fits within their capacious mouths, including rodents, young turtles, and birds. The frogs will be quite shy for some time and should be provided deep water in which to retreat. Many individuals become quite tame after a time, even to the extent of feeding from the hand. Adult bullfrogs will require a 20 gallon or, preferably, a 30 gallon aquarium to themselves. They can be fed earthworms, crickets, crayfish, and other insects as may be collected. Although bullfrogs will take rodents, they should not be fed mice regularly, as such has been shown to cause digestive problems.

Plan ahead if you decide to keep bullfrog tadpoles, because the adults require considerable space and care. If you do not intend to keep the frogs, arrange for a suitable adoption. Introduced populations of bullfrogs have caused considerable environmental damage, so they should never be released outside of their home range. Also, if you have purchased bullfrog tadpoles from a pet store, be aware that they have likely come from the southern part of the United States and may not survive the winters in the North if released.

Mexican Axolotl (Ambystoma mexicanum)

The Mexican axolotl is an aquatic salamander that has the distinction of being both a common laboratory animal and a species whose wild populations are in serious decline. This unique amphibian is native only to Lake Xochimilco and Lake Chalco, southeast of Mexico City. Both lakes have been drained and channelized, and although recovery projects are underway, it is feared that most or all of the native population is gone. The axolotl's plight is further exacerbated by the fact that local people find them quite tasty. It is said that some may survive in garden ponds in the area, but the majority today are to be found in laboratories and as pet or zoo animals.

The Mexican axolotl makes a fascinating aquarium animal. It is a neotenic species, meaning that the adult form of the salamander retains certain larval characteristics—in this case external lungs and an aquatic lifestyle. Adults have lungs as well and also breathe through the highly porous skin. Normally colored olive brown, with branching red gills, captive strains are now available in the leucistic, albino, black, yellow, and piebald patterns.

Axolotls require fairly cool temperatures, preferably less than 70°F (19°C), and soft water, with a pH of 6.9 to 7.2 (hard or acidic water damages the gills). They become quite bold in captivity, swimming to the surface like fish for floating food items. Although they will use shelters, these are not required, and they seem quite content to remain in view all day. Axolotls grow to a length of about 8 inches and are quite stocky but do not require a good deal of space. A pair can be comfortably housed in a 15 gallon aquarium.

FACT

The axolotl has long been a valuable laboratory animal, used in the study of human developmental biology and embryology. Animals that were originally collected, and that form the basis of today's captive populations, likely hybridized with closely related tiger salamanders collected at the same time. It is therefore unlikely that genetically pure specimens can be found in today's captive populations.

Axolotls breed quite readily if exposed to a period of cooler water temperatures (approximately 52°F, 10°C). Males are easily identified by their swollen cloacas, and the females are generally stouter in build. The several hundred eggs are laid on aquarium plants or other surfaces. The eggs should be removed to a mildly aerated aquarium as soon as possible, as the adults feed upon them quite readily. Newly hatched young require live food in the form of black worms. They are cannibalistic, but this can be prevented somewhat by giving them lots of hiding places. Eventually the young can be weaned onto commercial foods such as trout chow or other pellets designed for carnivorous fish. Such can form the basis of the diet, although they do appreciate the frequent meals of earthworms, black worms, and fish.

Threadfin Snapper

Yellow Tang

Hairy Crab

Blue Angelfish

Spotted Trunkfish

Yellow Seahorse

Clownfish sheltering in anemone

Scorpion Fish

Glass Catfish

Algae Eater (gold phase)

Common Octopus

Cleaner Shrimp

Flounder

Jellyfish

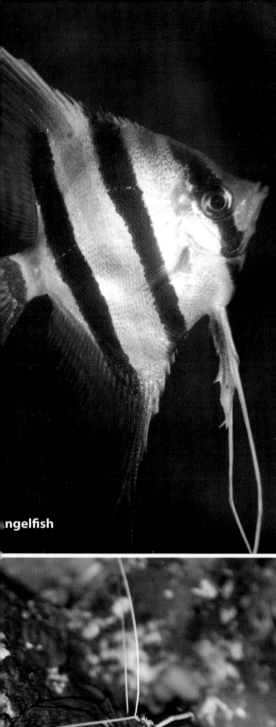

Malu Anemone

ngelfish

Unidentified Marine Shrimp

Powder Blue Surgeonfish

Photos by Darren Green

Banggai
Cardinal Fish

Queen Angelfish

Red-Bellied
Piranha

Pink Skunk
Clownfish

Sea Star

Pink Malu Anemone

Gold Gourami

Northern Pipefish

Photos by Darren Green

Copperband Butterfly Fish

Carribean Anemone

Green Moray Eel

Photos by Darren Green

Chapter 14

Brackish Water Aquariums

At the mouths of rivers the world over are unique habitats that are neither entirely freshwater nor marine. called "estuaries," these strange worlds are home to a variety of unusual animals. Despite this fact, brackish water habitats have been largely ignored by aquarists. In this chapter you will learn about some of the more interesting species that may be encountered in estuarine environments and how to keep them in captivity.

Estuarine Environments

The places where rivers empty into the sea are areas of wildly fluctuating environmental conditions. Depending upon the local tides, the entire habitat may be underwater for part of the day and completely exposed for another. As fresh river water encounters the marine water of an ocean or bay, a habitat is created that is neither fresh nor marine, but somewhere in between. The actual salinity of the water may vary widely each day, as saltwater enters the river during high tide, and then retreats to the ocean as the tide falls.

The Nature of Brackish Water Environments

Brackish water environments are found throughout the world, in temperate and cold places as well as in the tropics. Wherever freshwater encounters the sea, a unique habitat supporting a diverse array of organisms is formed. The influx of saltwater into a river at high tide may extend for miles in some cases. The denser saltwater sinks to the bottom, resulting in a stratified environment where, for a time, freshwater animals dwell at the surface while marine creatures live below. In the tropics, estuaries are often populated by mangrove trees. The long, exposed roots of the mangroves anchor the trees in shallow water. There they trap mud and detritus and, in the process, help to form new land. The trees create a complex environment populated by a unique assortment of fish, invertebrates, and birds. Temperate estuaries are also populated by plants and animals uniquely adapted to fluctuating levels of water specific gravity.

ALERT!

The mollie, one of the most commonly kept freshwater aquarium fish, actually hails from brackish water habitats in Mexico and Central America. Although this hardy species will adjust to freshwater, only in brackish water aquariums does it exhibit vigorous good health and vibrant coloration.

Estuaries are important nursery areas for the young of a number of commercially valuable fish and invertebrates. Also, especially where mangrove trees predominate, estuarine environments act as important buffer zones between land and sea and are vital in preventing erosion.

Sadly, estuaries and the coastlines adjacent to them are also highly desirable areas for real estate development. As the protective trees and grasses are removed, soil readily washes into the sea, often smothering offshore coral reefs in the process. Changes in the physical nature of the habitat also affect the salinity and other characteristics of the water itself, rendering it unsuitable for the myriad animals that dwell there. The destruction of mangrove forests and estuaries is an extremely serious but often overlooked environmental concern.

The Nature of Brackish Water Animals

Animals that thrive in an environment where the pH and water levels fluctuate on a daily basis can be quite hardy in captivity. Indeed, many seem to benefit from environmental changes that would kill creatures of a more delicate constitution. That being said, it is still safer to introduce fluctuations gradually, even as concerns estuarine species.

A good number of brackish water animals are equally at home in freshwater and marine habitats. Populations living in different environments face varying challenges and in many cases follow quite unique lifestyles. The diet of animals living in a shallow marine environment would, for example, likely be quite different than that of populations of the same species inhabiting a freshwater or tidal river.

Establishing a Brackish Water Aquarium

The basic rules that have been discussed concerning other types of aquariums apply equally to brackish water tanks. Just as freshwater aquarium experience is a useful asset for those seeking to keep marine animals, keeping estuarine species will help prepare you for the challenges posed by more delicate captives.

Environmental Parameters

In sharp contrast to the stable conditions encountered by marine organisms, brackish water fish and invertebrates experience daily changes in salinity, water level, and pH. These animals are, therefore, often quite resilient captives. As discussed in the species accounts, some such creatures actually benefit from salinity fluctuations. While few brackish water animals regularly breed in home aquariums, it does seem likely that such fluctuations might also be necessary to stimulate reproductive behavior.

Most brackish water animals will thrive at a specific gravity of 1.005. This should, for most organisms, be allowed to fluctuate from time to time. Safe parameters for the most commonly kept species seem to be between 1.002 and 1.007. Of course, these figures are general in nature, so be sure to learn as much as you can about the animals in which you are particularly interested. There is an array of fascinating estuarine fish and invertebrates that have rarely been maintained in captivity, so interested hobbyists have a real opportunity to add to our overall knowledge.

FACT

Although many estuarine animals can tolerate marine water, the most commonly kept species spend most of their time in water that is considerably less saline. The safest salinity level is approximately 1.005, which is roughly equivalent to 1 gallon of seawater dissolved in 4 gallons of freshwater.

Most brackish water fish are extremely active animals and, consequently, require highly oxygenated water. When setting up your filtration system, be certain that the water returned to your aquarium activates the surface well, or add additional air stones.

Estuarine animals generally fare well at a pH of 7.6.

Animals and Plants

Most dealers and pet stores maintain brackish water fish in either freshwater or saltwater, depending upon the species. Orange chromides are, for example, usually kept in freshwater aquariums, while monos are often exhibited with marine fish. Although they will survive under these conditions, most will not exhibit normal behavior or attain their brightest coloration. You should take note of how the fish that you purchase have been maintained, as the salinity and pH at your own brackish water aquarium will likely be very different. Even though most estuarine species are quite hardy, you should err on the side of caution and introduce them slowly into your aquarium.

Although plants specifically adapted to brackish water environments are not at all common in the trade, mangrove seedlings are becoming increasingly available. Certain aquatic plants that are usually grown in freshwater aquariums may also survive in mildly saline waters. In general, the freshwater plants that fare best are those with waxy leaf coverings, such as the various grasses of the genus Vallisneria, the giant sagittaria, *Sagittaria gigantea*, and Java moss, *Microsorium pterops*. You might also wish to experiment with various marine algae.

Creating Land Areas

A number of brackish water fish and invertebrates are best exhibited in aquariums only partially filled with water, and equipped with a land area. Fiddler crabs, archerfish, four-eyed fish and mudskippers will all exhibit their unique behaviors to their best advantage in such aquariums. There are a number of ways to establish a land area. The simplest is to create a land area of rock or coral. While this will suffice for some species, others do best when provided with an actual mud or sand beach.

A beach area may be established by installing a glass barrier in your tank to separate the substrate from the water, or by simply using a separate plastic container within the aquarium. Alternatively, a number of custom-made terrariums incorporating land and water areas are becoming increasingly available at pet stores. Be sure that the beach is readily accessible so that you are able to clean it and replace the substrate.

Mudskippers (Periopthalmus ssp.)

Those with an interest in a truly unique pet need look no further than the mudskipper. These truly bizarre little creatures exist at the limits of what is possible for a fish. In many ways, they seem to straddle the line between fish and amphibians, leaving the water for long periods of time to chase insects across mudflats and even up onto tree trunks.

Natural History

Mudskippers are fairly small fish, with the largest reaching a length of 12 inches. They occur throughout the tidal areas of East Africa, Southeast Asia, Australia, and along the Red Sea. Most species are associated with mud flats or mangrove swamps. Although populations can be quite dense under favorable conditions, their habitats are under a number of pressures and many species face an uncertain future.

The mudskipper's most distinguishing characteristic is its well-developed ability to move about on land. It is aided in this regard by highly modified pectoral, pelvic, and anal fins. These enable the fish to pull itself along and even to leap about quite rapidly. In addition, the fused pectoral fins form a suction disc that allows these little acrobats to climb up mangrove roots and tree trunks. The eyes are situated at the top of the head and are, for a fish, quite movable.

QUESTION?

Why don't mudskippers dry up and perish as do other fish that are removed from water?
Although they do leave the water for quite extended periods of time, mudskippers generally remain in fairly well saturated habitats, such as tidal mud flats. The skin is adapted to absorb water in these situations and the tightly fitting gill covers allow them to carry about a supply of water for breathing purposes.

Mudskippers are assisted in their terrestrial activities by covers that tightly seal the gill chambers, allowing the gills to stay moist. While on land, the fish utilizes oxygen in the water that is stored within these gill chambers. The most commonly available mudskipper in the pet trade is *Periopthalmus barbarus*, a fairly hardy species that reaches a length of 6 inches.

Captive Care

Most mudskippers do well in captivity if provided with a suitable habitat. The males are, however, very territorial and dominant specimens will make life miserable for others. Males of most species can be distinguished by their large dorsal fins and slightly brighter colors.

Mudskippers require a quite unique aquarium. They do best if provided with a "beach" area, as has been described earlier in this chapter. In the alternative, they can also be provided with small islands fashioned from nontoxic tree roots, coral heads, and rocks.

Mudskippers are fairly tolerant in their salinity requirements and will do well under typical brackish water aquarium conditions. They should be maintained at temperatures of approximately 75°F (24°C).

Feeding

Although adapted for capturing invertebrates such as crabs and insects, mudskippers adjust remarkably well to frozen foods such as prawns and clams. This food should be placed on land, as most species will not feed while submerged. They especially enjoy live insects such as crickets. Their frenzied hunting activities at this time will certainly delight you, as they charge about and even flip upside down in their rush to obtain this favored meal.

Archerfish (Toxotes chatareus)

Rivaling the mudskipper in uniqueness is another inhabitant of warm brackish waters, the archerfish. In the case of this interesting animal, the unique talent is the ability to knock insect prey from overhanging branches with a well aimed jet of water.

Natural History

There are six species of archerfish, the largest of which reaches a length of 16 inches. They are found throughout the Indo-Australian region, most commonly in association with mangrove swamps. Although most are creatures of shallow, coastal areas, some do enter freshwater environments as well.

Archerfish have developed a quite interesting method of securing their food. They spend most of their time scanning overhanging branches for insects. When a potential target is sighted, the fish stops, takes aim, and quite forcibly ejects a stream of water at the insect. The fish rarely misses, and the dislodged insect falls into the water and is consumed. The archerfish accomplishes this amazing feat by compressing its oral cavity and pressing the tongue against the grooved palate. These contractions force the water out of the mouth. The archerfish must allow for the distortion of light as it appears in the water when taking aim at its prey. The environments inhabited by the archerfish are home to an enormous number of insect-eating animals that compete with it for food. In such situations, animals often develop ways of exploiting food sources unavailable to similar creatures.

ALERT!

When opening your aquarium's lid to feed your archerfish, do not be surprised if they immediately stop swimming and begin focusing on you. In many cases, they will take aim at your eyes and will quite accurately squirt water at the movement they detect there!

Captive Care

Archerfish will do well in a typical brackish water aquarium set up. However, it seems a shame to house these unusual fish in a situation that does not allow for the use of their unique abilities. They are better exhibited in an aquarium that is half filled with water, over which has been positioned tree branches and plants. The set up as described earlier for keeping mudskippers will accommodate archers as well.

Archerfish thrive at water aquariums at temperatures of approximately 75°F (24°C). They can tolerate and even seem to benefit from fluctuations in salinity. They are very active and should be given as much room as possible. Archerfish get along fairly well with each other and with similarly sized species. Archers are quite accomplished jumpers, so their aquarium should be well covered.

Feeding

Although they are insect specialists, archerfish have expansive appetites and will readily consume all manner of fish foods. They do, however, relish live insects and will put on quite a show if crickets are released onto the branches overhanging their aquariums. Archers will also benefit from occasional meals of wild caught invertebrates such as grasshoppers, moths, small spiders, beetles, and earthworms.

Archerfish are aggressive feeders and will quickly out-compete most other tank mates. Therefore, pay particular attention to each individual at feeding time.

Mummichog (Fundulus heteroclitus)

Although typically encountered in bait shops rather than pet stores, mummichogs are quite interesting fish that deserve more attention from aquarists. The basic information provided here is also applicable to a wide variety of closely related species that are found throughout the world.

Natural History

Mummichogs are native to the coastline of the United States, from Maine to Texas. They belong to a group that is broadly termed the "killiefish." This order, Cyprionoformes, contains over 500 species, including such aquarium favorites as guppies, mollies, and swordtails.

FACT

Mummichogs are important research animals and have been utilized for many years in the study of genetics, behavior, and toxicology. Many of the results yielded by such research have, had, important implications for human health studies.

Mummichogs are commonly found at the mouths of rivers, in tidal streams, purely marine environments, and, occasionally, in waters that are nearly fresh in character. Female mummichogs reach a length of 5 inches, with the males being a bit smaller and more brightly colored.

Captive Care

Mummichogs take well to a wide variety of environmental conditions and seem equally at home in seawater or water that is only slightly brackish. Individuals that are slowly adjusted to freshwater aquariums will survive there quite well also. They are fairly tolerant of low levels of dissolved oxygen and are active at both cold and warm temperatures.

In nature and the aquarium, mummichogs form large schools, the behavior of which is quite interesting to observe. As is true with many such fish, captive mummichogs seem more comfortable in large groups. Males in breeding coloration are extremely attractive fish and, despite frequent courtship displays, rarely fight with each other.

Feeding

The mummichog's appetite knows no bounds. They do best on a varied diet of animal and plant based prepared foods. They also relish algae disks and vegetables and will become particularly ravenous when presented with live or frozen foods. Mummichogs are highly effective feeders and will easily overwhelm more passive species with which they are housed.

Four-eyed Fish (Anableps ssp.)

Yet another oddball in the seemingly unending parade of bizarre fish that inhabit brackish water environments, the four-eyed fish's protruding eyes give the animal a froglike appearance. Although not commonly available in the pet trade, this fascinating species is well worth learning about and searching for.

Natural History

Four-eyed fish are found along coastal areas from southern Mexico to northern South America. Unique among all fish, the eye is divided into two parts by a horizontal band of opaque tissue. The fish spends nearly all of its time at the surface of the water, and positions itself so that this dividing band of tissue is at the interface of the air and water. The upper portion of the eye then scans the air for prey and predators, while the lower half does the same below the water.

Captive Care

Four-eyed fish are best maintained in aquariums only partially filled with water. In this manner, you will more easily be able to observe their unique habits and lifestyle.

These fish are always on the move and therefore require an aquarium with a good deal of surface area. They are also quite skittish in captivity, and are prone to injuring themselves when startled. For this reason, four-eyed fish should be approached slowly and lights should never be suddenly turned on if the room is in complete darkness.

Four-eyed fish are best maintained alone or with noncompeting species such as mudskippers.

Feeding

Four-eyed fish have evolved to fit a very specific niche within their environments. In common with many such animals, their dietary requirements are fairly specific. Four-eyed fish definitely prefer live foods such as small shrimp and particularly insects. Some have acclimated to frozen foods, but they seem to thrive best when provided with a more natural diet.

Scat (Scatophagus argus *and* S. a. rubrifus)

Scats are among the most popular and widely kept estuarine fish. They are excellent starter animals for hobbyists setting up their first brackish water aquarium. Several species of scats are found throughout India, Southeast Asia, and Australia. They are schooling fish of shallow tidal areas, with the largest species reaching a length of 12 inches. Wild scats have been reported to consume mud, but it is more likely that they are taking up mouthfuls of mud and extracting the small invertebrates and organic detritus contained therein.

Scats are alert feeders, quick to take advantage of any opportunity that comes along. Schools of these fish are known to follow boats and to eagerly consume the contents of bilge and waste water that is flushed into the sea, a habit that gave rise to their Latin name.

Scats form large schools and are at home in environments ranging from river mouths to the open ocean. Large adults seem to favor marine habitats, while younger individuals tend to stay in estuarine areas.

The most commonly available species are green scats and red scats. Both have a shiny, almost metallic sheen, with the green species being particularly attractive in that the coloration does not fade with age. Red scats exhibit brown spots on a reddish background, the brightness of which tends to fade as the animal matures.

Captive Care

Scats do well in typical brackish water aquariums and coexist peaceably with other fish. They do best in small groups. Scats are quite active and require a good deal of room if they are to thrive and grow to full size.

Due to the peculiarities of their natural history, adults should be provided with water that is nearly marine in salinity. Younger specimens do well at lower salinities and seem to benefit from fluctuations in specific gravity.

Feeding

The feeding of scats in captivity presents no problems whatsoever. They will ravenously consume all manner of typical aquarium foods. Scats do seem to require a good deal of vegetable matter in their diet, so be sure to include greens and algae tablets.

Monos (Monodactylus argenteus)

Along with scats, monos are among the most popular of the brackish water fish. Their extended dorsal and anal fins render these beauties most "angelfish-like" in appearance. With their bright coloration and active lifestyles, monos are ideal subjects for larger aquariums.

Natural History

Various species of mono are found throughout a huge range extending from the east coast of India to Australia and New Guinea. The background color is silver, with areas of yellow on the dorsal, anal, and tail fins. A black line goes through the gill plate, and the eyes are often a startling blue in coloration. In body form, they much resemble fresh and saltwater angelfish.

Monos are fish of river mouths, protected bays, and sheltered coastlines and can tolerate fluctuations in salinity.

Captive Care

Monos are extremely active fish and require a large aquarium. In the wild they form large schools and should be maintained in groups of at least four. In smaller groups, distinct hierarchies form, and less dominant individuals are harassed and prevented from feeding.

ALERT!

Monos are often maintained in marine aquariums at pet stores. Be sure to determine the specific gravity at which your fish has been held, and make adjustments slowly if your own aquarium water is brackish.

Feeding

Captive monos are active feeders and may out-compete less aggressive species. They do best on a diet that contains a good deal of plant material, and particularly relish kale, dandelion, and other greens.

Other Brackish Water Fish

The world's estuarine environments are home to thousands of fish species, many of which make interesting additions to the brackish water aquarium. In this section you will learn about a number of other species that can be kept by those interested in this fascinating aspect of the hobby.

Bumblebee Goby (Brachygobius xanthozona)

This small (2 inches), orange and black striped fish is found throughout Southeast Asia, generally at the mouths of rivers. Eggs numbering 100 to 150 are laid in protected sites and are attended by the female. They hatch within four to five days at normal aquarium temperatures (75°F).

The pelvic fins of the bumblebee goby are fused and function almost like a suction cup. This adaptation is thought to allow the tiny fish to maintain its position in the fast flowing waters that it sometimes inhabits.

Bumblebee gobies do not swim so much as hop about the bottom of the aquarium. They are fairly slow feeders, rarely leaving the bottom in pursuit of food. As such, they do not compete well with aggressive fish. Bumblebee gobies will take prepared foods on occasion but prefer to feed upon live animals such as brine shrimp and black worms.

Siamese Tigerfish (Datnoides microlepis)

This fish is one of the larger species that may be maintained in brackish water aquariums. Commonly reaching 16 inches in length, the Siamese tigerfish is a powerful predator that will consume any animal that it can overpower. The body is attractively colored in yellowish brown with dark vertical bars. This coloration offers excellent camouflage in the weedy habitats that the tigerfish calls home.

Siamese tigerfish are found throughout Thailand, Borneo and Sumatra and do best when kept alone in heavily planted brackish water aquariums.

ESSENTIAL

Always research the habitats of the fish that you keep. Many species that are commonly kept in marine aquariums, such as pufferfish, are actually more at home in estuarine environments and brackish water aquariums.

Halfbeaks (Dermogenys pusillus)

Halfbeaks are small (3 inches), thinly built fish that occur throughout Southeast Asia. They lived mainly at the surface of the water, where they prey upon tiny insects. Halfbeaks are native to areas of fluctuating salinity and therefore are best maintained in brackish water aquariums. They are live bearers, with healthy females giving birth every thirty days or so. Unfortunately, the adults are quite cannibalistic, and the young rarely survive. Breeding traps do not work well, as the birthing process takes several days and females become stressed by long confinement in small areas.

Halfbeaks tend to be quite picky feeders and will, in general, consume only tiny invertebrates such as mosquito larva, brine shrimp, and the like. They do not do well with other fish and should be housed in single species groups.

Betting parlors throughout Thailand, Malaysia, and the Sunda Islands feature matches pitting male halfbeaks, known also as "wrestling halfbeaks" against each other. Fights rarely result in any damage being done, and halfbeaks kept in small groups coexist quite peaceably in the aquarium.

Pufferfish

A number of pufferfish species are well-suited for life in brackish water aquariums. Most commonly offered in the pet trade are the green pufferfish, *Tetraodon fluviatilis*, and the figure eight pufferfish, *T. palembangensis*, which is a truly gorgeous creature. Pufferfish are well known for their habit of inflating a sac within the stomach with air or water when threatened. This tactic causes numerous small spines to erect and makes them hard to swallow. Mainly carnivorous, pufferfish possess fused, beaklike teeth that enable them to feed upon hard shelled creatures. In fact, aquarists often use pufferfish to rid tanks of unwanted snails.

FACT

Aquarium pufferfish belong to the same family as the famed *Takifugu* spp. of East Asia. The toxin they produce, known as Tetradotoxin, is more potent than cyanide. Although generally served only by trained chefs who remove the venomous portions of the fish, mistakes are made, and a number of adventurous diners die each year.

Pufferfish quickly endear themselves to their owners by their comical mode of swimming (the tail steers, while the pectoral fins propel them forward) and their extreme alertness. They definitely seem to exhibit individual personality traits, and their large, movable eyes give the impression of being quite expressive.

Pufferfish can hold their own quite well with larger fish but are rarely aggressive toward each other. They can be quite gluttonous, stuffing themselves until they are unable to swim and are forced to lie on the bottom of the tank (do not encourage this!). Although they prefer live and frozen foods, pufferfish readily consume flakes and pellets, and some species also take plants and algae tablets.

Fiddler Crabs (Uca ssp.)

Fiddler crabs are among the most active and interesting crustaceans that may be kept in the aquarium. Although a bit of work must go into their care, the fascinating behavior exhibited by a colony of fiddler crabs renders the effort worthwhile.

Natural History

Fiddlers are semiterrestrial crabs that form huge colonies on tidal mud flats throughout the world. Either the right or left claw of the males is greatly enlarged and is used for territorial signaling and defense. These signaling motions seem reminiscent of a person playing the fiddle and have given rise to the animal's common name.

Each fiddler crab constructs a burrow into which it seals itself at high tide. As the tide recedes, the crabs leave their homes and forage in the mud for organic detritus, algae, and the remains of deceased animals. Fiddler crab colonies may contain millions of individuals.

Captive Care

A colony of fiddler crabs will present you with countless hours of entertainment. Once acclimated to captivity, fiddlers quite readily go about their usual activities, constantly foraging and squabbling over territories. Although males are intolerant of each other, they quickly establish territorial boundaries and fights are rarely serious.

To observe their natural behaviors, you should provide your fiddler crabs with a mud or sand beach. The substrate should be 6 to 8 inches deep so that the crabs may construct comfortable burrows. Newly introduced crabs may take several weeks to settle in and will only rarely show themselves during that time. Eventually, however, they will become quite bold and hearty captives. Strangely, fiddler crabs seem completely unaffected by the lack of tidal influences in captivity and soon establish their own pattern of active and resting periods.

ALERT!

The world's tidal areas are home to countless species of shrimp, crabs, oysters, spiny lobsters, and other invertebrates. These creatures are most often kept in marine aquariums but actually adapt to, and may even prefer, brackish water.

These crabs cannot swim but will enter shallow water and walk about on the bottom. It is critical that they are provided with simple methods of leaving the water section of their aquarium. Be sure to include a number of sloping areas and rocks. Fiddler crabs may also be maintained in a terrarium partially filled with mud that has been saturated with saltwater. A bowl containing saltwater for soaking should also be provided. This method of maintaining the crabs offers the advantage of providing them with a greater land surface and allows for a more expansive burrow system.

Feeding

Fiddler crabs find food by using their tiny claws to sift through the mud at low tide (the male's one large claw is not used for feeding). They do quite well on a diet of moistened fish flakes and pellets. Spread the food evenly around on the mud, because the crabs will exclude others from the immediate vicinity of their own burrows. Fiddler crabs also relish small bits of fish and shrimp. Mud collected at local shorelines will provide them with a valuable source of natural food items.

Chapter 15

Plants and Algae for Marine and Brackish Aquariums

Information concerning freshwater aquarium plants is readily available at aquarium stores and in a large number of publications. The culture of marine algae and brackish water plants is less well known and so will be the focus of discussion in this section. Keep in mind that most algae and aquatic plants require strong, full spectrum lighting. Review the chapter on lighting (Chapter 4) for a more detailed discussion of this topic.

15

General Considerations for Algae and Plants

Plants and algae should be added to your aquarium carefully. Just as with animals, sudden changes in environmental conditions can be harmful or fatal. Particularly important to consider is the pH of your aquarium. Plants that are not given time to adjust to changes in pH will experience fluctuations in osmotic pressure, which will result in the rupture of cells and the death of the plant.

Plants and algae utilize nitrates and phosphates in the aquarium water as nutrients. In this manner, they benefit the overall health of the environment and of the animals that live there. Although commercial fertilizers are available, such are rarely necessary and should only be added after consultation with an expert. Too much fertilizer in an aquarium will cause a decrease in water quality and will negatively affect fish and invertebrates. Certain calcareous algae may, however, require calcium supplementation or the addition of pH buffers.

In marine aquariums, certain types of hairlike green algae may establish themselves and spread rapidly. These, and also a deep purple type that forms a film on aquarium surfaces, should be removed via scraping with a blade or siphoning. Left unchecked, they may quickly cover and kill other algae species as well as sessile invertebrates such as corals. Fast growing species of marine algae may require trimming.

Marine Algae

In marine environments, the organisms that are most commonly referred to as "seaweed" are, in actuality, not true plants but rather marine algae. Found in both single celled and multicelled forms, marine algae are distinguished from plants by their absence of roots, stems, and leaves. They do, however, possess the equal ecological equivalents of these structures, although such may function somewhat differently. For example, the holdfast of a marine algae, superficially similar to a plant's roots, does not absorb nutrients but rather serves only to anchor the organism. Marine algae take in nutrients through leaflike structures that vary widely in shape from species to species.

ALERT!

Marine algae may leak various fluids during the pruning process and may not recover if pruned severely. Be sure to monitor algae growth carefully, so that only a small amount of trimming is necessary at any one time. Avoid chemical preparations designed to kill algae, because these will also destroy desirable species and may affect exhibit animals and beneficial bacteria.

One of the few true plants to be found in marine environments is eelgrass. Eelgrass beds are favored habitats for a wide variety of interesting creatures, but the plant itself has not often been established in aquariums. The aquarist with an interest in plants would do well to experiment with growing eelgrass in captivity.

Uninvited Species of Algae

Perhaps the first algae to establish itself in your marine aquarium will not be deliberately planted but rather will arrive attached to rocks, corals, or sessile invertebrates. Most commonly seen are various species of green algae that form a fuzzy coating on aquarium surfaces. These types greatly improve the appearance of artificial coral and plastic plants by lending them a realistic look and are an excellent food source for a variety of small fish and invertebrates. As described above, harmful species should be removed, lest they out-compete more desirable organisms.

Caulerpa *spp.*

Various species of Caulerpa are among the most readily available and resilient of the marine algae. This genus's members take on a variety of forms, depending upon the species. Some produced rounded leaves, while others grow blades that may be straight or fernlike in appearance. Most species can develop quite dense stands after a time and are useful as animal shelters and sight barriers.

Perhaps the most common species is *Caulerpa prolifera*, a native of warm waters extending southward from Florida. It is commercially cultivated in

Europe and is sold under a variety of common names. Other related species occur throughout Southeast Asia and in the Mediterranean Sea.

Caulerpa spp. spread via the use of runners, or rhizomes, that grow out over various substrates. Several species, such as *C. prolifera* and *C. asheadii* may grow very quickly and can overwhelm other algae and sessile invertebrates. To avoid shocking the algae, it is best to stay ahead of such situations by pruning in small amounts at a time so that a major cutting is not necessary.

Mermaid's Shaving Brush (Penicillus capitatus)

This aptly named marine algae belongs to a group known as the "calcareous algae." The leaflike structures of the mermaid's shaving brush and other calcareous species absorb calcium from the water. Such algae are, therefore, fairly rigid and stand up well to the attentions of herbivorous aquarium animals.

FACT

The shaving brush and similar algae require intense light and a high pH, and heavy growths may necessitate the use of a calcium supplement. The mermaid's shaving brush is, like similar species, fairly slow-growing but fairly hardy once established in the aquarium.

Sea Cactus (Udotea flabellum)

Sea cactus lack spines, but in their round, clustered appearance otherwise resemble their terrestrial namesakes. A calcareous algae, they are quite sturdy and therefore suitable for planting in aquariums that house large, active fish and invertebrates. The sea cactus is a warm water species and requires a fairly high pH but is otherwise undemanding and thrives well in marine aquariums. A number of other species of green algae, most often of the genus Halimeda, take the form of flat, platelike structures and are often sold in the trade under names such as "cactus algae."

Mermaid's Cup (Acetabularia spp.)

This algae forms a cluster of pale green, yellow-centered cups and is quite beautiful to look at. It is, however, very delicate and cannot withstand the nibbling of herbivorous fish or being trampled by vigorous invertebrates. The mermaid's cup requires placid waters and is best suited to aquariums housing sessile invertebrates and small, peaceful fish. It is a fairly slow grower and can be quickly overwhelmed by more vigorous species of algae.

Codiacea spp.

Members of this genus have been, in recent times, appearing more often in the pet trade. Most are at home in the warm waters of the Caribbean Sea and, being calcareous, are quite sturdy and fairly unpalatable to most aquatic creatures. Most Codiacea grow slowly but will do well if provided with intense light and suitably high pH levels. Various species may be reddish or brown in coloration.

Red Algae

While most of the commercially available species of marine algae are green, bright red or maroon specimens are occasionally offered for sale. Where this is legal, these may also be collected and established in the aquarium. Many types grow attached by thick holdfasts to small stones, and form dense thickets that are excellent shelters for many marine creatures. In the aquarium, their coloration offers a welcome bit of contrast to the more typical marine algae and corals.

Plants for Brackish Water Aquariums

With the exception of mangrove tree seedlings and Java ferns, few species specifically suited to brackish water aquariums are commercially available. However, many of the marine algae discussed earlier will adapt to brackish water aquariums, if introduced with care. Always remember that these algae are living organisms and will be injured or killed if suddenly exposed to drastic changes in pH, temperature, or other environmental conditions.

Many of the fish that are native to brackish waters feed voraciously upon plants and algae. Scats, in particular, are nearly impossible to keep in a planted aquarium. The vigorous swimming and digging activities of many mangrove fish also discourage the establishment of delicate plant and algae species.

The Java fern is the only true brackish water aquatic plant that you might find in the pet trade (mangroves are actually semiterrestrial in nature). It grows quite well under normal aquarium conditions, provided the tank is well lit. Although some fish will eat the leaves of the Java fern, it will regrow rapidly if maintained in a healthy environment.

Mangrove Seedlings

Mangrove tree seedlings are occasionally available from suppliers in the southern part of the United States. They should be planted in mud or a similar substrate and are best suited for the semiterrestrial aquariums housing creatures such as fiddler crabs and mudskippers. Mangroves are neither aquatic nor terrestrial and are generally to be found with the roots submerged and the plant itself growing above the water.

Freshwater Plants in Brackish Water Aquariums

Surprisingly, a number of well-known freshwater aquarium plants will adapt to brackish waters. In general, species best suited for this prospect are those with waxy coverings on their stems and leaves. Many of the plant species that will survive in brackish aquariums are quite hardy in general. However, it is important to bear in mind that the change from a freshwater to a brackish water environment is extreme, and the plants should be given plenty of time to adjust. Increasing amounts of brackish water should be mixed into the water in which the plants are growing or should be allowed to drip in slowly through an airline tube.

Anacharis densa

A longtime favorite of freshwater aquarists and much used in grade school science experiments, this plant is perhaps the hardiest of the freshwater plants that may be acclimated to brackish environments. Under conditions of strong light, Anacharis can grow in height by more than 1 inch each day, and cuttings taken anywhere along the stem will result in new plants. It survives quite well as a floating plant or in rooted form.

Hornwort, Ceratophyllum demersum

Hornwort is an extremely common freshwater aquarium plant, various species of which grow worldwide. Most specimens are quite tolerant of both cold and fairly warm water. This large (to 10 feet, 3 meters) plant adjusts well to brackish water conditions but will pale in coloration if not provided with adequate lighting.

Vallisneria *spp.*

This well-known freshwater aquarium grass does very well in brackish water and seems to prefer subdued lighting. Unfortunately, the delicate leaves are much favored by herbivorous fish and invertebrates.

Water Sprite (Ceratopteris thalicroide)

Water sprite reproduces quite prodigiously and can overwhelm slower growing species even in the foreign environment of a brackish water aquarium. Water sprite is an ideal plant to begin with, as it can take on entirely different forms in the same aquarium. It survives quite well as a floating plant and, in this form, has rounded leaves. If rooted, the leaves that develop can be either thick and bulky or almost fernlike in appearance. Water sprite requires bright light and warm temperatures and is, unfortunately, much favored by plant eaters.

Chain Swordplant (Echinodorus tenellus)

Deriving the "chain" part of its name from its reproductive strategy of using long runners, this plant grows rapidly and matures at a height of 4 inches. In common with most sword plants, the chain sword requires warm waters and bright light.

FACT

Hygrophila spp. is a plant that is well-known to freshwater aquarists as a hardy survivor and does equally well in brackish water aquariums. A native of India and Southeast Asia, *Hygrophila* produces large leaves when exposed to bright light and can be propagated from cuttings.

Cabomba aquatica

This delicate beauty is very popular with freshwater aquarists. It is a tropical plant, originating in South America and is, unfortunately, quite delicate. It cannot survive the attentions of herbivorous animals and is easily destroyed by the activities of vigorous fish. In brackish water aquariums, it is best-kept with small, peaceable species such as halfbeaks or those that will not come in contact with it, such as mudskippers.

Sagittaria *spp.*

Sagittaria, a commonly kept grass, is one of the best freshwater species to use in brackish water aquariums. It is not prone to salt damage as are other freshwater plants, and aquarium animals tend to find it unpalatable.

Chapter 16

Nutrition and Feeding Techniques

Proper nutrition plays a central role in the captive maintenance of all aquatic animals and affects every aspect of their lives. Although much improved in recent years, our understanding of the food requirements of most species of even commonly kept fish and invertebrates is still in its infancy. The hobbyist is, therefore, presented with a wonderful opportunity to learn and to add to what is known about this very important topic.

The Role of Nutrition

The importance of nutrition in certain areas, such as growth rate, and even to the overall survival of an animal, is obvious. Less obvious, however, is the effect that an animal's diet will play upon health and vigor in general. Many types of aquatic animals vary their diets throughout the year, in accordance with the demands imposed by their environments. Reproduction is, in particular, very much influenced by nutritional status, and it is the first function to cease when conditions are less than optimal. While some species may, in captivity, do well if offered a sound, unvarying diet throughout the year, others require certain types of foods or nutrients at specific times if they are to reproduce successfully.

Repercussions of a Poor Diet

Many of the maladies that plague aquatic animals can be directly linked to a poor diet. In some cases, the effect will be quite clear, where, for instance, a specialized feeder fails to adjust to a captive diet, refuses to eat, and dies. In other situations the link between poor nutrition and illness will be more difficult to assess. A deficiency in certain vitamins, minerals, or other nutrients can cause retention of body fluids, dull coloration, slowed or deformed growth, and a host of other conditions that may be difficult to link to dietary factors. Even less clear is the effect of diet upon a fish or an invertebrate's immune system. Animals that are able to survive on a suboptimal diet may nonetheless succumb to diseases or parasitic infestations that they might have resisted had they been fed properly.

FACT

Specific populations of individual fish or invertebrate species may have unique dietary requirements. One population may, for example, feed upon only one particular item, while animals living in another part of the range may have less demanding appetites. It is important to research carefully and to speak with others, especially if you plan upon maintaining delicate creatures.

Handwritten notes in top margin:
Nov. 16, Thurs.   11-16-2023
- Exercise
- ~~Bonus~~ Binnies
- ~~Milman~~ Groceries

cialized Diets

g the requirements of the animals that you are inter-
ping in our home, bear in mind that certain species that may
e nearly impossible to keep in captivity. Animals with
ts or those that will feed only when exacting environ-
met are among these. Many of the most gorgeously
desirable of the marine angelfish feed, for example,
living coral polyps—a diet that is nearly impossible to
these demanding creatures may consume food items
other than their natural diet, but such will not support them for long, and
most perish rather quickly in the average home aquarium. In some cases
this will be due to an inability to digest the foreign foods, while in others a
lack of key nutrients will be the deciding factor. For example, seadragons,
seahorses, pipefish, and related marine fish will all eagerly accept living
brine shrimp in captivity, but, with the possible exception of the dwarf seahorse, *Hippocampus zosterae*, few will survive for long if dietary variety is
not introduced.

The Ideal Approach

There are two basic ways of approaching the feeding of aquatic animals.
One school of thought holds that most fish and invertebrates should be
given as much variety as is possible, while the other leans toward the use
of standardized, prepared foods containing all or most of the animals' nutritional needs in one package. The main factors in guiding your decision in
this matter should be the natural history and specific food requirements of
the species that you maintain. Availability of the various food items will also
be important, but you should, of course, avoid animals whose nutritional
needs you will be unable to meet. In general, supplementation in the form
of added vitamins and minerals is more important for captive animals being
offered a limited number of food items than it is for those that receive a
good deal of variety in their diet.

E ALERT!

Even if your pets appear to thrive on a diet composed entirely of the flakes or pellets, you should provide occasional feedings of live or frozen foods and vegetables, where appropriate, as a safety measure. Even if such proves to be unnecessary, the animals will certainly appreciate the change and may benefit from it in ways that you cannot determine.

Current Advances

Great advances have been made in recent years in our understanding of the dietary requirements of captive fish and invertebrates. We are even beginning to grasp the subtleties of their requirements as concerns such important items as vitamins, minerals, and micronutrients. Along with this understanding has come an explosion in the varieties of prepared diets that are available to the hobbyist. Great strides were previously made in understanding the nutritional requirements of commercially imported food fish and invertebrates, such as trout, catfish, and clams. Much of what we have learned in those fields has been applied to ornamental fish and invertebrates and has provided the foundation for further research. In fact, the diets prepared for such commercially important animals are healthful dietary items for such relatives of those animals that may be kept by aquarists. Therefore, those who keep catfish would be well advised to use commercial catfish foods, and you will find that carnivorous freshwater fish often fare well on a diet consisting mainly of trout chow.

Choosing What Is Best for Your Pet

For certain species, foods such as trout or catfish chow or those specifically formulated for aquarium fish may provide all or most of the nutrition required for good health, and even for reproduction. Commercially available foods that fall into this category might include dry flake foods and pellets designed for use as staple diets for marine or freshwater fish. This would be especially true if the flake or pellet were fortified with vitamins and minerals. Unfortunately, a good deal of experimentation is required before you can determine if a particular fish can subsist on a diet comprised solely of flakes or pellets. Your best guide in this regard would be conversations with those who have successfully kept and bred the species in which you are interested.

Accommodating Live-Food Specialists

Aquatic animals that consume live food only may prove difficult to accommodate in captivity. Variety in the diet is often a key to success in maintaining such creatures. As has been mentioned earlier, many of these animals will accept whatever sort of live food you might provide, but they may fail to thrive without appropriate variety. Large cichlids such as the oscar, *Astronotus ocellatus*, for example, will readily consume goldfish throughout their lives. To remain in peak condition, however, these robust animals should also be offered other species of fish, shrimp, earthworms, crickets, and various frozen and pelleted foods. Fortunately, a wide variety of commercially cultured food animals are available to the aquarists today. See Chapter 17, devoted specifically to live foods, for further information.

One way to introduce dietary variety to animals consuming live or frozen foods is to insert tropical fish flakes or pellets into the gill flaps or body cavities of the food animals, or to inject liquid vitamins. This way, animals that are offered few food items in captivity will be supplied with important vitamins that might otherwise be missing from their diet.

One way to help ensure that those pets feeding upon live food are obtaining a balanced diet is to vary the species of food animal that is given to them. If, for example, you are keeping a pumpkinseed sunfish, *Lepomis gibbosus*, alternate the species of fish and insects that you offer to it. For example, readily available species such as guppies and crickets can form the basis of the diet, with small minnows, shiners, earthworms, and moths and other such insects when available. Also, bear in mind that commercially raised food fish will provide different nutrients than will those collected from their natural habitats. Wild-caught food fish will generally have been feeding on a wide variety of invertebrates and plants themselves and are therefore a more complete food item to offer to your pets. Bait stores often sell various species of minnows and shiners that have been seined from outdoor ponds, where they had been feeding upon a fairly varied natural diet. It is usually a simple matter to contact the supplier of such fish and to ascertain from where the stock originates.

An important point to remember is that the diet fed to the food animals will influence the quality of the nutrition that they supply to your pets. This topic is discussed at greater length in Chapter 17, which specifically concerns live foods.

Tailoring Feeding to Specific Situations and Behaviors

A variety of factors will influence the manner in which you will provide food to the animals living in your aquarium. In fact, as you learn more about your hobby in general and your animals in particular, you will become more aware of the importance not only of what you feed to your pets but also of how you present it. Whether an animal is active by day or night, the temperature at which it is kept (and therefore its metabolic rate), the type of community in which it lives, whether or not a food animal will survive in your aquarium—these and numerous other considerations will all influence the techniques that you will employ.

Feeding Strict Live-Food Specialists

Animals that refuse to accept nonliving food items present particular problems to the aquarist. Among the most difficult to keep are those that lure food to within striking range, such as the various anglerfish. For these, not only must the food be alive, but it must be well acclimated to the aquarium and itself interested in feeding (anglerfish wiggle worm like appendages to attract hungry fish). As always, there are methods you might employ to get around this situation. Particularly well-adjusted anglerfish might take small fish that are herded toward their mouths, but some individuals require food fish that approach slowly and attempt to take the bait. These and other confirmed live-food specialists might also be tempted to accept dead fish that are impaled upon glass or plastic rods. A transparent rod is used so as not to frighten or distract the fish. Greater success might be had in this undertaking if some live fish are introduced into the tank along with the dead one. As your pet becomes excited and begins feeding, it may be more likely to accept the impostor as well.

Feeding Seahorses

Seahorses and other species that normally consume tiny, living invertebrates are particularly difficult to acclimate to artificial diets. Some individuals may take frozen food that is circulated in front of them with a glass rod or via the currents created by the filtration system. As has been described above for anglerfish, you may have more success with this technique if you offer live food to the seahorses as well.

Filter Feeders and Sessile Invertebrates

Filter feeding organisms such as clams and sea cucumbers and sessile invertebrates such as sea anemones and tubeworms can offer unique feeding challenges, especially in large aquariums. In general, these animals are best fed by introducing the food directly over them, so that you are assured that the meal is within easy reach. You may also find it necessary to shut the pumps running the filtration system during feeding time so that the tiny food particles required by these creatures are not quickly removed from the aquarium.

One method of successfully keeping slow-moving or sedentary bottom feeders with more active surface dwellers is to choose species that prefer different foods. In this way, the more active surface dwelling fish, which are often carnivorous, will not bother with plant based pellets or vegetables offered to bottom feeders such as snails or herbivorous catfish such as *Plecostomus* spp.

Bottom Feeders

Bottom feeding fish and invertebrates made be deprived of food if the aquarium also contains active fish that feed at the surface. In these situations you may need to introduce food directly to the bottom feeders using forceps or a glass rod, preferably while the more aggressive feeders are occupied with their own meals. You can also adjust your feeding schedules to take into consideration the activity patterns of your pets, if, for example, you house nocturnal bottom dwellers with diurnal, surface feeding fish.

Frozen Foods

An enormous variety of frozen food items suitable for use with marine and freshwater fish and invertebrates are readily available in most pet stores. Among the many that you may find are plankton, krill, prawn, algae, fish of several species, clams and other mollusks, crab eggs, and squid. Pay particular attention to the various combination diets that include a number of ingredients, as these may more closely approximate a balanced diet for some species.

ALERT!

Frozen foods sold for feeding aquarium animals are usually exposed to gamma rays to kill potentially harmful parasites and other microorganisms. This irradiation may remove certain vitamins and trace elements from the food. Therefore, you may wish to soak frozen food items in a liquid vitamin preparation before feeding them to your pets.

Where legal, you may wish to collect your own food items and to freeze them for future use. Freshwater and marine habitats will yield an incredible wealth of suitable food animals such as small fish, crabs, insects, shrimp, amphipods, and the like, as well as numerous types of aquatic plants and algae. See the cautions mentioned elsewhere in this chapter concerning the possible transmission of disease organisms that may occur when using wild caught food animals.

Fresh Seafood and Vegetables

A wide variety of seafood and vegetables sold for human consumption are of great use to the aquarist in feeding aquatic animals. Particularly rich sources of fish of all sizes and shellfish are the markets serving Asian communities in large cities. If you are not familiar with the species offered, you will likely be pleasantly surprised with some new favorite meals for yourself as well! You may even be tempted to purchase additional pets from the live wells and tanks that are often maintained in such shops, but this is usually a risky proposition. Although much less expensive in price than animals sold in pet stores, those that make their way to food markets are generally in poor condition due to rough handling. You may wish to boil and then freeze any fresh foods that you purchase, particularly if the food item comes from a different part of the world than does the animals to which it will be fed. Often times, microorganisms that cause few or no problems to species that have evolved in the same habitat can be devastating to creatures from other parts of the world.

Another effective method of eliminating parasites and other microorganisms from fresh foods is to soak marine food animals in freshwater and freshwater food animals in saltwater. Doing this for a half-hour or so will kill most potentially harmful organisms.

Be cautious in feeding marine animals to your freshwater pets. Some freshwater species may not be able to properly digest marine food items. Occasional feedings are fine, but avoid diets consisting totally of marine species when feeding freshwater animals.

Many types of marine and freshwater fish and invertebrates relish vegetables and, less commonly, fruits. Kale, spinach, dandelion, cucumber, and zucchini are particularly favored. Most terrestrial plants contain a good deal more cellulose than do aquatic plants. This cellulose is, in general, indigestible to most fish and aquatic invertebrates. Therefore, you should break down the cellulose by soaking the vegetables that you use in hot water for approximately 5 minutes before introducing them into your aquarium. You will find that even the tiniest snails and shrimp will readily devour vegetables that have been treated in this matter. Be sure to thoroughly wash all green plants and vegetables before feeding them to your pets, so as to remove all traces of pesticides and fertilizers.

Naturally growing freshwater aquatic plants and marine algae are an excellent food source for your pets and should be utilized where their collection is legal. Be sure to wash them before use so as to remove potentially harmful microorganisms, or soak the plants as has been described in the section concerning fresh foods. Maintaining growing food plants within the aquarium will allow your pets to benefit from the plants' nutritional value as well as from their potential to produce oxygen and remove nitrogenous wastes. If your fish or invertebrates consume the growing plants too quickly, you may wish to culture the plants in a separate enclosure. Algae scrubbers are an excellent source of food for those keeping marine aquariums.

Dry and Freeze-dried Foods

Dry flakes are among the most commonly used foods by aquarists, especially for freshwater fish. A good deal of research has gone into the preparation of these and other similar foods such as various granules and pellets. The flakes, pellets, and disks come in a wide variety of sizes and so are suitable for animals ranging in size from tiny fry to large fish. Some brands of these may provide complete diets for certain fish species and may even support captive reproduction. Remember also to investigate chows and pelleted foods prepared for commercially important fish such as trout and catfish. These, too, are available in a wide variety of sizes and in floating and sinking forms.

ALERT!

If you base your pets' diets on commercially manufactured flakes, pellets and other such foods, be sure to feed them a variety of formulas and to use products from several manufacturers. In this way you are more likely to provide a balanced diet for your animals.

Freeze-dried foods are available in nearly as great a variety as frozen food items. All manner of small creatures such as fish, shrimp, worms, and even crickets are now available in freeze-dried form. One advantage of freeze-dried foods is that they can be stuck to the aquarium glass at various levels within the tank. By attaching the food to the glass at the level or location favored by each animal, you can cater to the specific feeding habits of your pets. The use of freeze-dried items also allows you to tuck food items into caves and under rocks, where it might be more readily accessible to shy or nocturnal species. As has been mentioned concerning frozen foods, be aware that the process of freeze-drying may remove certain important vitamins, minerals, and trace elements. Therefore, it is a good idea to occasionally soak freeze-dried food items in a liquid vitamin/mineral preparation.

Filter Feeding Organisms

Filter feeding animals such as corals, tubeworms, sea cucumbers, sponges, and related invertebrates have long been the bane of aquarists because of their unique and highly specialized diets. Most of these animals continuously pump or otherwise circulate water through their bodies, removing plankton and other microorganisms and detritus in the process. In the past, such species were kept mainly in public aquariums that were located close to an ocean, so that fresh seawater could be pumped into the tanks in which the animals were living (the circulating seawater provided the sponges, corals, and other creatures with a natural source of plankton and other food). Today, however, a number of liquid diets formulated specifically for filter feeding aquatic invertebrates are commercially available. Although such has by no means made the keeping of filter feeding organisms easy, it certainly has allowed for great strides to be made in the husbandry of these fascinating animals. In addition to liquid diets, you might consider the use of newly hatched brine shrimp when feeding such invertebrates. Finely meshed plankton nets may be purchased from biological supply houses by those with an interest in maintaining corals and other filter feeders. For the aquarist with ready access to a saltwater environment, the use of wild caught plankton provides perhaps the best opportunity for success in maintaining delicate sponges, corals, tubeworms, certain species of jellyfish, and similar creatures.

FACT

In addition to being a staple diet for filter feeding invertebrates, plankton collected from marine habitats is also an excellent food for the tiny young of many fish species, especially live-food specialists such as seahorses, seadragons, and pipefish.

Remember that many species of corals, clams, and other filter feeding invertebrates actually depend upon zooxanthellae (algae) living within their bodies for a good deal of their nutrition. The food is produced by the photosynthetic processes of these unique types of algae, and such can occur only in the presence of light of the proper wavelength and intensity. Without proper lighting, the host animals (the clams, corals, or sponges) will fail to thrive. Consult Chapter 4 about lighting before you consider maintaining animals that depend upon the presence of zooxanthellae for their survival.

Feeding During Your Absence

The commitment that you incur upon deciding to keep an aquarium will seem no greater than when you are away from your home for any length of time. In these situations, the best alternative is to have a trusted friend care for your animals in your absence. This person should be carefully instructed as to the care and feeding of your pets and should, if at all possible, be well experienced. For particularly sensitive creatures, you might consider measuring out daily food allowances beforehand. The person who will be responsible for your pets should also be familiar with basic maintenance and should be provided with the phone numbers of helpful experts for use in the event of an emergency.

In the alternative, a trusted pet store owner or supplier may be able to provide you with the names of people who set up and maintain home and office aquariums as a livelihood. One advantage of utilizing such people is that they often have a lot of experience. Of course, the references of all such people or businesses must be carefully checked.

In providing for the needs of your animals while you are away, bear in mind the differences between marine and freshwater fish. Most freshwater fish can survive for quite a bit longer on a limited diet than marine species of similar size and habit. Also, note that small, active fish generally require more frequent feedings than do large, predatory species, which have a tendency to eat heavily at one time and to store food.

For short periods away from home, battery or electrically operated feeders that dispense premeasured amounts of flakes or pellets into the aquarium are worth considering. Food tablets that dissolve in the water are also a possibility for certain species of freshwater fish but do not work well in marine aquariums. Follow the manufacturer's recommendations as to which species of fish will accept dissolving tablets.

Areas for Experimentation

In a hobby ripe for discoveries by interested aquarists, the area of nutrition offers near unlimited opportunities for new innovations. The introduction of new food items to the hobby, whether on a small-scale or, perhaps, on a commercial level, will benefit both those involved in the keeping of aquatic animals and the animals themselves. If you decide to experiment, be sure to consider species that have not been widely used as food sources. For example, in recent years a wide variety of fresh and saltwater invertebrates have been introduced to the hobby. Many of these, especially freshwater and marine shrimp, might be useful food sources for other animals if they can be easily bred in large numbers.

Those who collect invertebrates or plants for use as food for their pets must be completely familiar with the natural histories of the species that are to be collected. Many plant and insect species are toxic or otherwise harmful, and non-native pets may lack the instincts to discern this.

You may also wish to consider local species of small animals as food resources for your pets. Many types of insects, crayfish, sow bugs (which are actually crustaceans that live on land), and the like are easily collected or trapped and will readily reproduce if provided with the right environment.

Remember that the crickets, mealworms, and other animals that are now produced commercially were originally wild species that someone decided to study and eventually to breed on a large-scale.

If you do not have the time or interest to breed your own food animals, collecting may offer another option. Where such is legal, fish, insects, and aquatic invertebrates may be collected and will provide valuable dietary variety to your pets. Almost always, a new food item will elicit great interest from captive fish and invertebrates, and one cannot help but feel that the animals are benefiting from more than just the nutritional value of the food item.

One of the most effective ways to collect marine animals is through the use of a seine net, and terrestrial invertebrates can be captured in large numbers by running a butterfly net through high grasses. Crab traps, minnow traps, and insect traps are also available in a great variety of sizes and styles. See the chapter concerning live foods for a more complete discussion of this and related matters.

Whenever collecting food animals, be sure to check the laws in your area and be aware that the use of pesticides may compromise the value of the insects that you capture. Other dangers are the possibility of introducing parasites or predatory invertebrates to your aquarium. Be sure to very carefully check any living creatures that you collect, and to remove those that might bite, sting, or poison your pets.

Chapter 17

Live Food for Aquarium Inhabitants

Whole organisms can provide vital food elements missing from commercially prepared pet foods. The internal organs, bones, and other components of the prey of your pets may be nutritionally complete foods for certain species. Also, many interesting salt and freshwater aquarium animals will accept live food only, and it is often impossible to switch these species to substitute diets. In this chapter, you will learn about the natural histories of a number of species used as food for aquarium pets, and learn how they are obtained and raised in captivity.

Live-Food Specialists

A number of the most highly desirable freshwater and marine aquarium animals are confirmed live-food specialists. Although certain individuals of some of these species may be induced to accept nonliving food in captivity, in nearly all cases they fare much better on a diet that approximates that which would be consumed in the wild.

Live-Food Specialists Among Marine Fish

We find many live-food specialists among the marine fish that routinely appear in pet stores. Perhaps the best-known of these are seahorses and pipefish (other less commonly kept members of the order Syngnathiformes, such as shrimpfish, require live food as well). Most of these animals are extremely reluctant to feed upon nonliving food and require a varied diet of tiny living invertebrates if they are to do well in captivity. Closely related to the seahorses are the sticklebacks, family Gasterostidae, a largely marine assemblage of tiny fish that are characterized by the fascinating habit of constructing enclosed nests of plant material. These also need a varied diet of small living shrimp and other such creatures, although certain species can be habituated to a diet of flake and frozen foods.

Anglerfish, order Lophiiformes, well known for their use of wormlike lures to attract prey, require as food living fish that are themselves well-adjusted to the aquarium and, therefore, interested in the angler's lure. Many, if not most, of the marine angelfish, which are among the most colorful and highly desirable aquarium inhabitants, feed exclusively upon coral polyps and the tiny animals that live among them.

Hardy fish that thrive and reproduce when fed exclusively on commercially prepared diets will none the less benefit from an occasional meal of live food. Observing the frenzied reaction of even the most passive of species to such foods will leave no doubt in your mind as to the benefits that your pets derive from such treats.

A number of interesting fish that are usually collected rather than purchased by aquarists, such as the lizardfish, family Synodontidae, also are stimulated to feed only by the movement of prey.

Invertebrate Live-Food Specialists

Filter feeding invertebrates such as corals, tubeworms, sponges, and sea cucumbers feed nearly exclusively upon living plankton, although they do likely take in some nonliving particulate matter as well. Commercial diets have now been formulated for many of these invertebrate species, but most fare much better in captivity when supplied with living planktonic organisms. As you will see in the discussion of fish breeding in Chapter 20, many species are brought into breeding condition by an abundance of live food in the diet.

Freshwater Fish That Require Live Food

Although most freshwater aquarium fish seem less discerning when it comes to dietary matters than do their marine relatives, many of the most interesting ones do prefer or even require live foods. Among these are the bizarre elephant-nosed mormyrid, *Gnathonemus petersi*, whose elongated lower jaw allows the fish to effectively snap tiny worms from the substrate. This fish is also unique in that it discharges electrical impulses to navigate the murky waters of its West African range and, perhaps, to communicate with others of its kind.

Hailing from the same waters as the elephant nose is the butterfly fish, *Pantodon bucholzi*. This oddly shaped fish is specifically adapted to float at the water's surface, where it catches insects with a uniquely upturned mouth. Expertly camouflaged as a dead leaf, the butterfly fish's large pectoral fins assist it in leaping from the water to catch low flying insects as well.

The interesting spiny eels and their brightly colored relatives the fire eels of the family Mastagembelidae are also reluctant to consume anything other then tiny worms, brine shrimp, and similar invertebrates. Indeed, their body shapes and uniquely formed mouths ideally suit them for borrowing under rocks and through the substrate where such prey is to be found.

Gar, ancient predatory freshwater fish of the family Lepisosteidae, can rarely be induced to feed upon anything other than small live fish.

Fish That Prefer Live Food

In addition to live-food specialists, there are a number of fish species that, while not reliant on it, prefer live food, or that are hard to maintain without it. The aquarist who keeps sizable predatory fish will find that it is difficult to provide a complete diet to such animals without the use of live food, even if the fish themselves will readily take commercial diets. For example, a number of the extremely interesting freshwater fish of the family Centrarchidae, such as the North American sunfish, basses, and perch, do best when fed earthworms, insects, and small fish. Nearly all of these animals will accept cut pieces of fish and other meats, and some will even take commercially available pellets, but these do not supply all of the nutrients required for optimal health.

ALERT!

The feeding habits of many live-food specialists commonly offered for sale are not well known. In addition, those who sell these fish may be reluctant to inform prospective purchasers of the difficulties inherent in keeping such animals. Therefore, you should always deal with trusted, knowledgeable suppliers when purchasing aquarium animals.

Brine Shrimp (Artemia salina)

These tiny crustaceans are members of the large order Eubranchipoda. While they do, at first glance, resemble tiny shrimp, they are not shrimp at all but quite different animals.

Natural History

Brine shrimp were one of the first aquatic invertebrates to be widely raised as food for aquarium fish and remain one of the most popular today. They reside in lakes whose waters are highly salty in nature and reach only 0.33 to 0.5 inches in length. Brine shrimp are adapted to environmental conditions of extreme severity, and their tiny eggs can remain viable during prolonged droughts. This characteristic is behind their popularity as food items, as the dried eggs can be packed into containers, shipped around the world, and left to sit on pet store shelves for years until purchased.

FACT

The nutritional quality of brine shrimp may be improved by allowing them to feed for two or three days upon algae pellets (sold as food for a variety of herbivorous fish) or the liquid foods formulated for filter feeding invertebrates. Products specifically intended for use in nutrient loading brine shrimp are also available.

Brine shrimp are eagerly accepted by nearly all small predatory fish and are nearly indispensable and raising the tiny fry of many species and in keeping seahorses and pipefish. They are, however, an inadequate diet in and of themselves and should never be fed to the exclusion of other foods.

Raising Brine Shrimp

Brine shrimp eggs and adults can be purchased at most pet stores, so there really is little need to keep breeding colonies of these animals. The hatching time is dependent upon temperature, with the young, known as "naupli," emerging within 24 hours at 85°F (29.4°C). The eggs and shrimp do best in clean, well-aerated marine water.

Commercial Shrimp Hatcheries

A variety of shrimp hatcheries are available if you wish to hatch the eggs. When raising large numbers of baby fish you may find it necessary to purchase several of these, so that a variety of different sized brine shrimp will be available at all times. The hatcheries make use of the fact that the hatched eggs float, and that the brine shrimp are attracted to light. A series of plastic dividers are used to exclude the hatched eggs and the live shrimp are attracted to a collection chamber by the presence of light.

Homemade Shrimp Hatcheries

You can also fashion your own brine shrimp hatcheries from a variety of materials. Perhaps the easiest method is to use an inverted soda bottle that is covered in black paper except for the very top of the bottle, near the cap. The hatched eggs will float, and the brine shrimp, drawn by the light, will gather at the top of the bottle. There they may be easily collected by simply unscrewing the cap. Remember that both homemade and commercial shrimp hatcheries should be provided with vigorous aeration in the form of a battery operated air stone.

Do not hatch brine shrimp eggs in the aquarium where your pets live. In their mad rush to catch this favored food, your fish will consume the eggshells along with the brine shrimp. Although quite small, the hatched eggs are very tough and indigestible to most fish and have been implicated in digestive disorders.

Learning More

You should make every effort to observe the behavior and reproductive strategies of the food animals that you maintain. Many such creatures, especially the smaller crustaceans, have been little studied, and any information that you might acquire would be most helpful. You will also undoubtedly find much of great interest in observing the lives of the fascinating creatures.

Earthworms and Black Worms

Any number of worm species may be readily cultured in captivity or purchased for use as food for your fish and invertebrates. All provide excellent nutrition for your animals, especially if the worms are fed a nutritious diet before being used.

Earthworms

Nearly all predatory fish and invertebrates go into a feeding frenzy when presented with earthworms, quite an unusual phenomenon considering that earthworms are basically terrestrial creatures. Many aquarists have had excellent results when using earthworms as the major portion of the diet of large freshwater fish such as bullhead catfish and invertebrates such as crayfish. In one study, a nutritional analysis of earthworms showed that they provide beneficial levels of Vitamin E and Vitamin A for a wide variety of aquatic creatures.

Using Earthworms

Earthworms of the species *Lumbricus terrestris* and a number of others may be broken into small pieces to provide appropriately sized meals for nearly any sized animal. The larger species, often called "nightcrawlers," are substantial enough to tempt even large fish such as adult oscars and other cichlids.

Although earthworms can be broken into pieces so as to be readily swallowed by your smaller pets, a whole, small earthworm will provide more complete nutrition than will a small piece of a larger worm. Therefore, you may wish to purchase earthworms in various sizes or maintain a breeding colony of this very important food animal.

Uneaten earthworms will remain alive in aerated freshwater for up to eight hours, but they decompose rapidly upon death. They may also be fed to marine animals, but be aware that earthworms die and decay rapidly in saltwater.

Obtaining Earthworms

Earthworms may be purchased at bait stores and some pet stores, or ordered in large quantities from commercial breeders (check the classified ad sections of magazines or publications devoted to aquariums or to the keeping of reptiles and amphibians as pets). Earthworms are, however, such a useful food item for so many creatures that you may wish to establish a breeding colony. The only drawback to this endeavor is that earthworms are, in general, fairly intolerant of warm temperatures and so are best raised in a cool basement or a similar area. Earthworms that are purchased and stored for later use do best when kept in a refrigerator.

Raising Earthworms

Earthworms can be easily cultured in a garbage can or similar container filled with alternating layers of good-quality soil and dead leaves. The earthworms will consume the leaves as well as tropical fish food flakes, vegetables, oatmeal, cornmeal, and breadcrumbs. Collection of the worms can be simplified by feeding them on the surface of the soil, below a layer of damp burlap.

ALERT!

Earthworms consume large amounts of soil while feeding and thus likely take in pollutants, pesticides, and other harmful substances that may be present in the earth. Therefore, wild-caught earthworms should be used with caution. You may wish to consider purchasing your earthworms from commercial farms rather than collecting them.

Black Worms

Black worms are small, aquatic relatives of earthworms and are readily available in the pet trade. They should be stored in a refrigerator, where they will live for at least two weeks if the water is changed daily. To change the water, run cold tap water into the container so as to agitate the worms, which tend to clump together. Pour off the excess water along with the dead worms, which, conveniently, float after being stirred up by the new water.

Using Black Worms

Black worms will live well in freshwater aquariums, where they burrow into the substrate and provide foraging opportunities for bottom dwellers such as catfish, spiny eels, crayfish, and other such animals. In fact, many aquarists "seed" their tanks with black worms so as to keep their animals busy and to provide for interesting observations.

Black worms are readily accepted by nearly all fish and invertebrates that consume live prey. They are an excellent food source for elephant-nosed mormyrids, *Gnathomenus petersi*, and other narrow mouthed specialists. The worms are also excellent scavengers, burrowing under rocks and deep into the substrate to consume uneaten food and wastes.

Black worms tend to clump together, a habit that often results in one animal obtaining a lion's share of the meal. To prevent this, you can purchase a stationary or floating worm feeder. These handy devices dispense individual worms through tiny holes, thereby allowing a greater number of animals to feed at one time. Worm feeders are also useful when feeding animals that may not be able to extract the black worms from the substrate of the aquarium.

Tubifex worms, which superficially resemble black worms, should not be used as a food for your pets. Formally a pet trade staple, they are harvested from heavily polluted waters and have been implicated in the intestinal disorders of fish and in human skin infections. Fortunately, most pet stores had replaced tubifex with black worms, but question the store's employees if you are unsure.

Marine and Freshwater Fish

Fish of appropriate size are excellent food sources for predatory species. Many types of small- to medium-sized freshwater fish, including guppies, goldfish, fathead minnows, and golden shiners are sold by pet stores specifically for use as food fish.

Freshwater and Marine Candidates

Several species of freshwater live-bearing fish are very hardy and, if maintained properly, will produce large numbers of young that can be used as food for other pets. An advantage of maintaining a colony of such fish is that you will always be assured of a supply of food fish of varying sizes. Ideal candidates for captive breeding include guppies, mollies, swordtails, and platys.

ESSENTIAL

Suppliers do not always house food fish under the best of conditions. Carefully examine their condition and avoid tanks containing individuals with obvious signs of disease. It may be prudent to treat incoming food fish with methelyne blue or a similar medication before feeding them to your pets.

Currently there are no marine species that can be easily bred in large numbers as a food source for other animals. However, the very fruitful mollies are, in actuality, brackish-water fish. When properly acclimated, mollies will live in marine aquariums and can be hunted by the inhabitants at will. This is an especially important consideration for those maintaining marine species such as anglerfish, which will often consume only prey that shows an interest in the angler's lure.

Raising Live-bearers

Guppies and similar live-bearers should be housed in a well filtered aquarium at a ratio of one male to every three or four females. At temperatures of 73°F to 77°F (22.7°C to 24.9°C), these fish will reproduce quite rapidly. Breeding success can be increased by feeding a well-balanced diet of tropical fish food flakes, pellets, and live foods such as brine shrimp and black worms. In addition to allowing for larger and more vigorous broods, such a feeding strategy will also greatly enhance the nutritional value of the food fish. Pregnant females can be readily identified by their swollen abdomens and should be placed in breeding traps. These devices hang within the aquarium and have a sloped, slotted false bottom that allows the young to escape the ravenous appetites of their mothers. Babies can be housed in the same aquarium with adults if provided extremely dense cover in the form of living plants or commercially available breeding grass, but in such situations you will likely lose a good number to predation.

Minnows and Shiners

The commercial suppliers of golden shiners and fathead minnows usually seine them from outdoor ponds in the southern part of the United States.

Although these fish are fed a commercial diet, a good portion of their food comes from native plants and invertebrates. Animals consuming a well-balanced and fairly natural diet will likely provide your pets with good nutritional value. You should, therefore, consider using farmed or wild caught fish along with the other species mentioned above.

Bait Stores and Wild Caught Fish

You may also wish to stop in at bait shops in your search for additional food animals for your pets. These establishments, as well as commercial dealers that advertise in the classified section of fishing magazines, often stock fish and invertebrates unavailable in the pet trade. Purchasing such animals will add important variety to the diet of your aquarium's inhabitants and may tempt reluctant feeders.

ALERT!

Wild fish are frequently infested with fish lice (*Calgus* spp. and *Argulus* spp.) and may also carry contagious diseases. Broad-spectrum medications are now formulated for use in treating food fish. Feeding freshwater fish to marine species and vice-versa is another way to lessen the possibility of disease and parasite transference.

A wide variety of freshwater and marine fish suitable for use as food may also be seined or trapped in the local ponds, rivers, and oceans. As always, be sure to check applicable laws and regulations before collecting any fish.

Marine and Freshwater Shrimp

An enormous variety of shrimp species are to be found in fresh and marine waters throughout the world. Many of these make nutritious meals for a wide variety of other invertebrates and fish. Indeed, delicate captives such as seahorses do very well on a diet composed almost entirely of small marine shrimp.

Collecting Shrimp

Shrimp such as *Peneus* spp., *Crago* spp. and *Palaemonetes* spp. may be quite easily collected by seining through eelgrass or by searching stands of marine algae. Marine and freshwater shrimp species will also readily enter commercial traps baited with dead fish. Freshwater shrimp are not usually found in the dense populations that occur in marine species. In some habitats, however, adequate numbers may be obtained by seining along shorelines or with baited traps.

You should also check bait stores and commercial shrimp farms for suitably sized species. These sources may well carry types unavailable elsewhere, thereby providing nutrients that might otherwise be missing from your pets' diets.

Keeping and Breeding Shrimp

You may find that local shrimp species are quite hardy and will even reproduce in captivity. The aquarium housing your shrimp colony should be filtered and well planted with marine algae or freshwater plants. Because some species are cannibalistic, be sure to provide numerous hiding places in the form of empty shells, rocks, or bits of crockery flowerpots.

Most shrimp have hearty appetites and will consume tropical fish food flakes, algae tablets, trout chow, and frozen foods. Many will also take bits of fish and most relish an occasional meal of black worms or brine shrimp.

Be sure to investigate the possibilities of breeding shrimp that are sold for use as aquarium animals. Tropical freshwater and marine species grow quite large and when given proper care will produce large numbers of young in captivity. Even if large-scale breeding of these animals proves unfeasible, you will no doubt enjoy the effort and learn quite a bit in the process.

Marine and freshwater shrimp and other crustaceans such as crabs travel well packed in wet marine algae without standing water, especially if they are kept cool. If water is used, be sure to aerate it with a battery powered air pump, lest the animals use up the available oxygen and perish.

Insects

As the most numerous animals, in terms of both species and individuals, insects form a large part of the diet of a wide variety of freshwater fish. Many insect species are also readily taken by marine fish and invertebrates. Fortunately for the aquarist, a number of insect species are commercially bred and many others are quite easily collected.

House Crickets (Acheta domestica)

House crickets have been commercially bred for use as food for pet reptiles and amphibians for many years. Their use as a fish food has, however, been largely overlooked. Many freshwater fish eagerly accept crickets, and they should figure highly in the captive diets of such species. Freshwater invertebrates such as crayfish and aquatic insects, as well as many marine fish and invertebrates will also eagerly accept this nutritious insect. Even tiny fish such as guppies will relish a cricket that has been crushed to provide them access to the body cavity.

FACT

Crickets are possessed of a seemingly suicidal impulse when it comes to water and will seem to rush to drown themselves in a water bowl if one is provided. Commercial cricket water drinkers are available, but a slice of apple or orange works just as well as a water source.

Obtaining Crickets

Many pet stores stock crickets in several sizes, including newly hatched (called "pinheads"), 10 day old, ½" size, and adult. Commercial cricket farms, which usually advertise in magazines devoted to reptile and amphibian husbandry, will ship large quantities of whatever size you might need. Purchasing crickets in this manner will generally be much less expensive than buying from pet stores.

Nutrient Loading

Unless you are certain that your supplier has fed the crickets well, you should keep your crickets on a high quality diet for two days or so before feeding them to your pets. This step will ensure that your pets will obtain optimal nutrition from the crickets that are consumed. The crickets should be fed tropical fish flakes, trout chow, or a commercial cricket diet. Apples, carrots, oranges, and banana skins should also be provided as a source of water as well as nutrition. Note that house crickets require water to drink but are generally tolerant of damp conditions and will quickly die if not kept dry. Normal room temperatures are adequate for their maintenance but be aware that they can be quite noisy.

Using Crickets

Crickets may be fed to all manner of fish and invertebrates but are especially favored by insectivorous freshwater species such as sunfish. They should compose a large part of the diet of insect specialists such as the West African butterfly fish, *Pantodon bucholzi*. In cases where crickets are used as the basis of a fish's diet, it is especially important that the crickets themselves are maintained on high quality food, as described above.

Breeding Crickets

House crickets may be bred in captivity, but the task is labor-intensive. Crickets are ravenous predators of their own eggs, so the egg laying sites (plastic containers containing damp soil) must be removed often. In most cases, it is preferable to buy the crickets, feed them for several days and then use them as food for your pets.

Collecting Crickets

Free living crickets of many species are common worldwide and will provide an excellent treat or dietary supplement for your aquatic pets. Crickets may be collected by overturning boards and rocks in grassy areas or by luring them into cans buried flush with the earth and baited with a small amount of molasses or ripe banana.

Mealworms, Tenebrio molitor *and* Zoophobia *spp.*

Long a dietary staple for captive reptiles, amphibians and birds, mealworms are of much use to the aquarist as well. They are commercially available in sizes ranging from hatchling to adult. Fully grown Zoophobias, sold as "super mealworms," are large enough to tempt such sizable fish as the largemouth bass, Jack Dempsey, and oscar.

Colonies of mealworms are fairly easy to maintain. The worms themselves are actually the larvae of various species of beetle. They should be kept in several inches of oatmeal, cornmeal, and dry baby food. The colony should be kept dry, with the only moisture being provided in the form of slices of orange, apple, and potato. The adult beetles may be retained as breeding stock or fed to larger fish.

Tenebrio molitor, the smaller of the mealworm species, may also be stored in a refrigerator until needed. The largest species, Zoophobia, is native to warm areas in South America and does not tolerate refrigeration well.

ALERT!

Mealworm exoskeletons, especially those of the smaller *Tenebrio molitor*, are thick and have been implicated in digestive disorders in reptiles and amphibious. It might therefore be prudent to use mealworms only as an occasional supplement. If you maintain a colony of mealworms, you can avoid problems by selecting soft, newly-molted individuals. These are readily identifiable by their white color.

Waxworms (Galleria mellonella)

Superficially resembling legless maggots or beetle grubs, waxworms are actually caterpillars that live a unique and specialized existence within beehives. They are a pest on commercial honey farms, where they are harvested for use as fishing bait. In recent years waxworms have become quite popular as food for pet reptiles, amphibians, and birds and are now readily available in pet stores.

Due to their specialized diet, waxworms are quite difficult to raise (unless, of course, you happen to own a bee farm!). They do, however, survive for quite long periods in the refrigerator. Waxworms are eagerly accepted by all manner of freshwater fish and invertebrates, and by some marine species as well. The exoskeleton is fairly thick, so you may need to crush the waxworms when feeding small fish.

Waxworms are supplied packed in sawdust or wood chips. Unfortunately, these materials stubbornly adhere to the insects themselves. You should, therefore, be careful to brush the sawdust from each insect before feeding your pets, lest they ingest this potentially harmful material or it blocks filter intake tubes.

Chapter 18

Maintaining Your Aquarium

Along with care and research during the creation of your exhibit and the installation of the life support system, a schedule of routine maintenance is essential to the establishment of a successful aquarium. Do not be tempted to ignore regular maintenance when your aquarium water is crystal clear and animals are in excellent health. It is precisely at this time that small changes in water parameters may go unnoticed, leading to a catastrophe in the future.

18

Checking the Animals

The physical condition of each of your pets should be checked every day. The most convenient time to do this is generally during the morning feeding, because most of the animals will be hungry and therefore active at this time. Your most important ally in detecting illness and disease among aquatic animals is your own familiarity with their normal behavior, feeding habits, and positions within the aquarium. All wild animals, fish and invertebrates included, possess an uncanny ability to hide signs of sickness and injury. In the wild, this strategy serves a very useful purpose in that predators almost always focus on animals that stand out by appearing weaker and thus less able to escape or fight back. In captivity, however, the propensity of animals to hide their discomfort complicates the work of the hobbyist in evaluating their health. Any unfamiliar behavior or posture should be thoroughly investigated.

ALERT!

When checking your fish, be especially alert for behaviors that indicate a deterioration in water quality or oxygen levels, such as clamped fins, flared gills, or gulping at the surface of the water.

When you observe your pets as they feed, be sure to check that all are getting a sufficient portion of the food, as dominant animals will inhibit others from feeding properly. This behavior is not always readily apparent, especially during the frenzied feeding activities of a good number of fish in a large aquarium. Therefore, you must pay particular attention to each individual. You should also learn to recognize what a healthy individual fish looks like. This varies greatly for each species, but even fish that are naturally thin or elongated in shape will show pinched bellies or other signs that they are not feeding well. Observing healthy animals in public aquariums or reliable pet stores will go a long way toward helping you in this regard.

It is important to remember that signs of illness will be even harder to notice in less active fish and, especially, in sessile invertebrates. Therefore, be sure to check carefully each sponge, clam, coral, and other such creature that inhabits your aquarium. The deaths of such animals are easy to overlook. Decaying corpses that go unnoticed can quickly pollute your aquarium and kill the other animals living there. Water quality can deteriorate rapidly upon the death of an organism within the aquarium, even if the creature is quite small in size. Be sure to perform an ammonia test immediately upon the discovery of any dead fish or invertebrate in your aquarium.

The Importance of Regular Water Changes

Regular water changes are an indispensable key in maintaining aquarium water quality. This holds true for all aquariums, even those equipped with the most advanced, expensive, and effective filtration systems available. Regular water changes will also relieve your filtration system of a good deal of work, thereby increasing its overall efficiency. The frequency of the water changes and the amount of water that should be replaced each time will vary greatly depending upon the size of the aquarium, the number and types of creatures that are kept within, and the stage of the nitrogen cycle that is in progress at the time.

Full Tanks Versus Lightly Stocked Tanks

Obviously, heavily stocked tanks or those with large animals that produce a good deal of waste will generally require more frequent changes than will lightly stocked tanks housing live rock, plants, and small animals. Water changes may also be required more frequently during the early stages of the establishment of your aquarium, before large populations of beneficial nitrogenous bacteria have become fully established.

FACT

Invertebrates, both freshwater and marine, are nearly always more sensitive to water quality than are most fish. Unfortunately, invertebrates do not usually make it obvious that they are in distress due to poor water quality. Therefore, it is important that you observe them carefully and always maintain your water within safe parameters.

In all cases, however, water changes are the most effective means of removing ammonia and other harmful nitrogenous wastes and in maintaining the overall quality of the water and, therefore, the health of your pets. It is especially important to remember that organic debris, such as animal waste, uneaten food, and decaying plant material will release carbon dioxide during decomposition. This will buffer the water, lowering the pH, and, eventually, compromising the health of your pets.

Removing Water

The best way to remove water from the aquarium during a water change is to use a "gravel cleaner" attached to a siphon. These are available in a variety of models, including ones with very long hoses that attach to a sink and utilize pressure from the sink to draw water from the aquarium. The end of the siphon is thrust into the substrate, where it draws out trapped detritus while leaving the substrate in place. Such cleaners are not practical in heavily planted aquariums where the entire substrate is covered by living plants. In such situations, merely siphoning water from directly above the substrate should suffice. Do not use a siphon that expels aquarium water into a kitchen sink or in other areas where food is prepared. Always drain water into a utility sink or out of a door or window.

Except for unique situations, such as during the early stages of the establishment of your aquarium, or when you are keeping large animals or large numbers of animals in a tank, a monthly change of 20 to 25 percent of the aquarium's water should be sufficient to maintain water quality. A more effective schedule would be to change 10 percent each week, but this is not always practical.

Added Water After Water Change

The water to be added to the aquarium after the water change should be prepared beforehand and aerated overnight, if possible. Although chlorine will generally evaporate from water within 24 hours, it is a good idea to use commercially available preparations to be sure that all chlorine and chloromine is removed from the water before it is added to your aquarium. Most preparations available today act instantly and are harmless to fish and invertebrates.

Water lost through evaporation from a marine aquarium should be replenished with freshwater, not saltwater, because sea salts are not lost during evaporation. Adding more saltwater would raise the overall salinity of the aquarium's water. Water removed from a marine aquarium during a water change should, however, be replaced with saltwater of the same specific gravity.

The makeup water should be poured slowly into your tank or onto a sheet of glass held on the water's surface, so as not to disturb the substrate or your pets. The water added to the aquarium after a water change should, of course, be of approximately the same temperature as that in the aquarium. If you are keeping a marine aquarium, be sure to add trace elements to the replacement water as per the schedule recommended by the manufacturer.

The Importance of a Logbook

One of the most enjoyable aspects of aquarium keeping is the learning process that accompanies this fascinating hobby. A logbook conveniently located near the aquarium and used to record your behavioral observations will vastly increase your enjoyment of your hobby and, in the long run, will add to your knowledge of the creatures that you keep. The logbook should also be used to record your measurements of such environmental parameters as temperature, pH, and ammonia levels. Do not trust your memory in regard to such details. Notes accumulated over a long period of time will give you insights into aquarium functioning and animal behavior that are simply not possible to gain by relying upon your memory or by reading the words of others. Each aquarium is unique, and each hobbyist is unique in what he or she can observe and analyze.

Be sure to share your insights with others, and to publish what you have learned whenever possible. The newsletters of local aquarium societies offer the easiest and quickest way of getting your observations into print. The people who manage such societies, or any professionals that you may be in touch with, will also be able to guide you as to publishing your observations in books and magazines. Bear in mind that nearly all of what we know about the earth's living creatures originated as someone's simple observation, and that the original observations of a hobbyist are no less valuable than are those of a scientist.

Daily Maintenance

You should visually inspect each of your pets, including all sessile invertebrates, each morning. The functioning of all the electrical equipment such as lights, heaters, and filters should also be visually checked each day. Be sure to ascertain that water is flowing freely and at its usual rate from the filter. Any decrease in your filter's output may indicate that the pads or filter materials are becoming clogged with debris or that the motor itself is slowing down due to some malfunction. It is a good idea to have backups of each piece of important electrical equipment on hand at all times.

ALERT!

Because water is an excellent conductor of electricity, it is very important that all pieces of electrical equipment, including lights, be disconnected before any type of servicing or adjustment is done.

Any visible debris at the bottom of the aquarium should, ideally, be removed each day. This is best accomplished through the use of a fine net moved back and forth in a figure eight motion just above the aquarium's substrate. The nets commonly sold as "brine shrimp nets" are the most useful for this purpose, as they trap even the tiniest bits of detritus. Check also that any aerating equipment is functioning properly. An accumulation of algae, or, in marine tanks, of salt, will inhibit the action of air stones and will slow the flow of air through plastic air hoses.

Temperature and Light

The temperature of your aquarium's water should be checked each day and you should ascertain that your backup heater has not come on. A functioning backup heater may indicate that your main heater has failed or that temperatures have fallen to an unacceptably low level for some reason.

Visually inspect the intensity of all light bulbs used over your aquarium. Be aware that full spectrum and other fluorescent lamps will lose their effectiveness over time, even though they continue to remain lit. In other words, they will light your aquarium but may not, as they age, provide the specific wavelengths needed for plant or algae growth or for normal animal behavior.

The effective life of fluorescent lamps is generally listed by the manufacturer. It is important that you calculate your lamp's effective life, based upon its daily hours of operation, and that you note the expiration date on a calendar or in your logbook.

Water Quality

Water quality is best monitored by chemical tests, but be sure to take note of any visual change in the condition of your water each day. A buildup of foam at the water's surface or a cloudy or yellowish tint to the water is an indication of a problem. Often the source of the change will be a dead organism, so be sure to search carefully for those animals that usually remain hidden, or those invertebrates that are normally immobile. A filter malfunction or a sudden die-off of plants or algae are other possible causes of overnight changes in the water's appearance. In all cases, it is important that you determine the source of the problem and correct it. Of course, you will also need to take a short term measure to remedy the situation, such as a water change, but the most important factor is that you learn why the water quality has deteriorated.

Is it advisable to use preparations that promise to "clear up cloudy aquarium water immediately"?
The use of such preparations is a bad idea because they treat the symptoms of the problem only, and water conditions worsen. When your water becomes cloudy, you must discover the cause of the problem and then take appropriate steps to remedy it and to prevent its reccurrence.

Removing Salt

If you maintain a marine aquarium, you will need to use a damp sponge to remove the salt that will accumulate on the hood of the tank and on various other surfaces. Water that evaporates from a marine aquarium does not contain dissolved salts, but water that leaves as a fine mist, due to the aerating action of air stones or filter outputs, does contain salts. Over a long period of time, the removal of salt from the aquarium in this manner will lower the specific gravity of the water, so be sure to monitor it carefully.

Getting Rid of Dust and Algae

You may be quite surprised at how quickly the interior and exterior of your aquarium glass becomes clouded due to the accumulation of dust and a near invisible film of algae and other organic material. Clean glass will make a remarkable difference in the appearance of your aquarium, so be sure to clean the outside and inside surfaces each week. The outer glass may be cleaned with a commercial glass cleaner, as long as you are careful not to spray any into the aquarium.

Sponges designed specifically for glass cleaning are available at all pet stores, and can be used to clean the interior glass surfaces. If you own an acrylic tank, make sure that the sponge or pad you choose is specifically approved for use on acrylic, as this material is easily scratched. Razor blades are very efficient at the removal of algae from glass but should never be used on acrylic aquariums. Algae removed in this manner may be fed to a wide variety of freshwater and marine animals. Do not leave a large amount of algae scrapings in a tank where they will not be consumed, as they may quickly clog your filter's intake strainer.

The fluorescent lamp above your aquarium will be shielded by a pane of glass or plastic. It is very important that you clean the surface of this material, because it will quickly become coated with algae or, in marine aquariums, with salt. Even a light covering of salt or algae in this location will drastically cut down on the intensity of light that reaches your aquarium. The reduced light level will detract from the aquarium's overall appearance and will, over time, negatively affect plant growth and the health of your animals.

ALERT!

When cleaning the inner surface of your tank's glass, be especially careful as you near the substrate, because any gravel or sand that you may inadvertently rub against the glass or acrylic will cause scratches.

Testing pH

The water's pH should be tested weekly. Minor changes in pH can be corrected by a water change or with commercially available preparations. Be aware, however, that rapid or major changes in pH indicate a problem whose source needs to be investigated. The specific pH that you will need to maintain in your aquarium will depend on the species of animals that you keep. Freshwater fish and invertebrates vary greatly in their pH requirements because they come from a wide variety of habitats with pH values ranging from basic to quite acidic. Marine systems, on the other hand, tend to be very stable in terms of pH. Therefore, most saltwater organisms will fare well at a pH of 8.1 to 8.3. Remember that most marine fish and invertebrates are relatively intolerant of pH changes, especially if they occur within a short period of time. Certain hardy species of freshwater organisms may be more resilient in this regard, but in all cases, aquatic animals will fare better if not subjected to drastic changes in pH or any other water quality parameters. Reread the section on pH in Chapter 2 for a more complete discussion of this topic.

In marine aquariums, specific gravity (salinity) should be tested weekly with a hydrometer. The evaporation of water will cause an increase in the water's salinity, and the loss of salt from the aquarium through water mist will lower the specific gravity.

In marine aquariums, it is difficult to estimate the amount of salt needed to make up for that lost in association with mist from aerating devices. Therefore, do not attempt to mix the salt directly into the aquarium, because mistakes cannot then be corrected. Prepare your makeup water in a separate vessel, check the salinity, and then add the water to the aquarium.

Monthly Maintenance

Depending on a variety of factors, including the number of animals kept, the size of your aquarium and the type of filtration used, filter pads and other filter materials may need to be cleaned or replaced on a monthly basis. An easy way to check if the activated carbon in the filter is still effective is to release a few drops of methylene blue (available as a fish medication at pet stores) near the filter's intake. If the water leaving the filter shortly thereafter is blue, you will know that the activated carbon is exhausted and needs to be replaced. Clear water exiting your filter will indicate that the carbon is still effectively removing pollutants from the water. You should also perform a partial water change on a monthly basis, or more frequently.

FACT

Many fish can tolerate nitrate levels of at least 30 mg/liter, but, ideally, the levels in your aquarium should be maintained below 5 mg/l and certainly no higher than 10 mg/l. This is especially important with invertebrates. While sublethal levels of nitrate may not kill your pets, they can subject them to stress and may inhibit growth, breeding, and overall health.

The condition of aquarium decorations such as plastic plants and coral skeletons should be observed at this time also. Any materials that are porous or that contain numerous crevices, such as coral skeletons, may need to be rinsed or more thoroughly cleaned. If the organic debris that has accumulated within a coral skeleton cannot be removed by simple rinsing, the material may be immersed in a solution of 8% bleach and water overnight and then carefully rinsed with fresh water before being returned to the aquarium.

Nitrate, ammonia ,and nitrite levels should also be taken on a monthly basis. In the early stages of your aquarium's establishment, these tests should be made more frequently, as outlined in Chapter 2. As you become more familiar with your aquarium and its specific water chemistry, you may be able to monitor it adequately by testing nitrate levels on a monthly basis and ammonia and nitrite levels on a bimonthly basis.

Emergency Maintenance

If you stay with the hobby long enough, you will likely be faced with emergencies of one type or another, no matter how carefully you plan. Being prepared ahead of time can make the difference between an inconvenient situation and the loss of your entire collection.

One of the most useful pieces of emergency equipment available to the aquarist is the battery operated aerator. Originally sold to keep baitfish alive on fishing trips, units of all sizes are now available in pet stores as well as in bait shops. Be sure to purchase enough units to supply oxygen to all of your tanks in the event of a power failure (because when filters shut down due to an electrical failure your pets will be denied the oxygenating effects of water movement). Pet stores also sell tablets that dissolve in water and release tiny bubbles in the process, but these seem not nearly as effective as battery operated aerators. Aquariums may also be manually aerated by scooping out water and pouring it back into the tank from above the water's surface.

In the event of a thermostat malfunction that overheats your water, a partial water change with water of a cooler temperature may be necessary. Be sure that the water you add is not so cold as to cause an extremely rapid change in temperature. A gradual temperature change, even if it takes a longer time to reach the ideal temperature level, is preferable to a drastic drop in temperature. Aquarium water may also be cooled by floating hot water bottles filled with ice or cold water in the tank. In all cases, be sure to carefully monitor the temperature with an accurate aquarium thermometer.

If your pets have survived a temperature emergency and are living in water that is too hot or too cold, be sure to readjust the water's temperature gradually. A sudden change will stress most aquatic animals and may kill them outright or leave them open to disease and parasitic infection in the near future.

If a power failure during cold weather renders your aquarium temperatures too low, the water should be gradually reheated through the addition of warmer water or by floating hot water bottles in the tank. Water loses heat fairly slowly, so you may be able to offset a short term power loss easily in this matter. In the event of a longer emergency, keep on hand enough insulating material to wrap completely around all of your aquariums. By doing this you will greatly reduce the rate of heat loss from the water.

Chapter 19

Health and Disease

All types of wild animals do their utmost to hide outward signs of sickness. Predators single out animals that appear weak and unable to defend themselves, so it is always in an animal's best interest to appear healthy, even when it is not. This particular fact often makes it difficult for you to detect a pet's illness until an advanced stage, at which point it will be harder to cure. It is therefore important to understand the normal behaviors of each of your pets, and to recognize changes that might indicate a problem.

Stress

An important key in avoiding potential health problems among aquarium animals is to understand the role that stress plays in this area. An animal that is under stress will succumb to disease or parasites much more rapidly than will a well-adjusted individual. A wide variety of parasites are nearly always present in the captive environment and they are quick to take advantage of immune systems weakened by stress. A healthy animal might be able to tolerate suboptimal captive conditions, while a stressed one of the same species might be killed by the very same circumstances.

Stress and the Immune System

All animals employ a variety of chemicals that enable them to deal with stressful conditions. This process is often referred to as the "flight or fight reaction," in that adrenaline and other substances prepare the animal to defend itself or to escape from a situation. This reaction is a necessary survival tool in the wild. In captivity, however, what often happens is that environmental stressors persist for unnaturally long periods of time, and the animal is unable to escape from them. The bodies of most animals are not designed to withstand long-term exposure to stress-induced chemicals. Over time, the immune system will be weakened, and the fish or invertebrate will readily succumb to disease or parasitic infection.

Sources of Stress

Factors that cause stress to aquarium animals may arise from any number of conditions that originate outside of the animal itself. The most common stress-inducing factors are poor water quality, improper diet, aggressive or threatening tank mates, and a captive habitat that does not meet the animal's needs.

The animals that you purchase will almost certainly have experienced a range of stress causing conditions in their transit through various stops along the way to your home. Wild caught animals, particularly those from distant locales, may have had an especially difficult journey. You should, therefore, take care in establishing and observing newly purchased pets.

ESSENTIAL

One of the most effective ways of eliminating stress from your pet's life is to learn as much as you can about its biology, diet, methods of reproduction, and natural habitat. You will then be able to provide captive conditions that are conducive to natural behavior and good health. Read widely and learn from others whenever possible.

Aquarium Design

Your aquarium must be designed to meet the environmental needs of your pets. Many animals are extremely specific in their requirements and will fail to thrive if they are not given a close approximation of their natural habitat. For example, retiring animals such as octopus require shelters, active bottom dwellers such as stingrays require expanses of flat, sandy areas, and large, surface dwelling fish such as arawona need to swim unencumbered. Providing suitable hiding places and densely planted aquariums for shy animals will enable them to live in comfort and to exhibit their natural behaviors.

Temperature and Other Parameters

It is very important to keep your pets in an environment that provides them with proper temperatures and appropriate levels of salinity and pH. Even if an animal survives under conditions that are not to its liking, its immune system will certainly be weakened, and this may prevent the animal from fighting off disease and parasites. You must also be careful to avoid rapid fluctuations in water quality parameters. This can best be accomplished by regularly monitoring nitrates, ammonia and pH levels, and by installing a backup aquarium heater, so that temperatures will not plummet if your main heater fails.

Tank Mates

The animals with which your pet shares the aquarium have an important effect on its overall health. Aggressive individuals may prevent others from feeding properly or may attack more passive creatures outright. Even in the absence of actual hostilities, a dominant animal can be a significant source of stress to others in the aquarium. The mere presence of a potentially aggressive individual can trigger stress reactions in others that will, in the long run, compromise their health. Even creatures that normally live together in the wild may not coexist within the confines of an aquarium. It is also important to ascertain that the animals are compatible in terms of their activity patterns. Shy, retiring creatures may be disturbed by actively swimming tank mates, even if there is no actual aggression between them. Likewise, nocturnal animals such as catfish may become very active at night and disturb diurnal species.

Diet

Unfortunately, we know little about the nutrients required by many commonly kept fish and invertebrates, especially marine species. An inappropriate or incomplete diet is one of the most common long term stresses that aquarium animals are forced to endure. Over time, even individuals that feed vigorously and appear well will weaken if essential nutrients are missing from their diets. You should, therefore, learn all that you can about the nutritional requirements of the animals that you keep. Do not attempt to keep animals that, while interesting and desirable, require foods that you may not be able to provide.

Identifying Diseases

Although some diseases of aquarium animals are indicated by very specific and easily recognizable symptoms, in many cases you will need to rely upon generalized changes in behavior or condition when attempting to diagnose an illness. As always, you will need to understand your pets' normal behaviors to be able to quickly recognize any deviation from them.

General Symptoms of a Problem

Even allowing for the vast differences in the behavior of the many species of fish and invertebrates, certain general patterns may indicate to you that a closer look is necessary. Animals that swim about without normal pauses or sedentary creatures that suddenly begin to wander about rapidly may be indicating that the water quality is poor or that they are under pressure from an aggressive tank mate. At the other end of the spectrum, sluggishness or the adoption of an unusual posture may also signal that something is amiss. Seahorses, for example, usually remain anchored to coral or plants, even when feeding. Seahorses that spend a good deal of time swimming about the aquarium, Even though this is behavior that is quite normal for many other fish), are definitely under some type of stress.

QUESTION?

Is it safe to medicate fish or invertebrates if I cannot determine the exact nature of their illness?

Broad-spectrum medications that treat a variety of commonly encountered diseases are available for marine and freshwater aquariums. Be sure, though, that a disease and not an environmental condition is involved. If the distress is caused by a factor such as improper water temperature, medications will do more harm than good.

Take note of the usual respiration rates of the fish that you keep. Any increase in this rate, especially if the fish gulps air at the surface of the tank, may indicate that the oxygen content of the water is too low. A number of factors can cause a drop in oxygen levels, including overcrowding, a filter that is malfunctioning or too small, or a sudden spike in temperature (water's ability to hold oxygen decreases as the temperature rises). Similarly, you should be familiar with each of your pets' modes of feeding and the usual states of their appetites. In most cases, a reluctance to feed indicates illness or, in the case of females, it can indicate that she is developing eggs or young.

Prevent and Learn

Although the diagnosis and treatment of the diseases of fish and invertebrates has come a long way in recent years, knowledge in this area is still far from complete. Therefore, prevention of disease will be a far more effective tactic than looking for a cure. Fortunately, by careful research and discussion with others, you will likely be able to avoid many of the pitfalls that befall those who do not take the time to learn about their pets.

Be sure to take careful notes concerning your experiences, and do not be afraid to engage in "educated experimentation" when it comes to diagnosing and treating disease. Especially for those conditions that people are currently unable to cure, you would do well to apply your interest and knowledge to serious experimentation. Above all, remember to share the results of your work.

Quarantine

Several factors must be considered when deciding whether or not to quarantine an animal before introducing it into your aquarium, or when providing medication. The use of a quarantine aquarium requires the animal to adapt to an additional change in environment and water conditions. Such changes are stressful in and of themselves and may make recovery from illness more difficult.

The Quarantine Aquarium

Many hobbyists keep newly acquired animals separated from their collection for a three to four week period to assess the animals' health and to be sure that they will not introduce disease or parasites into the main aquarium. In general, quarantine aquariums should be sparsely furnished so they can be easily cleaned when new animals are introduced, and so the confined creature is more readily observed. However, you must be sure to meet the quarantined animal's environmental needs and to provide it with shelter, if necessary. For this reason, animals that require complex, well planted exhibits are more difficult to quarantine than are less sensitive species.

It is vital that the quarantine aquarium's physical parameters, such as temperature, pH, and specific gravity be very close to those that the animal will experience once it is introduced into the main aquarium. One exception to this rule might be in the case of salinity when dealing with marine animals. While most marine fish can tolerate a slightly lower than usual salinity, such as 1.018, most of their parasites cannot. Especially when keeping wild caught marine species, therefore, you might consider quarantining the animals at this lower salinity.

ALERT!

Any change in environment is a potential stress, so fish and invertebrates that have been kept in a quarantine aquarium must be very carefully introduced into the main aquarium, even if water quality conditions are similar. This is especially true if you have kept marine fish at a low salinity to combat parasites.

Filtration for the Quarantine Aquarium

The quarantine aquarium must, of course, be kept extremely clean. Therefore, you should employ an effective but easily maintained filtration system. Since aesthetics are not your main concern here, a simple box filter placed within the aquarium may suffice. Be sure that the biological capacity of the filter is maintained. To do this, the beneficial aerobic bacteria in the filter must be provided with a food source. During periods when the quarantine aquarium is empty, be sure to add commercial preparations that provide food for the beneficial bacteria, or introduce commercially available aerobic bacteria before adding fish to the tank.

Medications and the Quarantine Aquarium

It is sometimes possible to treat an ailing fish within the main aquarium. This is especially possible if the animal is the aquarium's sole inhabitant, or if its tank mates will likely be affected by the disease as well.

Often, however, it is advisable to isolate a sick fish before trying to cure an illness with medication. Isolation will often be necessary when you are medicating fish housed in aquariums that contain invertebrates as well. Copper is the most common ingredient in medications designed to kill fish parasites. Most aquarium invertebrates cannot, however, tolerate even the slightest bit of copper in the water, so you will need to remove either them or the fish that is being treated before using such medications.

Certain medications will kill the beneficial aerobic bacteria living in your filtration system. To avoid a crash of your main tank's system, ill fish should be removed from the tank and treated separately if these medications are required. Of course, bear in mind that the quarantine aquarium's beneficial bacteria will also be killed off, so be sure to keep an eye on water quality.

ALERT!

Fish that lack scales may be weakened or even killed by certain medications that are safe for other fish. Loaches and both freshwater and marine catfish and eels are particularly sensitive to a wide variety of chemicals. Be sure to read all directions carefully before medicating tanks containing such species.

Another factor to consider is that certain filtration materials, most especially activated carbon, will effectively remove medications from aquarium water, thereby negating their effect upon the sick fish. Read the directions carefully to determine whether or not you should remove activated carbon and other such materials from the filter before using the medication in question.

Parasitic Diseases

A large number of species of parasitic invertebrates plague both marine and freshwater aquarium animals. Some are quite specific in their hosts, affecting only one species, for example, while others are opportunistic and attack a wide variety of animals. Entire volumes are devoted to these successful but troublesome creatures, so only the more commonly encountered types will be discussed below.

Coral Reef Disease

In common with many parasitic diseases, coral reef disease is fatal if left unchecked. The parasite that causes the disease, a protozoan known as *Amyloodium ocellatum*, has both a free swimming and a cyst stage. The parasite affects a wide range of marine fish species and is not specific in its attachment site. The tiny white and yellow spots that are indicative of this parasite may be found on the gills, fins, or body of the fish that is affected. Fish suffering from coral reef disease that has taken hold in the gills will increase their respiration rate and may gulp air at the water's surface.

A variety of copper-based medications are effective in the treatment of coral reef disease. As with all medications containing copper, it is important that invertebrates are not housed in the tank to be treated, or they will be killed. Note also that copper is toxic to many fish species at high levels, so be sure to follow the manufacturer's directions carefully.

The medication must be continued for at least two weeks after the parasitic cysts have disappeared, because the parasite is quite resilient during this stage and will only succumb to treatment when in its free swimming form.

Fish parasites are usually resistant to medication during the cyst and egg stages of their life cycles, and must be killed during their free swimming stage. It is, therefore, important to know how long the cyst or egg stage lasts and to follow the manufacturer's recommendation concerning treatment duration.

Ick

Also known as white spot disease, ick is transmitted by protozoans of the genus Crytocarya. These organisms are widespread in both freshwater and marine environments and are often present in aquariums. They generally affect only animals whose immune systems have been compromised by exposure to rapidly fluctuating temperatures. Once the disease takes hold, however, it is readily transmitted to healthy individuals. White spot disease most commonly occurs soon after fish are introduced into a new aquarium, such as when they arrive at a pet store or pet owner's home. It is during these times that the animal has most likely experienced stresses due to changes in environment or temperature fluctuations while in transit.

Ick is diagnosed by the presence of large white spots on the fish's body. A number of readily available medications effectively treat this condition. The protozoan species that causes the disease has a life cycle that averages twenty-one days in length. Because the parasite is resistant to treatment during the cyst stage, medication should be continued for at least twenty-one days. The contagious nature of this disease usually dictates that all animals living with the affected individual be treated.

Gas Bubble Disease

A variety of conditions caused by several parasites are commonly termed "gas bubble disease." Although the process of infection is not completely understood, it seems that air bubbles attach to the bodies of affected fish and create conditions favorable to bacterial growth. Water that is supersaturated with oxygen or nitrogen has been implicated in certain, but by no means all, cases.

In its early stages, gas bubble disease can be treated by pricking the affected area with a sterilized needle and releasing the enclosed air bubble through massage (the fish should be carefully held underwater during this process). A wide spectrum antibacterial should then be swabbed on the wound site. Advanced cases are nearly always fatal.

A related ailment specific to male seahorses is the buildup of gases within the brood pouch. Affected animals float to the surface of the aquarium in a head down position. This condition, the cause of which is as yet unknown, may sometimes be cured by gently massaging the inside of the pouch with a tiny, sterile pipette. After the gas has been expelled, the pouch should be flushed with a broad-spectrum antifungal medication.

Clown Fish Disease

Although marine clown fish are particularly susceptible to the protozoan that causes this disease (*Brooklynella hostilis*), they are by no means its only victims. The protozoan is microscopic in size and may be contracted by many types of marine fish. In some species, the skin color of affected specimens becomes quite pale, and most also exhibit skin lesions and an increase in respiration rates. The lesions themselves are frequently colonized by opportunistic bacteria, the presence of which further weakens the host fish.

FACT

Disease organisms affect different species of fish in varying ways. While some may respond to treatment long after symptoms have appeared, others may expire within a day of encountering certain parasites. As with most aquarium problems, vigilant observation and sound husbandry is your best defense.

A variety of medications, usually containing some form of malachite green, can be used to treat clown fish disease. However, action must be taken quickly. Unfortunately, by the time symptoms appear, the disease is often well advanced and not responsive to treatment. It is, therefore, extremely important to carefully monitor your pets so as to detect changes in their condition as soon as they occur.

Flukes

Flukes are fairly large trematode worms that are usually readily visible to the naked eye. They are quite mobile and may move about the aquarium from fish to fish. Flukes are external parasites that use their hooked mouth parts to attach themselves to the skin or scales of their hosts. The resulting lesions may, as with any injury, give rise to secondary bacterial infections that further complicate treatment. In addition to direct observation of the flukes, infestations may be diagnosed by increased rates of respiration, and in some fish species, by a paling of the skin coloration. Affected fish also will be seen to frequently rub themselves against rocks and the substrate in an effort to dislodge the parasites.

Formalin based medications are most commonly used to treat fluke infestations. Other medications may be required to assist with wound healing and to kill opportunistic bacteria.

Copepods

While some copepod species are important food items for small fish, others are dangerous parasites that attack a wide variety of marine and freshwater species. They are external parasites, attaching to numerous locations on the body, and most are visible to the naked eye.

A number of copper based products will effectively eliminate copepods from the aquarium. The eggs are, however, unaffected by most medications, and so treatment must continue for the parasite's entire lifecycle. Depending on the species, eggs may take up to five weeks to hatch. It is, therefore, important to follow the manufacturer's directions as to the length of the medication period.

Fungal, Bacterial, and Viral Diseases

Microorganisms such as fungi, bacteria, and viruses are present in most aquariums but are invisible to the naked eye. Many of these only rarely attack animals directly. They are opportunistic in nature and become established following some other condition that paves their way. Such conditions may be a wound or other injury, a parasitic infestation or a general decline in the immune system due to poor environmental conditions.

Fungi

Fungal infections most commonly manifest themselves as a fuzzy coating on the afflicted animal's body. In some species of fish, discolored patches, usually darker than the fish's normal color, may also appear. Fungi of one type or another are present in nearly all marine and freshwater aquariums and generally cause problems only after a fish's or invertebrate's immune system has been compromised.

A wide variety of fungicides are available for treating fungal infestations. Most contain malachite green or methylene blue and, being fairly broad spectrum in nature, will kill a number of troublesome species.

ESSENTIAL

Bacteria, fungi, and viruses frequently afflict aquarium animals during or immediately following parasitic infestations. Therefore, when treating for parasites, you should be particularly alert for symptoms of other related conditions. Often, a second medication may be required to combat opportunistic pathogens.

Bacteria

While certain bacteria directly cause disease, the vast majority manifest themselves after injury or parasitic infection has weakened the infected animal. Bacteria often cause skin ulcerations and the loss of fin and tail tissue.

Bacterial infections are most effectively treated with antibiotics. Unfortunately, most antibiotics will rapidly decimate the population of nitrifying bacteria in the filter. This will result in a sudden rise in ammonia levels, a condition that can weaken and eventually kill even healthy animals.

Viruses

The viruses that affect fish and invertebrates are, at this point, largely incurable. Viral infections may be diagnosed by the presence of hard white nodules on the body. Other symptoms will vary widely according to the internal organs that are affected by the virus.

A good deal of research is being conducted on the treatment of the viruses that affect commercially valuable fish and invertebrates, such as salmon and lobsters. Hopefully, knowledge gained in these areas will someday translate into medications suitable for treating viral infections in home aquariums.

If opportunistic microorganisms such as viruses seem to be affecting your fish, check for other diseases as well because virues and other diseases usually go hand-in-hand. Fungi, bacteria, and viruses also take hold when animals are stressed by environmental conditions, so be sure to monitor temperature, pH, and ammonia carefully.

Water Quality and Illness

High ammonia levels and other symptoms of poor water quality are common causes of illness in fish and invertebrates. Even if these conditions do not kill the animals outright, they stress the immune system and allow parasites and opportunistic microorganisms to establish themselves.

Nitrogenous Wastes

Ammonia is the most toxic of the nitrogenous compounds to be found in the aquarium, but high levels of nitrites and nitrates are also of concern. Invertebrates are, in general, extremely susceptible to ammonia and may perish rapidly when levels rise. Fish vary in their resistance to this toxin. High levels of ammonia will impair a fish's ability to transport oxygen to its cells, a symptom of which will be rapid respiration followed by listlessness.

FACT

A water change is the quickest and most effective way to deal with a spike in ammonia levels. Once this has been accomplished, it is critical that you identify the cause of the problem. An accumulation of uneaten food, a dead organism or a malfunctioning filter is usually behind a sudden increase in ammonia levels.

Nitrates and nitrites are less toxic than is ammonia but will also negatively affect the health of aquatic animals. Fish not immediately killed by high nitrate or nitrite levels will, nevertheless, suffer reduced growth rates and may exhibit labored breathing. Long-term exposure to high levels of any nitrogenous compound will also inhibit reproduction in most animals.

Chlorine and Chloramine

Chlorine, chloramine, and related chemicals are added by municipal authorities to our water supply to render it safe for drinking. They are, however, toxic to most freshwater and marine organisms. Both chlorine and chloramines may be removed instantly via the use of commercially available drops. Chlorine also evaporates from water that is left uncovered for 24 hours or so, especially if it is aerated.

Be aware, however, that chloramine detoxification may result in the formation of ammonia, which is toxic to fish and invertebrates. If you treat large quantities of water containing chloramine, be sure to filter the water through commercially available ammonia removing resins before using it in your aquarium.

Your local water authority should be able to provide you with the names of the chemicals that are added to your water.

Heavy Metals

Although heavy metals exist in natural bodies of freshwater and saltwater, they are extremely toxic, even in small amounts, in the aquarium. Copper is the heavy metal most commonly encountered by aquarists. Water that has passed through copper pipes, which today are most often found in older buildings, may pick up enough copper to kill fish and especially invertebrates.

Copper accumulates in water that has remained in the pipes for some time. If your water supply passes through copper pipes, you should allow the water to run for 15 minutes or so before using it. This will flush most of the copper from the system, but tests should be conducted until you are sure. You may also wish to consult your local water authority if you are experiencing an unexplained rise in copper levels, because many agencies use copper to control algae and parasites in reservoirs.

Certain rocks may contain heavy metals such as lead and aluminum. These may not cause problems in a natural environment but can, within the confines of an aquarium, poison your pets. Although live rock and gravel is often collected and used by aquarists, you may wish to be on the safe side and purchase these materials from reputable dealers.

Plastic plants that are placed in the aquarium must be designed specifically for use with living animals. Plastic plants, even flexible ones, may have internal metal supports that can rust if placed in either fresh or saltwater.

Fish and invertebrates poisoned by heavy metals may exhibit a wide variety of reactions, ranging from escape attempts to lethargy and increased respiration rates.

ALERT!

The use of aquarium medications must be considered in conjunction with other husbandry practices, because each change affects something else. For example, aquarium water containing safe levels of copper may be rendered toxic if copper based medications are introduced.

Other Toxins

Many commonly used household products, such as air fresheners, glass cleaners, paints, and varnishes may be toxic to aquarium animals. Covering the aquarium may not necessarily exclude such materials, because fumes can be introduced into the water via the aquarium's air pump. If toxic chemicals must be used in the same room as your aquarium, be sure to cover the tank well and to disconnect any pumps that might introduce air into the water. Of course, the beneficial anaerobic bacteria in the filter will not survive long without oxygen, so it is best not to use toxic chemicals in close proximity to your aquarium.

Nutritional Deficiencies and Euthanasia

Nutritional deficiencies are difficult to diagnose in most aquatic creatures. An improper diet may manifest itself in poor or deformed growth and a failure to reproduce. Unfortunately, we know little of the nutritional requirements of many fish and even less concerning invertebrates. See Chapter 16 for more information about nutrition.

Unfortunately, many of the diseases that affect captive fish and invertebrates cannot, at this point, be cured. Because many such conditions can lead to a lingering and painful death, you may wish to consider euthanasia for your terminally ill pets. Fish anesthetics can be used to quickly and humanely euthanize animals afflicted with incurable diseases. At present, these are available only through veterinarians.

Chapter 20

Breeding Fish and Invertebrates

The captive reproduction of fish and invertebrates is one of the most rewarding and important projects you can explore. Such undertakings can be quite simple or extremely complex, depending upon the species chosen. In all cases, observing the courtship and breeding behavior of your pets and raising the young will be a learning experience. Faced with rapidly dwindling habitats and the loss of species, it is vital to reduce pressure on wild populations by learning to breed more species in captivity.

Breeding Strategies of Fish and Invertebrates

Fish and invertebrates employ a countless array of reproductive strategies. We know little about this phase of the life history of many species, especially invertebrates and marine fish. For a more complete discussion of specific breeding strategies employed by aquatic creatures, see the descriptions of the various families and species elsewhere in this book.

Invertebrate Reproduction

The untold millions of invertebrate species have evolved some unique reproductive methods, some of which dispense with the notion of separate sexes altogether. As many species still await discovery, we will likely in the future find entire modes of reproduction that are as yet unimagined. Invertebrate reproduction takes forms that differ widely from the reproductive strategies of more familiar animals. Invertebrates ranging in size from tiny brine shrimp to large crabs carry their eggs about with them and protect them from predators. Others, such as the highly complex octopus, deposit their eggs in a shelter, stand guard, and then perish shortly after the young emerge.

The larvae of both marine and freshwater invertebrates may float about as plankton for a long time before settling down to resume an adult lifestyle. Marine invertebrates in particular may be carried many miles from their hatching site, allowing for the establishment of new colonies.

Many invertebrates pass through several life stages, some of which are completely unrecognizable when compared to the adult form. In fact, the larvae of many even quite common invertebrates have been accidentally classified as separate species from the adult.

Live-bearing (Viviparous) Fish

A surprising number of fish utilize internal fertilization and give birth to living young. Females of some such species, such as the freshwater guppy, may produce viable offspring for many months or even years after a single mating. More commonly, the female needs to mate repeatedly if fertile eggs are to develop. Many of the most common freshwater aquarium fish are live-bearers, such as platys, mollies, and swordtails. In most of these species, gestation averages three to four weeks at average aquarium temperatures (the length of the gestation period is affected by the temperature at which the female is maintained). Although the actual internal development of the babies varies greatly among the many fish species, most seem to provide nourishment to the young through a placenta-like organ.

FACT

Male live-bearing fish inseminate females using a modified anal fin known as the gonopodium. Fertilization generally takes place after a somewhat frenzied chase by the male, in contrast to the more ritualized mating displays of many egg-laying fish.

In the aquarium, live-bearing fish lessen the aquarist's workload in that there is no need to care for delicate eggs. The hard part of the process is done by the female. Live-bearing fish are often born at a fairly large size, thus making them easier to feed and raise than their egg-laying counterparts.

Egg-laying (Oviparous) Fish

Fish employ a great number of strategies to help ensure that their eggs hatch and the fry survive. Perhaps the simplest is the scattering of eggs and milt (sperm) into the water column, resulting in many eggs being simultaneously fertilized. Fish employing this method of reproduction, such as the freshwater white cloud, generally lay a great number of eggs, because fertilization of all is not guaranteed. Depending on the species, the eggs may float about in the current, or settle onto the substrate or among aquatic plants.

A great many of the eggs produced in this manner are consumed by other fish, and in some cases are consumed by the parents. In many environments, resident fish recognize the courtship behavior of egg-laying species and follow pregnant females in the hopes of acquiring a tasty meal. The enormous number of eggs produced by fish that reproduce in this manner is a strategy adopted to offset such predation.

Some fish take greater care in choosing an egg laying site than do the egg-scatterers. Such species may utilize surfaces such as plants or rocks, or caves and other protected sites. In many cases, one or both of the parents will remain to guard and aerate the eggs, and to keep the clutch free of debris.

One of the more unique strategies employed by egg laying fish is that developed by certain fresh and brackish water killiefish of the order Cyprinodontiformes. Loosely termed "annual killiefish" for their habit of laying eggs at the end of each rainy season, these fish inhabit water bodies that dry out each year. At the end of the rainy season the females deposit their eggs in the mud, after which they and the adult males die. The eggs are drought resistant and remain viable until the pools refill. The fry hatch nearly instantly upon the resumption of the rains and, in many species, are ready to reproduce within one week.

ESSENTIAL

Killiefish, especially males in breeding condition, are quite beautifully colored creatures. Dealers take advantage of the eggs' tenacity by shipping them, in dried form, to hobbyists throughout the world. Killiefish interest groups, whose members exchange eggs by mail, are popular in several countries.

Egg-laying fish are, in some senses, more difficult to accommodate in captivity than are most live-bearers. The eggs are often extremely delicate and require special care. In many cases, the young hatch out at an extremely tiny size, making it difficult for hobbyists to provide them with suitable foods. However, these factors are somewhat offset by the fact that many egg-laying fish take very good care of their eggs, and, in some cases, of the young. In fact, given the proper environment, pairs of many egg-laying fish will do all the hard work for you. Freshwater discus, while by no means easy to maintain, go as far as feeding their young with specially produced mucus. Because the vast majority of fish are egg layers, it is very important that we learn as much as we can about them to encourage captive reproduction and discourage the taking of wild specimens.

Mouth-Brooding

A large number of freshwater and marine fish incubate fertilized eggs in their mouths or throats. It many cases the attentive parent, often the female, forgoes feeding until the eggs hatch. The fry of mouth-brooding fish remain in close proximity to the parent and quickly swim back into the mouth when danger threatens. One of the first mouth- brooding fish to be introduced into the aquarium trade was the Tilapia, an African species known to hobbyists in past years as the "Mozambique mouth breeder." Interestingly, the Tilapia's highly effective reproductive strategy and its resistance to both high water temperatures and low dissolved oxygen levels have today rendered it an extremely important food fish.

For a variety of reasons, certain habitats seem to have given rise to a large number of fish species that utilize mouth-brooding as a reproductive strategy. Particularly well-known in this regard are many cichlids that are endemic to the various African Rift Lakes.

Nest-Building

A great many fish are accomplished nest builders, and the resulting structures are a fascinating study in and of themselves. Well-known to European aquarists are the sticklebacks, tiny marine and freshwater relatives of the seahorse that construct intricate nests consisting of plant material.

FACT

To attract females, males of several cichlid species native to Africa's Lake Malawi construct sand "castles" greater than 3 feet in diameter at their base, while others evacuate pits up to 10 feet in width. Amazingly, the individual architects are only 6 inches in length. Breeding aggregations, or leks, may contain more than 50,000 nests.

Another well-known nest builder is the beta, or Siamese fighting fish, whose males build floating nests of air bubbles into which the females are induced to lay their eggs. In North America, many people are familiar with the circular pits evacuated in sandy substrates by various species of sunfish. Like many nest builders, male sunfish guard these nests jealously, aerate the eggs with fin movements, and periodically remove fungus and debris from among the clutch.

General Breeding Considerations

The breeding of fish and invertebrates is never as simple as placing two individuals of the opposite sex together. A host of other very important factors should be carefully considered before you embark on a breeding project. The production of eggs or young is really only the first step in this fascinating but often labor-intensive aspect of your hobby.

Experience

Animals employ a wide variety of breeding strategies and certain strategies are easier to accommodate in an aquarium than others. In general, experience with freshwater fish and invertebrates will greatly increase your chances of success with the less-studied marine species. Also, when working with freshwater species, you would be well-advised to begin with well-known live-bearers such as guppies and then go on to some of the hardy egg-layers, such as the zebra danio. Eventually, you may want to work with fish that form pairs and utilize courtship rituals, nest building, and other more complicated reproductive patterns.

Marine fish and invertebrates in general reproduce far less commonly in captivity than do freshwater fish. However, advances in this area are becoming more and more common, with over 100 species of marine fish having been bred in home aquariums to date. Marine invertebrates are less well studied, but their reproductive husbandry is also being explored by many hobbyists. One of the first marine species to be successfully bred was the dwarf seahorse, followed shortly thereafter by the ever popular clown or anemone fish, and by several species of goby and blenny. Of the marine invertebrates, only the banded coral shrimp reproduced in aquariums with any regularity in the early years of the hobby.

The hobbyist who seeks to work with marine species might consider keeping a large, hardy native species at first. Native species are more easily accommodated in terms of natural foods, light cycles, and water quality. Also, you might be more familiar with their actual habitats as a result of personal observation, a situation that will greatly increase your chances of success.

QUESTION?

What species might I consider as a beginner in marine fish breeding?
The toadfish (*Opsanus tau*) makes an ideal candidate. Females guarding eggs may be collected by checking within jars, shoes, and other debris. Carefully transferred to a large aquarium, the eggs will usually hatch and the sizable young are fairly easy to rear. Mated pairs have also bred in captivity.

Food

Keep in mind that young fish of all types require enormous quantities of food, usually several times each day, and that much of this food is difficult to procure. Although commercial preparations have made the hobbyist's work easier, live foods such as daphnia and infusoria are often the essential. The culture of such food items will require additional time and space. Also, while some fish species will reproduce while being fed their normal diet, many require a special conditioning period during which they should be fed a variety of live foods or fresh vegetables. See Chapter 16 for additional information on this topic.

Aquarium Design and Size

In nearly all cases, mated pairs of fish or invertebrates will fare better in a tank by themselves. Even those fish species that breed in large aggregations will do so more successfully if other species are excluded from their aquarium. This will necessitate a separate aquarium as well as additional life-support systems, lights, and related accessories.

Also to be considered is the fact that many animals will not reproduce unless they are given suitably-sized aquariums. Some species need the security of a tank that approaches the size of their natural territory if they are to breed successfully. Water depth is also a consideration, especially for certain marine fish. As always, careful research is required, but you should be aware that maintaining animals in breeding condition may be quite different from keeping them for exhibit purposes.

ALERT!

Commercial breeding operations producing freshwater species such as crayfish and tilapia or marine species such as clams and shrimp may be sources of information beneficial to those seeking to reproduce similar or related animals in home aquariums. The economic value attached to such creatures ensures that a good deal of research has gone into their captive husbandry.

Aquarists who have bred both marine and freshwater fish and invertebrate species often comment that they achieve greater successes, overall, by maintaining animals in somewhat "naturalistic" aquariums. A heavy growth of plants or algae seems almost essential for many species. Filtration systems employing live rock and sand, with little water disturbance from external filters, are also mentioned time and again as helpful or even necessary. You may wish to learn more about such aquarium systems when seeking to breed delicate species.

Selecting a Mated Pair

Fish and even invertebrates can be extremely picky when it comes to a mate choice. In some cases, you may notice that two fish in a dealer's tank or in your own will spend a good deal of time together or engage in what appears to be courtship rituals. Such fish are ideal candidates for transference into a separate aquarium for breeding purposes. Pairs of freshwater angelfish are often identified in this matter.

Although little is known about the natural or captive reproduction of most invertebrates, a few species do appear to establish long-term pair bonds. Banded coral shrimp, for example, seem to be particularly devoted to each other, with males having been observed to feed pregnant females. As usual, close observation will be your key ally in identifying a pair.

A surprising number of fish can change their sexes in response to a variety of environmental conditions. Obviously, this may complicate the task of identifying a pair. However, in some cases this reproductive strategy may simplify matters. Marine clownfish, or anemone fish, for example, all begin life as males. The largest and most dominant in any group eventually changes sex and becomes a female. Therefore, any small group, or even any two fish, will likely provide you with a pair suitable for breeding.

A further complication to captive breeding efforts is the fact that many fish and invertebrates do not exhibit sexual dimorphism, or, more likely, aquarists have not yet learned to identify the dimorphism that does exist. In such cases, the behavior of the animals themselves may give you a clue as to whether or not they are a compatible pair. In fact, your studies of this matter may lead to reliable ways of differentiating the sexes in animals that currently baffle aquarists.

As with most endeavors involving captive animals, extensive research and discussions with serious hobbyists and professionals will increase the chances of success and will greatly increase the pleasure that you derive from the hobby.

Manipulating Conditions to Induce Breeding

Many if not most aquatic animals are brought into breeding condition by environmental changes that occur within their habitats. In some cases, the change involved may be quite subtle, such as a short-term drop in temperature. In other cases, dramatic events such as the changing of a season may be necessary to induce breeding.

Parameters Involved

It is nearly impossible to describe the range of factors that influence the reproductive strategies of the world's aquatic animals. What is known is that many require delicate manipulations of certain conditions if they are to breed in captivity. As has been mentioned, corals over huge sections of the Great Barrier Reef in Australia reproduce simultaneously, somehow brought into condition by as yet little understood factors. What is apparent, however, is that the complex system of environmental cues is involved.

In some areas of the world, falling water levels induced by drought concentrate food animals, resulting in a bonanza for predatory creatures that, under these conditions, are brought rapidly into breeding condition. Over large tracts of the Amazon River basin, seasonal floods allow fish and invertebrates to enter forests that are normally above the river's water level. There they feed ravenously upon fruits, plants, and animals that are otherwise unavailable to them. This glut of seasonally available nutrients likely stimulates reproduction in some species.

Chemical Changes

In cases like those previously mentioned and countless others, complex chemical changes to the water are also no doubt taking place. As water levels drop, salts and minerals become concentrated, causing the pH and specific gravity to change. Similarly, floods might dilute these elements while introducing others that were missing previously.

In seeking to learn more about captive reproduction and other aspects of aquarium keeping, be sure to consult older books and publications. In the days before advanced life-support systems were readily available, aquarists generally paid great attention to the daily lives and habits of their pets. Sadly, such vital information is often bypassed today.

Perhaps the most common reproductive cue is temperature change. Temperate species often require a "cooling down" period if they are to reproduce successfully. Along with this period of reduced temperatures, these species generally must experience a change in day length. Manipulation of light cycles in the aquarium is often an important aspect of husbandry.

Nutrition and Reproduction

A well-balanced and complete diet is necessary for the successful maintenance of all aquatic creatures. In some hardy and readily bred species, a solid diet may be enough to support captive reproduction. However, many animals require additions to their diet as breeding time approaches.

Conditioning Animals for Breeding

In certain species, the presence of a certain type of food may actually be a stimulus for reproduction. Unfortunately, specifics in this area are lacking. As you read and research, be sure to note the environmental changes that your pets experience in their wild state. If drastic changes such as floods or droughts regularly occur, it is likely that the animals will be exposed to important dietary fluctuations that may influence reproduction.

The specific facts will vary from species to species. In general, it pays to play it safe by increasing the amounts and varieties of foods fed to pets that appear to be approaching breeding condition. Live foods work well for many species, even those that do not necessarily prey upon other creatures on a regular basis. The addition of growing aquatic plants or algae, or fresh vegetables, may well be the key for herbivorous species. You might also try varying the usual diet by including new foods such as fish roe or small, whole shrimp.

Planning Ahead

When contemplating the birth of a brood of fish, it is important to plan ahead to acquire the foods that will be necessary. There are currently available a wide variety of foods designed especially for young fish. For many, however, tiny live food items such as rotifers and infusoria are preferable and, in many cases, necessary. This holds especially true for the young of predatory species, which may not recognize nonliving foods.

One of the most important steps that you can take to ensure success in raising large numbers of small fish is to establish a thriving colony of infusoria. Freshwater or saltwater infusoria can easily be cultured in a well lit aquarium or one placed in a sunny location. The water should be gently aerated and a bit of yeast, shrimp, and hay should be added to the aquarium.

Many of the tiny creatures that will develop are nearly invisible to the naked eye, so you may wish to confirm their presence by using a magnifying glass or microscope. A number of algae species should also establish themselves, and their presence will be beneficial to the culture. Even the tiniest of fish species will readily consume infusoria and will grow rapidly on this rich diet. As the fry increase in size, enriched brine shrimp and other suitably sized foods can be introduced.

Lesser Known Live Foods

The use of alternative food items and smaller invertebrate species takes on greater importance when you are maintaining small, specialized animals or raising particularly delicate fry. The commercially available diets for such creatures might be limited to one or two items, so you must look elsewhere to arrange a balanced diet. For less demanding captives, live foods are less critical, but they do provide much-needed dietary variety and may help stimulate reproduction. Experiment, if possible, with untried food animals and attempt to establish breeding colonies of those that show promise.

Tadpole Shrimp, Triops spp.

Tadpole shrimp are tiny crustaceans that superficially resemble shrimp and, much like brine shrimp, are adapted for survival in extremely harsh environments. Some species complete their entire life cycles within one week, because they live in desert pools where water may collect only once every three or four years. Tadpole shrimp are generally considered to be freshwater animals, but the tiny pools that they inhabit may contain a good deal of salts and other minerals. Many species will therefore survive for a time in saltwater aquariums. Tadpole shrimp cultures may be purchased from biological supply houses but are generally not available in pet stores.

Fairy Shrimp, Suborder Anastraca

Fairy shrimp are closely related to tadpole shrimp and also dwell in temporary freshwater pools. Although not commercially unavailable, large numbers may be collected when conditions are right. In temperate areas, they gather in huge breeding groups during the late winter and early spring. You may be surprised by the very cold temperatures in which they will remain active. As always, check into the legality of collecting fairy shrimp before doing so.

Seed Shrimp

Seed shrimp, also known as Ogtracods, are worldwide in distribution and are among the most common crustaceans to be found in fresh, marine, and brackish waters. They do not so much swim as bounce along the bottom of the aquarium, close to the substrate. This habit renders them an ideal food for small, bottom dwelling fish and invertebrates. Although not often bred as a food source for aquarium animals, seed shrimp are resilient in captivity and will thrive on a diet of algae pellets, liquid invertebrate food, and finely ground tropical fish food flakes.

Plankton

An innumerable variety of tiny animals and plants, many of them invisible to the naked eye, form the basis of the food chain in the world's fresh and marine waters. This conglomeration of diverse organisms is loosely referred to as "plankton" and the larger species are an excellent and often vital food for tiny fry and filter feeding invertebrates. Plankton is most easily collected by using a mesh plankton net. Available through biological supply houses, these nets can be used from the shore and are also manufactured in styles that can be towed behind a boat. The use of plankton as a food source will greatly improve your success in breeding and raising a wide variety of otherwise delicate aquatic creatures.

Daphnia

Daphnia are tiny crustaceans that may be collected using a plankton net or purchased from biological supply houses. In the alternative, you may start a culture by adding pond water and some dead leaves or hay to a jar or aquarium that is placed in a sunny location. The largest and most often available species, *Daphnia magna*, reaches a length of 0.25 inches and does best at temperatures of 75°F to 80°F (23.6° to 26.6°C). Most species of daphnia mature within one week, with adult females being capable of producing 100 or so eggs every few days. Daphnia can reproduce without the presence of males. Daphnia can be fed algae tablets and liquid foods sold for filter feeding invertebrates. They do best in aerated aquariums that support a growth of algae. Due to their small size, daphnia will be drawn into the intakes of most filters, so filtration is best achieved using live plants and algae, water changes, and possibly a sponge filter.

If you use pond water and bottom debris to establish your daphnia colony, check for the presence of the larvae of dragonflies and other predatory insects, and for pests such as fish lice.

Copepods

Copepods are another of the many crustaceans that are excellent food sources for the smallest of aquarium inhabitants. Copepods may be found throughout the world in both fresh and marine waters, with more than 5,000 species having been described to date. One of the most commonly encountered species is Cyclops fuscus, which grows to 0.125 inches in length.

Copepods may be collected and cultured in the same manner as has been described for daphnia.

Sandworms and Other Marine Worms

A number of large marine worm species are seasonally available at bait stores. Unfortunately, these worms are not cultured in captivity and thus are wild collected and quite expensive. You might consider their use, however, as a supplement for particularly valuable large marine fish. Be aware, however, that several types possess very sharp mouth parts that can deliver a painful bite to yourself and your pets. Ask the dealer about this and remove the heads of any potentially dangerous species before feeding them to your pets. Marine worms may also be collected by searching under rocks at the very edges of bays, lagoons, and oceans. Most marine worms will survive for several weeks if kept refrigerated and packed in damp marine algae.

Microworms

Microworms, *Anguillula silasiae*, are not true worms but rather invertebrates known as nematodes. They require temperatures of approximately 75°F (23.6°C) and will feed upon vegetable-based tropical fish food flakes. Microworms thrive well in damp peat moss.

Grindalworms, Enchytraeus bucholizi

Grindalworms are annelids and are closely related to earthworms. They can be cultured as has been described for microworms.

Whiteworms, Enchytraeus albidus

Whiteworms are also available commercially and do well when kept in peat moss and fed on a diet of moistened oatmeal and fish food flakes. They require cooler temperatures than do the species formerly described, faring best at 50°F to 55°F (9.9°C to 12.7°C).

Bloodworms, Chironomus spp.

Looking much like small aquatic worms, bloodworms are actually the larval stage of insects known as midges. The adults, winged creatures sometimes referred to as "gnats," often swarm on warm summer nights. The larvae are aquatic and may be purchased from some pet stores or ordered from dealers that advertise in aquarium hobbyist magazines. Blood worms utilize a form of hemoglobin very similar to that possessed by humans. It fulfills the same function in insects, namely carrying oxygen in the blood, and imparts to the larvae their bright red color. It is not practical to raise blood worms, but they survive for long periods under refrigeration. Blood worms are relished by many fish and invertebrates, but they die and spoil quickly in saltwater.

Mysid Shrimp

Despite their external appearance, mysids are not shrimp but rather are unique Crustaceans that are placed within their own order, Mycidea. Mysids are valuable food animals and may completely meet the nutritional requirements of a number of highly specialized marine animals. Seahorses and seadragons, for example, languish when fed only brine shrimp but thrive on a diet composed entirely of mysids. Mysids are best considered indispensable to the captive husbandry of seahorses and their relatives.

Mysids are commercially available, but they tend to be quite expensive. Although they breed readily in captivity, their culture is a bit complicated. The adults are cannibalistic and are very adept at locating smaller individuals, even in a well planned tank. To maintain a thriving colony, you need a series of aquariums, preferably 20 gallons in size, so that the young can be removed (siphoning is the easiest way to do this) and established in separate enclosures. Adults live for several months only, so ongoing production can only be assured by having a series of tanks housing individuals of different ages.

At 75°F, mysids will become sexually mature at one month of age. Unfortunately, the captive breeding of mysids is further complicated by the fact that they do best on a diet of live brine shrimp.

Larger Crustaceans and Mollusks

A wide variety of crabs, snails, clams, mussels, oysters and similar creatures may be collected or purchased in fish markets and bait shops. Crack the shells of mollusks such as clams to render the meat accessible to your pets. You may be surprised at the feeding frenzy that will erupt upon the introduction of a cracked clam or mussel into the aquarium.

Bait stores stock seasonally available species such as fiddler crabs and green crabs, both of which are readily accepted by many aquatic creatures.

Take care when feeding freshwater animals to your marine pets, and vice-versa. Most food animals die rapidly in alien environments, and uneaten ones will decompose quickly and foul the water. Be particularly cautious when using soft-bodied creatures such as worms because they break down very rapidly in saltwater.

Flour Beetle Larvae

The larvae and adults of several species of beetles, known collectively as "flour beetles" are an easily raised source of food for small fish and invertebrates. Because they represent a species of insect different from those normally fed to aquatic animals, these beetles may provide important nutrients that might otherwise be missing from the diet.

Flour beetles may be found in old boxes of cereal or old boxes of dog biscuits. The colony should be housed in a dry container partially filled with dog biscuits. Flour beetles will reproduce quite rapidly at room temperature, and even faster if kept in a warm location. To use the beetles, simply break open a dog biscuit and tap it over the aquarium. Flour beetles need not be provided with a water source, and the colony should never be moistened or exposed to water.

Appendix B

Additional Resources

Books

Amos, William Hopkins. *Wildlife of the Rivers.* 1981: Harry N. Abrams, Inc.

Arnett, Ross H. and Richard L. Jacques. *Simon and Schuster's Guide to Insects.* 1981: Simon and Schuster.

Bartlett, Richard D. *Frogs, Toads and Treefrogs.* 1996: Barron's Educational Series, Inc.

Bertin, Leon. *The New Larousse Encyclopedia of Animal Life.* 1980: Bonanza Books.

Blasiola, George C. II. *The New Saltwater Aquarium Handbook.* 1991: Barron's Educational Series, Inc.

Burgess, Warren. *An Atlas of Freshwater and Marine Catfishes.* 1989: TFH Publications, Inc.

Campbell, Andrew C. *The Larousse Guide to the Seashore and Shallow Seas of Britain and Europe.* 1980: Larousse and Company, Inc.

Center for Marine Conservation. *The Ocean Book: Aquarium and Seaside Activities and Ideas for all Ages.* 1989: John Wiley and Sons, Inc.

Cousteau, Jacques Yves. *The Cousteau Almanac.* 1980: The Cousteau Society, Inc.

Dakin, Nick. *Complete Encyclopedia of the Salt Water Aquarium.* 2003: Firefly Books, Inc.

Frank, S. *The Pictorial Encyclopedia of Fishes.* 1971: The Hamlyn Publishing Group, Ltd.

Indiviglio, Frank. *Newts and Salamanders.* 1997: Barron's Educational Series, Inc.

———.*Seahorses.* 2002: Barron's Educational Series, Inc.

Mills, Dick. *Aquarium Fish.* 1993: Dk Publishing, Inc.

Miner, Roy Waldo. *Field Book of Seashore Life.* 1950: Roy Waldo Miner.

Moe, Martin A. *The Marine Aquarium Reference.* 1993: Green Turtle Publications.

Moore, Clifford Bennett. *The Book of Wild Pets.* 1954: Charles T. Bradford Co.

Obst, Fritz J., Klaus Richter, and Udo Jacob. *Atlas of Reptiles and Amphibians for the Terrarium*. 1988: TFH Publications, Inc.

Paxton, John R. and William N. Eschmeyer (Ed.). *Encyclopedia of Fishes*. 1995: Academic Press, Inc.

Pennak, Robert W. *Fresh Water Invertebrates of the United States*. 1989: John Wiley and Sons, Inc.

Scott, Peter W. *The Complete Aquarium*. 19097: Penguin Books, Ltd.

Straughan, Robert P. L. *The Salt Water Aquarium in the Home*. 1970: A. S. Barnes and Co.

Thompson, Gerald and Jennifer Coldrey. *The Pond*. 1984: The MIT Press.

Magazines

Tropical Fish Hobbyist
www.tfhmagazine.com
TFH Publications, P.O. Box 427
Neptune, New Jersey 07754

Seascope
8141 Tyler Boulevard
Mentor, Ohio 44060

Aquarium Fish Magazine
www.aquariumfish.com

Freshwater and Marine Aquarium Magazine
www.famamagazine.com
144 West Sierra Madre Boulevard
Sierra Madre, CA 91024

Organizations

Coney Island Aquarium/Aquarium for Wildlife Conservation
Brooklyn, New York 11224
718-265-3400

American Museum of Natural History
www.amnh.org
Central Park West at 77th Street
New York, New York 10024

Science Development, Inc.
400 Riverside Drive
Suite 4A
New York, New York 10025

American Aquarist Society
205-386-7687

Brooklyn Aquarium Society
718-837-4455

Greater City Aquarium Society
718-846-6984

Long Island Aquarium Society
www.liasonline.org

Index

THE EVERYTHING SERIES!

BUSINESS & PERSONAL FINANCE

Everything® Accounting Book
Everything® Budgeting Book
Everything® Business Planning Book
Everything® Coaching and Mentoring Book
Everything® Fundraising Book
Everything® Get Out of Debt Book
Everything® Grant Writing Book
Everything® Home-Based Business Book, 2nd Ed.
Everything® Homebuying Book, 2nd Ed.
Everything® Homeselling Book, 2nd Ed.
Everything® Investing Book, 2nd Ed.
Everything® Landlording Book
Everything® Leadership Book
Everything® Managing People Book, 2nd Ed.
Everything® Negotiating Book
Everything® Online Auctions Book
Everything® Online Business Book
Everything® Personal Finance Book
Everything® Personal Finance in Your 20s and 30s Book
Everything® Project Management Book
Everything® Real Estate Investing Book
Everything® Robert's Rules Book, $7.95
Everything® Selling Book
Everything® Start Your Own Business Book, 2nd Ed.
Everything® Wills & Estate Planning Book

COOKING

Everything® Barbecue Cookbook
Everything® Bartender's Book, $9.95
Everything® Chinese Cookbook
Everything® Classic Recipes Book
Everything® Cocktail Parties and Drinks Book
Everything® College Cookbook
Everything® Cooking for Baby and Toddler Book
Everything® Cooking for Two Cookbook
Everything® Diabetes Cookbook
Everything® Easy Gourmet Cookbook
Everything® Fondue Cookbook
Everything® Fondue Party Book
Everything® Gluten-Free Cookbook
Everything® Glycemic Index Cookbook
Everything® Grilling Cookbook

Everything® Healthy Meals in Minutes Cookbook
Everything® Holiday Cookbook
Everything® Indian Cookbook
Everything® Italian Cookbook
Everything® Low-Carb Cookbook
Everything® Low-Fat High-Flavor Cookbook
Everything® Low-Salt Cookbook
Everything® Meals for a Month Cookbook
Everything® Mediterranean Cookbook
Everything® Mexican Cookbook
Everything® One-Pot Cookbook
Everything® Quick and Easy 30-Minute, 5-Ingredient Cookbook
Everything® Quick Meals Cookbook
Everything® Slow Cooker Cookbook
Everything® Slow Cooking for a Crowd Cookbook
Everything® Soup Cookbook
Everything® Tex-Mex Cookbook
Everything® Thai Cookbook
Everything® Vegetarian Cookbook
Everything® Wild Game Cookbook
Everything® Wine Book, 2nd Ed.

GAMES

Everything® 15-Minute Sudoku Book, $9.95
Everything® 30-Minute Sudoku Book, $9.95
Everything® Blackjack Strategy Book
Everything® Brain Strain Book, $9.95
Everything® Bridge Book
Everything® Card Games Book
Everything® Card Tricks Book, $9.95
Everything® Casino Gambling Book, 2nd Ed.
Everything® Chess Basics Book
Everything® Craps Strategy Book
Everything® Crossword and Puzzle Book
Everything® Crossword Challenge Book
Everything® Cryptograms Book, $9.95
Everything® Easy Crosswords Book
Everything® Easy Kakuro Book, $9.95
Everything® Games Book, 2nd Ed.
Everything® Giant Sudoku Book, $9.95
Everything® Kakuro Challenge Book, $9.95
Everything® Large-Print Crossword Challenge Book
Everything® Large-Print Crosswords Book
Everything® Lateral Thinking Puzzles Book, $9.95
Everything® Mazes Book

Everything® Pencil Puzzles Book, $9.95
Everything® Poker Strategy Book
Everything® Pool & Billiards Book
Everything® Test Your IQ Book, $9.95
Everything® Texas Hold 'Em Book, $9.95
Everything® Travel Crosswords Book, $9.95
Everything® Word Games Challenge Book
Everything® Word Search Book

HEALTH

Everything® Alzheimer's Book
Everything® Diabetes Book
Everything® Health Guide to Adult Bipolar Disorder
Everything® Health Guide to Controlling Anxiety
Everything® Health Guide to Fibromyalgia
Everything® Health Guide to Thyroid Disease
Everything® Hypnosis Book
Everything® Low Cholesterol Book
Everything® Massage Book
Everything® Menopause Book
Everything® Nutrition Book
Everything® Reflexology Book
Everything® Stress Management Book

HISTORY

Everything® American Government Book
Everything® American History Book
Everything® Civil War Book
Everything® Freemasons Book
Everything® Irish History & Heritage Book
Everything® Middle East Book

HOBBIES

Everything® Candlemaking Book
Everything® Cartooning Book
Everything® Coin Collecting Book
Everything® Drawing Book
Everything® Family Tree Book, 2nd Ed.
Everything® Knitting Book
Everything® Knots Book
Everything® Photography Book
Everything® Quilting Book
Everything® Scrapbooking Book
Everything® Sewing Book
Everything® Woodworking Book

Bolded titles are new additions to the series.
All Everything® books are priced at $12.95 or $14.95, unless otherwise stated. Prices subject to change without notice.

HOME IMPROVEMENT

Everything® Feng Shui Book
Everything® Feng Shui Decluttering Book, $9.95
Everything® Fix-It Book
Everything® Home Decorating Book
Everything® Home Storage Solutions Book
Everything® Homebuilding Book
Everything® Lawn Care Book
Everything® Organize Your Home Book

KIDS' BOOKS

All titles are $7.95

Everything® Kids' Animal Puzzle & Activity Book
Everything® Kids' Baseball Book, 4th Ed.
Everything® Kids' Bible Trivia Book
Everything® Kids' Bugs Book
Everything® Kids' Cars and Trucks Puzzle & Activity Book
Everything® Kids' Christmas Puzzle & Activity Book
Everything® Kids' Cookbook
Everything® Kids' Crazy Puzzles Book
Everything® Kids' Dinosaurs Book
Everything® Kids' First Spanish Puzzle and Activity Book
Everything® Kids' Gross Hidden Pictures Book
Everything® Kids' Gross Jokes Book
Everything® Kids' Gross Mazes Book
Everything® Kids' Gross Puzzle and Activity Book
Everything® Kids' Halloween Puzzle & Activity Book
Everything® Kids' Hidden Pictures Book
Everything® Kids' Horses Book
Everything® Kids' Joke Book
Everything® Kids' Knock Knock Book
Everything® Kids' Learning Spanish Book
Everything® Kids' Math Puzzles Book
Everything® Kids' Mazes Book
Everything® Kids' Money Book
Everything® Kids' Nature Book
Everything® Kids' Pirates Puzzle and Activity Book
Everything® Kids' Princess Puzzle and Activity Book
Everything® Kids' Puzzle Book
Everything® Kids' Riddles & Brain Teasers Book
Everything® Kids' Science Experiments Book
Everything® Kids' Sharks Book
Everything® Kids' Soccer Book
Everything® Kids' Travel Activity Book

KIDS' STORY BOOKS

Everything® Fairy Tales Book

LANGUAGE

Everything® Conversational Chinese Book with CD, $19.95
Everything® Conversational Japanese Book with CD, $19.95
Everything® French Grammar Book
Everything® French Phrase Book, $9.95
Everything® French Verb Book, $9.95
Everything® German Practice Book with CD, $19.95
Everything® Inglés Book
Everything® Learning French Book
Everything® Learning German Book
Everything® Learning Italian Book
Everything® Learning Latin Book
Everything® Learning Spanish Book
Everything® Russian Practice Book with CD, $19.95
Everything® Sign Language Book
Everything® Spanish Grammar Book
Everything® Spanish Phrase Book, $9.95
Everything® Spanish Practice Book with CD, $19.95
Everything® Spanish Verb Book, $9.95

MUSIC

Everything® Drums Book with CD, $19.95
Everything® Guitar Book
Everything® Guitar Chords Book with CD, $19.95
Everything® Home Recording Book
Everything® Music Theory Book with CD, $19.95
Everything® Reading Music Book with CD, $19.95
Everything® Rock & Blues Guitar Book (with CD), $19.95
Everything® Songwriting Book

NEW AGE

Everything® Astrology Book, 2nd Ed.
Everything® Birthday Personology Book
Everything® Dreams Book, 2nd Ed.
Everything® Love Signs Book, $9.95
Everything® Numerology Book
Everything® Paganism Book
Everything® Palmistry Book
Everything® Psychic Book
Everything® Reiki Book
Everything® Sex Signs Book, $9.95
Everything® Tarot Book, 2nd Ed.
Everything® Wicca and Witchcraft Book

PARENTING

Everything® Baby Names Book, 2nd Ed.
Everything® Baby Shower Book
Everything® Baby's First Food Book
Everything® Baby's First Year Book
Everything® Birthing Book
Everything® Breastfeeding Book
Everything® Father-to-Be Book
Everything® Father's First Year Book
Everything® Get Ready for Baby Book
Everything® Get Your Baby to Sleep Book, $9.95
Everything® Getting Pregnant Book
Everything® Guide to Raising a One-Year-Old
Everything® Guide to Raising a Two-Year-Old
Everything® Homeschooling Book
Everything® Mother's First Year Book
Everything® Parent's Guide to Children and Divorce
Everything® Parent's Guide to Children with ADD/ADHD
Everything® Parent's Guide to Children with Asperger's Syndrome
Everything® Parent's Guide to Children with Autism
Everything® Parent's Guide to Children with Bipolar Disorder
Everything® Parent's Guide to Children with Dyslexia
Everything® Parent's Guide to Positive Discipline
Everything® Parent's Guide to Raising a Successful Child
Everything® Parent's Guide to Raising Boys
Everything® Parent's Guide to Raising Siblings
Everything® Parent's Guide to Sensory Integration Disorder
Everything® Parent's Guide to Tantrums
Everything® Parent's Guide to the Overweight Child
Everything® Parent's Guide to the Strong-Willed Child
Everything® Parenting a Teenager Book
Everything® Potty Training Book, $9.95
Everything® Pregnancy Book, 2nd Ed.
Everything® Pregnancy Fitness Book
Everything® Pregnancy Nutrition Book
Everything® Pregnancy Organizer, 2nd Ed., $16.95
Everything® Toddler Activities Book
Everything® Toddler Book
Everything® Tween Book
Everything® Twins, Triplets, and More Book